DISCOVERING ORGANIZATIONAL IDENTITY

DISCOVERING ORGANIZATIONAL IDENTITY

Dynamics of Relational Attachment

Michael A. Diamond

UNIVERSITY OF MISSOURI PRESS
Columbia

Copyright © 2017 by

The Curators of the University of Missouri

University of Missouri Press, Columbia, Missouri 65211

Printed and bound in the United States of America

All rights reserved. First printing, 2017

ISBN: 978-0-8262-2098-1

Library of Congress Control Number: 2016945534

♾™ This paper meets the requirements of the

American National Standard for Permanence of Paper

for Printed Library Materials, Z39.48, 1984.

Typefaces: Frutiger and Minion Pro

For my brilliant and extraordinary daughters, Simone and Tova Diamond, who share my aspiration for a more humane, respectful, diverse, and democratic workplace. With love . . .

CONTENTS

Preface   ix

Acknowledgments   xiii

Introduction   3

PART ONE / THEORY

Chapter 1   Psychoanalytic Organizational Theory   19

Chapter 2   Self Identity and Organizational Identity   39

Chapter 3   Group Dynamics   55

PART TWO / KEY CONCEPTS AND APPLICATION

Chapter 4   Intersubjectivity and Potential Space   81

Chapter 5   Repetition, Remembering, and Change   97

Chapter 6   Metaphor and Metaphoric Processes   119

Chapter 7   The Unthought Known   129

PART THREE / REFLECTIVE PRACTICE

Chapter 8   Narcissistic Organizational Leadership   147

Chapter 9   Executive Coaching: A Critical Psychoanalytic Perspective   163

Chapter 10   Conclusions   183

Appendix   191

Notes   195

References   207

Index   221

PREFACE

When the heart speaks,
the mind finds it indecent to object.

—**Milan Kundera**
The Unbearable Lightness of Being

W HILE COMPLETING MY doctorate at the University of Maryland in College Park in 1980–1981, I was asked to participate as a researcher in a study of the senior executive service (SES) of the federal government. The project was headed by organizational psychologist Lyman Porter of the University of California, Irvine. Since I was writing my dissertation on the psychology of bureaucracy, I thought it might provide an interesting opportunity to go inside and learn more about the bureaucratic experience. So I enthusiastically joined the research team.

While much of the SES study involved administering survey questionnaires, I took the opportunity to walk around and interview many of the SES personnel in a variety of federal agencies, including the USDA. To my surprise I found many executives who were pleased to find in me someone with whom they could share their disappointments with a career that left them joyless and dissatisfied. Notwithstanding their feelings of gratification at being appointed to a coveted executive level of public service, many described an oppressive bureaucratic culture with limited opportunity to innovate and participate in solving problems. One illustration from an executive in one of the federal government's largest departments stuck with me and was a significant factor in shaping the direction of my academic writing, teaching, and organizational research.

During an interview memorable for its simultaneous tediousness and heaviness, the government executive drew my attention to a framed picture over his desk. It was a photo not of family or a prominent politician or cabinet secretary. Rather, it was a photo of his tiny, inconspicuous sailboat on the sea. He explained to me that he attributed to this photo his capacity to emotionally cope and survive in an otherwise disappointing and gloomy career. The transformation of his feelings from weightiness to lightness and frivolity while describing the effect of this symbol to me was stunning. It was as if the photo took him away from the doldrums of the office and into the "oceanic feeling" Freud spoke of in *The Future of an Illusion* (1927) and *Civilization and Its Discontents* (1930). No survey questionnaire, I thought, could capture the emotional distress and suffering experienced by many of these federal executives. No experience-distant research methodology could hear the distress and isolation communicated by these leaders of government.

It was simply assumed by many that by virtue of their membership in the senior executive service and the presumed recognition and higher pay scale afforded these leaders of government agencies, they would be sincerely grateful, motivated, and content. Beyond the Likert-scale surveys, my observations and the stories shared with me, after a promise of anonymity, signified a darker and hidden psychological reality of work life inside the federal government. Then and there, I knew that this thinly veiled darker dimension of organization was precisely what I wanted to explore further and better understand.

My graduate studies in critical theory, political philosophy, psychoanalysis, and political and organizational psychology had led me to the Washington School of Psychiatry, in Washington, DC, where I participated in several workshops and seminars. There I met psychoanalysts Michael Maccoby and Douglas LaBier, among others. Maccoby, who had been mentored by Frankfurt School critical theorist, philosopher, and psychoanalyst Erich Fromm, was the director of the Project on Technology, Work, and Character in Washington, DC, and wrote the bestseller *The Gamesman* (1976). LaBier published an article in 1980 in the *Washington Post Magazine* about federal government workers entitled "Uncle Sam's Working Wounded." In 1983, he wrote "Emotional Disturbance in the Federal Government" in the academic journal *Administration & Society* and "Bureaucracy and Psychopathology" in *Political Psychology*. His book entitled *Modern Madness: The Emotional Fallout of Success* was published in 1986.

Simultaneously, I was working with the organizational psychologist Harry Levinson at Harvard and had been working for more than a few years with the political philosopher James M. Glass at the University of Maryland, where under his supervision I was writing my dissertation on bureaucracy, applying Harry Stack Sullivan's interpersonal theory of psychiatry to organizations. In

1984 I published "Bureaucracy as Externalized Self-System" in the journal *Administration & Society*, and in 1985 I wrote "The Social Character of Bureaucracy: Anxiety and Ritualistic Defense" in *Political Psychology*, among other articles dealing with bureaucracy and psychopathology.

Sullivan's pioneering legacy in American psychiatry began at the Washington School of Psychiatry and at Sheppard and Enoch Pratt Hospital in Baltimore, and he, along with Erich Fromm, Clara Thompson, and Frieda Fromm-Reichmann, cofounded the William Alanson White Institute in New York City. Sullivan's interpersonal theory and the British School of Kleinian object relations theory influenced in large part what is contemporary relational psychoanalytic theory, as well as the framework for studying organizational identity explained in this book.

In 1993 I published *The Unconscious Life of Organizations: Interpreting Organizational Identity*. In that book, I defined organizational identity as "the unconscious foundation of organizational culture . . . the totality of repetitive patterns of individual behavior and interpersonal relationships that, when taken together, comprise the unacknowledged meaning of organizational life" (p. 77). In this book, I reexamine the concept of organizational identity after thirty-five years of writing, teaching, studying, and consulting for large public and private organizations. In particular, this book advances our understanding of organizational identity as located in intersubjectivity and potential space and as rooted in the infantile tension between attachment and separation, membership and separateness. This book is addressed to readers interested in transcending the limitations of organizational culture and in thinking more deeply about organizational membership.

Throughout this book, I integrate the action-research, relational psychoanalytic, participant-observation, and fieldwork approaches to the study of organizations with the combined goals of understanding them and changing them. Thus, when I use the terms *organizational researcher* and *organizational consultant*, it ought to be understood that, given the combined goals of understanding and change, these terms are referring to two dimensions of the same process and that they are intimately linked and not mutually exclusive. Whether using the term *consultant* or *researcher*, I am describing the process of immersion and fieldwork by team members (outsiders) engaged in organizational assessment/diagnosis and feedback as precursors to intervention. I often use the terms synonymously because the psychoanalytic model of organizational research/consultation is a scholar-practitioner model. Similarly, I use the terms *participant* and *research subject* to refer to the subject of a psychoanalytic study of organizations wherein fieldwork and participant observation occur along with interviewing and collection of varied data; they can be interpreted as synonymous with the term *client* since the same methodology is applied in either a formal study of organizations without intervention or a contracted consultation comprising a formal organizational study, feedback, and intervention.

The true identities of all the organizations discussed in this book have been changed, and certain facts have been altered so that the subjects' (clients') anonymity and confidentiality are protected. Any resemblance to a particular organization is coincidental as the narratives each represent parts of several different cases with similar psychodynamics. Common themes and psychodynamics confirm and validate shared experiences and observations.

ACKNOWLEDGMENTS

I WISH TO THANK my friends and colleagues Drs. Seth Allcorn, Howard F. Stein, and Carrie M. Duncan for their enthusiastic support for the conceptualization and writing of this book. Working outside the academic mainstream of the social and behavioral sciences requires a solid group of enthusiasts and collaborators. I am forever grateful to Professor James M. Glass of the University of Maryland for his encouragement and confidence early in my academic career. The late Dr. Harry Levinson was always a generous critic and compassionate supporter of my work; he is greatly missed. I also want to acknowledge my good friends and professional colleagues Drs. Shelley Reciniello and Karen Poulin. I miss the presence of my dear friend and colleague the late psychoanalyst and organizational psychologist Dr. Laurence Gould. I also wish to acknowledge the late Drs. Alex Rode Redmountain and Paul T. King, both extraordinarily compassionate and insightful human beings. Also, I wish to express my gratefulness to Dr. Mary M. Dick. I wish to thank my friends and colleagues Professors Guy B. Adams, Robert B. Denhardt, Barton Wechsler, Howell Baum, David Levine, Howard Schwartz, and the late Ralph Hummel. Also, I want to express my gratitude to David Rosenbaum, director of the University of Missouri Press, for his intellectual curiosity, open-mindedness, and enthusiastic support.

DISCOVERING ORGANIZATIONAL IDENTITY

INTRODUCTION

Man, being torn away from nature, being endowed with reason and imagination, needs to form a concept of himself, needs to say and to feel: "I am I." Because he is not *lived,* but *lives,* because he has lost the original unity with nature, has to make decisions, is aware of himself and his neighbor as different persons, he must be able to sense himself as the subject of his actions. (Fromm, 1955, p. 62)

For psychoanalyst, philosopher, and critical theorist Erich Fromm, identity and awareness of "I" are vital to being human: one must be able to send oneself as the subject of one's actions. Similarly, the ethos of psychoanalytic organizational action research and consultation offered in this book has as its aim to promote a work environment of claimed action and mutual responsibility. I view organizations as the context within which true self and authenticity can potentially live and breathe, and I see organizational identity, as defined in this book, as hypothetically valuing true self and authenticity in theory and practice. Viewing organizations as transformational objects[1] is possible but requires rejection of the positivists' trap of objectification of the human subject in organizational science. In this book, I provide an in-depth description of psychoanalytic organizational theory and the concept of organizational identity.

The theoretical framework for the study of organizations envisioned here for organizational scholars, practitioners, and advanced graduate students interested in learning a contemporary psychoanalytic approach to organizational dynamics is intended to promote healthier and more humane work environments. In particular, I present organizational identity as a psychodynamic concept for understanding the relational forces at work between individual members and their organizations. I provide in this section an introduction to organizational identity and some key psychoanalytic concepts, which are then discussed in greater depth in chapter 1.

In this book, I describe and apply organizational identity using the theories and language and governing assumptions of psychoanalytic theory. Readers unfamiliar with psychoanalytic theory or its contemporary and competing paradigms might be puzzled as to how individual psychology could explain and transform groups and organizations. The framework for organizations presented here assumes that infantile, primitive, emotional, and relational experiences of attachment significantly influence adult character and accompanying relationships. The emotional roots of organizational membership, central to organizational identity, are located in the metaphor of the mother-baby union. In contrast with the view of classical psychoanalysis as an individual psychology, contemporary psychoanalytic theory is a relational, developmental, experiential, and perceptual framework. Its interpretive focus is in understanding the meanings and motives behind human actions. Psychoanalytic theory acknowledges that human cognition and emotion operate at various levels of consciousness and that individuals are repeatedly unaware and unconscious of the reasons for many of their actions. "Why did I say that?" "Why did I do that?" "What has gotten into me?" and "I just wasn't thinking" are common thoughts that people have about their own actions.

Explaining and unpacking the mystery of organizational dynamics requires a theory that, on the one hand, acknowledges conscious, rational, formal, and intentional influences of structure, strategies, processes, and technologies, and that, on the other hand, attends to unconscious, nonrational, informal, and ostensibly unintentional dimensions of group emotions and associated psychological defenses. For example, one common dynamic is the mistreatment of subordinate members of groups and organizations by tyrannical and emotionally blinded leaders. Members of such groups feel vulnerable and anxious as a result of their exposure to intimidation and emotional abuse. Under these circumstances, workers feel victimized and under attack, so they retreat in self-defense into primitive emotional and nascent cognitive states that result in their viewing the external world as composed of us against them, allies and enemies, a Manichean organizational mind-set of mistrust, paranoia, and fragmentation.

The Essence of Organizational Identity

The philosophy of psychoanalysis is centered on exposing the individual proclivity for self- and other-deception. Consequently, it requires unpretentiousness and a surrender to unconscious processes and the idea of not knowing. In that spirit, organizational identity is a relational theory of mind, meaning, and motive that transcends superficial appearances and defensive routines.

Organizational identity is the result of an investigative process that exposes the collective, compliant, and submissive false self and replaces it with an authentic, spontaneous, and relational true self.

In the exploration of organizational identity through a psychoanalytic organizational framework, I encourage action researchers and consultants to assume balance in taking seriously the effects of leaders' personalities and their exercise of power and authority while not underestimating the formal and informal role and function of followers. In the model presented here, organizational researchers analyze cognitive, emotional, experiential, and associational patterns of networked relationships. These make up the structure and culture of group and organizational systems, or what I call *organizational identity*. As this term suggests, researchers can capture organizational life as a moment in time and space. This snapshot of the meaning and significance of relational experiences, perceptions, narrative patterns, and structures that embrace the passions and desires of participants' language and actions advances our understanding of organizations and the workplace.

The idea of organizational identity is epistemologically grounded in contemporary relational psychoanalytic organizational theory. The discovery of organizational identity demands focus on the intersubjective structure of self and other, subject and object. Seen, heard, and felt by way of metaphor, repetition, and the unthought known, organizational identity is the intersubjective relational patterns revealed in organizations beneath the surface of organizational cultures. We can locate organizational identity by focusing attention on intersubjectivity and potential space.[2] Researchers and consultants (I use both terms because the psychoanalytic model of organizational research/consultation is a scholar-practitioner model) concentrate on group dynamics, transference and countertransference patterns, and narcissism in positions of leadership, power, and authority to understand organizational life.

Analyzing historical, observational, associative, experiential, and transferential/countertransferential data is essential for psychodynamically informed organizational scholars. In collaboration with organizational participants, action researchers should strive to bring to awareness the tenacity of deep nonverbal, sensational levels of experience in groups and organizations. This recognition is intended to facilitate participant awareness of self and object[3] as a precursor to insight and fundamental organizational change.

This book presents a coherent and in-depth psychoanalytic theory of organizational identity grounded in the evolution of object relations, self psychology, and attachment theory. Next, I summarize the relevant psychoanalytic schools of thought and explain their applications for the purposes of this book.

Theories of Influence on Organizational Identity
Winnicott and Childhood

In chapter 1, I offer the metaphor of the mother-infant bond as a psychosocial benchmark for assessing the health, well-being, and integrity of the workplace. In particular, I use Winnicottian object relations theory[4] to understand organizational identity. Psychoanalyst and pediatrician D. W. Winnicott's theory, like Kohut's theory below, emphasizes empathy and introspection as a way of accessing and assessing workplace well-being. Is the workplace a *good enough* or a *not good enough holding environment*? Do workers feel secure enough to raise operational problems and invent solutions to them? Is *potential space* present? Is there a safe enough area in which workers can experiment and be creative? These concepts and others will be defined shortly. As with any new theory, one has to learn the language used in reference to it, and to do so requires understanding its premise, assumptions, and key concepts. I make a special effort throughout the book to clarify these ideas for the reader. Winnicott's hermeneutic ideas covered here are instrumental to assessing the capacity of organizational leaders to create a playful, imaginative, creative, inventive, and humane workplace. These workplace attributes are critical to reflective functioning, learning, innovation, and progressive change.

Infant Research and Attachment Theory

Infant researchers such as Mahler, Pine, and Bergman (1975); Stern (1985, 2004); Bowlby (1969, 1973, 1980); Fonagy (2001); and Jurist, Slade, and Bergner (2008), among others, write about secure versus insecure, and nonanxious versus anxious early attachments (mother-infant bonds) that are critical to the cognitive and affective processes of individuation and separation, and the emerging sense of self. In addition to contributing to a paradigmatic shift in psychoanalysis, these developmental findings shaped the ways in which organizational identity contributes to understanding the tension between matters of membership and separateness.

Kohut and Self Psychology

Psychoanalyst and pioneer of self psychology Heinz Kohut (1977, 1984) regards the presence or absence of early narcissistic gratification, as opposed to narcissistic deprivations between parent and child, as critical to self-cohesion and integrity. This developmental phenomenon is viewed as consequential for later adult manifestations of constructive versus destructive narcissism in organizational leaders and followers. For instance, among mirror-hungry narcissistic leaders with inordinate power and authority, the desire and demand for adoring and idealizing followers can be extreme and can take precedence over all other matters. Simultaneously, ideal-hungry followers search and frequently locate mirror-hungry leaders. This phenomenon and other patterned and repetitive psychodynamics, both destructive and constructive, shape organizational identity and the meaning of membership through the shared emotions of transference and countertransference relations among organizational participants, leaders and followers, and superordinates and subordinates.

Ogden and the Dialectical Modes of Experience

Psychoanalyst Thomas Ogden's (1989, 1994) dialectical modes of experience and self-organizing perceptions are critical to observing, experiencing, and interpreting, through empathy and identification, psychological regression in groups and organizations. I present the three modes of experience in the early chapters of this book: (1) the depressive, (2) the paranoid-schizoid, and (3) the autistic-contiguous. I discuss these modes at greater length in chapter 1 and how they can be observed, experienced, and interpreted from the vantage point of intersubjectivity and potential space, as outlined in chapter 4.

For now it is important to stress to the reader who is unfamiliar with these concepts and with the application of psychoanalytic theory to organizations that these modes of experience and the use of relational concepts throughout the book are meant to be descriptive and interpretive, not to be taken as clinical diagnoses or as judgments. In fact, organizational identity is in part a psychosocial construct that assists our understanding of the psychodynamics common to relationships, groups, and organizations.

Discovering Organizational Identity

Psychoanalytic approaches to organizations typically consider group dynamics as a critical level of analysis for understanding larger organizational dynamics. Organizational identity is shaped by up to three defensive work-group subcultures and one nondefensive work-group subculture; these group dynamics support dysfunctional and functional organizational performance, respectively. These work-group subcultures represent elements of organizational identity and are discussed at length in chapter 3. The typology of work groups includes (1) homogenized, (2) institutionalized, (3) autocratic, and (4) resilient. Each of these work groups is a consequence of compromise formations, where group subcultures coexist and may come into conflict with one another, resulting in one dominant group subculture. This group typology is paradoxical, each group defining, confirming, and negating the other and vice versa. Like Ogden's modes of dialectical experience, the work-group subcultures are parts of a larger interactive and paradoxical model of organization.

Intersubjectivity and Reflective Practice

Psychoanalytic researchers and consultants must acknowledge their trusted role in the experience-near study of organizations. To do so, they must consider the concepts of intersubjectivity and potential space. The intersubjective framework enables an attentive and observing outsider to promote participants' consciousness of relational psychodynamics. These efforts can promote shared and claimed mutual acts within organizations. This potentially transformative and linking work role of researchers (as fieldworkers, participant-observers, and action researchers) arouses the reflectivity and consciousness that are necessary for insight and change from stagnant, unconsciously embedded, regressive, and defensive routines.

Attentiveness to intersubjectivity and potential space organizes researchers' observations, permitting interpretation of self-sealing patterns of transference and countertransference. Called into question is the proclivity for repetition and the compulsion to repeat individual and group dynamics regardless of their dysfunctionality or oppressiveness. Organizational participants' resistance to insight and change is predictable and unavoidable. Resistance to change is fundamentally a defensive response to anxiety about a loss of familiar routines and attachments. It is not abnormal or pathological, nor is it stubborn or thick-skulled. Rather, resistance to insight and change is a profoundly human feature and more importantly a key to unlocking personal and interpersonal defensive and anxious repetitive responses to change.

The Language of Metaphor

When considering the unconscious dimensions of organizations, such as the human compulsion to repeat, one must realize that there are varied and primitive layers of consciousness at work. Awareness of linguistic transitions and affective communications results from organizational researchers' attention to participants' use of metaphors and metaphoric processes, as discussed in chapter 6. For example, in the construction of frozen and fluid metaphors, personal and interpersonal learning and reflectivity evolve from deeper levels of members' consciousness and emotionality. Thus, metaphor comes to signify a linguistic competency, which, in addition to promoting understanding, can assist in repairing conflicts and fragmented relational experiences between groups within organizations. Fluid metaphoric processes depend on mature separation, differentiation, and diversity between self and others, transcending rigid and defensive boundaries rooted in separation anxieties.

Fluid metaphoric processes assist in the capacity to move away from fragmentary or paranoid-schizoid modes and toward more holistic, integrative, depressive, and reparative actions. Much like metaphor, organizational storytelling as a form of communication and feedback to participants can promote movement from frozen relational patterns to more fluid work in the present. Organizational identity is often partially constructed on the basis of metaphor and metaphoric processes, where communication and feedback with organizational participants promotes consensual validation of collective experience and awareness of the previously unthought knowns.

The Unthought Known and Consensual Validation
Psychoanalyst Christopher Bollas's (1987) idea of the unthought known is illustrated by participants' responses to researchers' feedback as presented in the narrative form of organizational storytelling and construction of organizational identity. In chapter 7, I describe how research participants, upon hearing the organizational story of fragmentation and dysfunction and following several minutes of group silence, proclaimed, "I knew that, I just never thought of it." It was as if the organizational members were carrying "it" around with them and just needed someone such as the consultants to give "it" voice and meaning.[5]

By coming out in their stories of a fragmenting organization, members' previously unarticulated feelings acquired a meaningful shape and sensible linguistic form, which is part of organizational identity. Mutual validation of experience materialized with individual resonance and recognition of the collective sense of "we-ness" and shared identity. The narrative provided by the consultants and validated by the participants' experiences and associations verbalized the unthought known. Psychoanalytically oriented action researchers' diagnostic feedback of what they saw, what they heard, what they felt, and what they associated to it gave voice through language to what participants knew to be real at a deeper and unspoken level of consciousness—at the level of the unthought known.[6]

Organizational Identity and Potential Space
From the standpoint of psychoanalytic organizational theory, organizational intervention produces potential space that enables psychodynamically informed researchers and consultants to explore patterns of intersubjectivity and

organizational identity. By opening potential space, the action researcher is able to reach a deep understanding of the organization, with particular focus on group dynamics, the unthought known, repetition, metaphor, and narcissism and leadership. Figure 1 is meant to illustrate these interactive parts of the conceptual model for discovering organizational identity located in intersubjectivity and potential space. The reader might find it helpful to keep this conceptualization in mind throughout this book.

Narcissism at Work and Executive Coaching

The goal of psychoanalytic organizational theory presented throughout this book is to discover organizational identity, the collective "we-ness" and intersubjectivity, the common ground located in the potential space between groups and divisions, leaders and followers. A part of this discovery process is identifying the attributes of destructive narcissistic leadership that are critical to organizational diagnosis and to the discovery of organizational identity, and are thereby central to eventual reparation, reconciliation, and the development of organizational health and well-being.

FIGURE 1 Conceptual Model for Discovering Organizational Identity

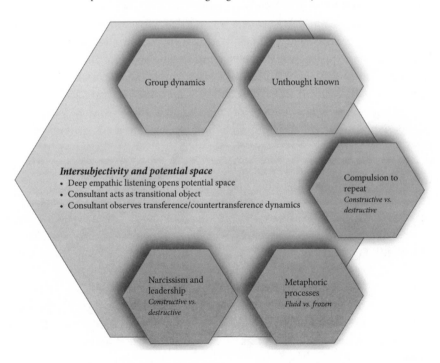

Narcissism is acknowledged as a critical factor in healthy early human development and is therefore a necessary ingredient for the emergence of a worthy, lovable, confident, and secure sense of self. However, when primary narcissistic needs are unmet or frustrated, and the holding environment of early childhood is generally inadequate, infantile narcissistic hunger for omnipotence and grandiosity lingers and crushes the formation of healthy attachments and significant adult relationships.

Hence, one frequently observes organizational leaders and followers locked in a repetitive and self-perpetuating dance of mirroring and idealizing transferences. These emotional knots of transference bind leaders and followers to meet disproportionate demands for narcissistic gratification. Leaders propagate organizational identities characterized by relational submission and dominance. Thus, assessing and recognizing destructive narcissism in leadership as a central feature of culture and identity is crucial in transforming toxic and emotionally unhealthy workplaces into emotionally healthy and humane organizations.

I discuss the detection and management of narcissistic leadership for executive coaching late in the book. Consultants' and coaches' providing a holding environment that contains executives' anxieties over uncertainty and change is helpful and constructive. The coaching process discussed in chapter 9 focuses on helping leaders cope with an evolving organization where power and authority are shared with knowledgeable and competent workers and where workers are encouraged to be reflective practitioners and discouraged from aggrandizing and idealizing the leadership. Table 1 illustrates the key features and concepts of the model for discovering organizational identity. It outlines essential concepts, how they are applied in practice, and their representation as dimensions of organizational identity.

Audience

I wrote this book for organizational scholars and theorists who are interested in organizational psychology and change, particularly from the perspective of contemporary relational psychoanalytic theory, application, and practice. It will appeal to academics and scholar-practitioners interested in considering the nexus between psychoanalysis, organizational politics, culture, and change. Finally, this book is also intended for thoughtful and reflective leaders and consultants who share the larger vision of a fair, respectful, and humane workplace.

TABLE 1 Key Features of the Model for Discovering Organizational Identity

Concept	Theory/definition	Practice	Feature of organizational identity
Intersubjectivity and potential space	Dialectical modes of self-organizing: depressive, paranoid-schizoid, autistic-contiguous Movement between positions Intersubjective framework	Researcher-consultant role, position, and attention	Locating organizational identity in transitional and potential space Awareness of self and self-other repetitions and their meaning
Group dynamics	Compromise formations: homogenized, institutionalized, autocratic, resilient group subcultures	Collection of data through observation, feedback, and confirmation Transference and countertransference dynamics	Group subculture shapes experience and sense of membership
Unthought known	Feedback and unconscious processes: "I knew that, I just never thought of it"	Attends to levels of consciousness and unconscious processes Interpretive tool for insight and change	Identity located in organizational story and its confirmation through feedback
Compulsion to repeat	Destructive and constructive forms of repetition, transference trap	Narrative structure Understanding via repetition, resistance to insight and change	Organizational identity discovered through the narrative pattern of repetitive and relational dynamics
Metaphoric processes	Frozen and fluid organizational metaphors and images	Organizational participant's use of language and its meaning for organizational identity	Articulation of experience and perception
Narcissism and leadership	Destructive and constructive: influence of power and authority on the social character of leaders and followers Holding, containing, and the intersubjective and organizational context	Role and function in organizational narrative and diagnosis Role and position defined in terms of process of executive and leadership consultation	Key element in overall experience and perceptions of organizational members The impact of leadership in shaping the organizational identity

Organization of This Book
Part One: Theory

In part 1, I explain the combined theoretical foundation for analyzing and transforming organizations rooted in relational psychoanalytic theory and organizational theory, and I present the interpretive, relational, and experiential psychoanalytic framework for organizational studies. I also explain the central psychoanalytic idea of self and organizational identity and the psychoanalytic theory of group dynamics and psychological regression.

Introduction

Chapter 1: Psychoanalytic Organizational Theory
Chapter 1 provides the articulation of a contemporary psychoanalytic organizational theory assembled around the construct of organizational identity.
It begins with a discussion of the relevance of Freud's original thinking as the
basis for a school of thought that has evolved over the last hundred years. The
chapter discussion then moves from a classical application to a contemporary
psychoanalytic application to organizations, moving from ego psychology to
object relational theory and a tripartite model that describes dialectical modes
of organizing experience and perception.

Chapter 2: Self Identity and Organizational Identity
In chapter 2, the psychoanalytic concept of organizational identity is defined
and articulated. The self-object relational interplay between membership and
separateness is key. Locating organizational identity necessitates the organizational theorist's capacity for empathy and identification with organizational
participants. It also requires learning and understanding members' experiences and perceptions. "The *sense of identity,* a subjective experience, begins with
the child's awareness that he or she exists as an individual in a world with
similar objects, but that he has his own wishes, thoughts, memories, and appearance distinct from that of others" (Moore & Fine, 1990, p. 92). This sense
of self-identity is compromised to varying degrees when individuals are employed or when they join groups, associations, and organizations.

Chapter 3: Group Dynamics
Chapter 3 discusses the key concepts of transference and countertransference,
and introduces a model or typology of defensive work groups in organizations
that captures the common phenomenon of collective psychological regression,
adults in childlike roles, in groups and organizations. A crucial differentiating
assumption of the contemporary psychoanalytic approach to the study of organizations is the hermeneutic importance placed on psychological reality and
intersubjectivity, where groups evolve and change as a consequence of unconscious compromise formations between leaders and followers.

Part Two: Key Concepts and Application
In part 2, I present key concepts and ideas of contemporary psychoanalytic
theory and their application to organizations. Each chapter develops and ap-
plies primary concepts starting with the larger idea of intersubjectivity and
potential space and followed by repetition, metaphoric processes, and the unthought known. Each idea represents a component part of the whole of relational psychoanalytic organizational theory and application.

The knowledge of organizational identity results from members' participation in an experience-near hermeneutic approach, which requires the researcher's immersion in organizational culture. This reflective inquiry elicits for the researcher the capacity to observe what is similar about organizations regardless of sector, mission, or profession as well as what is unique and peculiar to each organization. This applied relational psychoanalytic method is illustrated through the theory and application of intersubjectivity and potential space.

Chapter 4: Intersubjectivity and Potential Space

This chapter examines the idea of intersubjectivity and potential space, which is a representation of the psychoanalytic consultant's frame of reference as located between subject and object, self and other, leader and follower, supervisor and subordinate. Also known as the intersubjective third, it signifies the presence or absence of a transitional and potential space for reflective inquiry. In due course, it becomes the psychological location of organizational identity.

Intersubjectivity and potential space assist in building a competency and cognitive-emotional capacity among participants for reflectivity and consciousness of otherwise unconscious and taken-for-granted relational dynamics. I summarize a case example of a department frozen by dysfunction and conflict in this chapter to illustrate the concepts of intersubjectivity and potential space.

Chapter 5: Repetition, Remembering, and Change

This chapter examines a specific type of repetition—the compulsion to repeat. This dimension of human action is central to the interpretation of transference and countertransference dynamics in organizations. People are habitual creatures who engage in repetition and routine. Despite the mindless character and experience of repetition, it serves a defensive function against anxieties of separation and uncertainty. Organizations are designed bureaucratically and with varying degrees of routinization and rationalization of work processes. Consequently, they foster self-sealing, repetitive, and perpetual defensive actions. Bureaucratic repetition can foster a frozen-metaphor, silo mentality, as depicted in the subsequent chapter on metaphoric processes.

Chapter 6: Metaphor and Metaphoric Processes

In chapter 6, I discuss the concept of metaphor and metaphoric processes in organizations and organizational change. In particular, I discuss the commonly used silo metaphor as symptomatic of rigid and routinized unconscious organizing. I present the challenges of moving from frozen and self-sealing metaphoric processes such as silos to fluid and dynamic metaphoric states. The latter, a fluid metaphoric process, as one might imagine, lends itself to change in the status quo.

Chapter 7: *The Unthought Known*

This chapter depicts the unthought known as a conceptualization of unconscious processes in individuals and organizations. I suggest that, due to undigested and unarticulated feelings and experiences from the past, individuals and organizational participants frequently know at a preverbal emotional state of consciousness what they feel but not what they think about it. Thus, participants require an intervener or invited intruder (such as an organizational researcher or consultant) to disrupt the defensively repetitive and siloed status quo. They require someone to listen to them and assist them in articulating what they as participants know but have not thought. Feelings are not always easy to understand and contextualize. This process of gaining knowledge and insight is necessary for change and for overcoming the inclination to compulsively and unknowingly repeat the past. Emotions rooted in infancy are by their nature preverbal and therefore require formulation into language before insight into and change related to their causes can occur. Organizational identity is discovered through these experience-near processes of intervention and disruption.

Part Three: *Reflective Practice*

The final section links back the idea of organizational identity to contemporary psychoanalytic organizational theory and practice. First, I discuss the theory and practice of psychodynamic consultation, narcissism, and leadership and illustrate them with case examples. The review of narcissistic personality and leadership is a critical dimension of this book, given the inequities of power and authority in most contemporary hierarchic organizations. Next, I discuss psychodynamic executive coaching and consider the importance of context. Finally, I offer concluding thoughts on organizational identity and the psychoanalytic model of organizational research and consultation.

Chapter 8: *Narcissistic Organizational Leadership*

This chapter considers the critical role of leadership in managing the boundary between siloed subcultures and larger organizational cultures. Leadership promotes its own narrative of superiority versus inferiority, greatness versus smallness, and this social and psychological structure frequently opposes strategies for more integrative work-group processes. This chapter includes two cases of executives, first in a department of behavioral health and second in an international music and entertainment company. In both cases, I present the negative impact of destructive narcissism on management and workers and their capacity for solving problems and promoting productive change.

As a manifestation of destructive narcissism and leadership, organizational identity is intimately woven into the fabric of executive personality-in-role and the use of power and authority for abuse and intimidation rather than as a vehicle to enhance and enrich the potential of workers. In some cases leadership and organizational change is possible, while in others, change in the leader and her organization is unlikely. The departure of a leader is sometimes required for authentic and humane organizational transformation. This chapter's two cases have different outcomes.

Chapter 9: Executive Coaching: A Critical Psychoanalytic Perspective
In this chapter, I critique psychodynamic approaches to executive coaching and then offer a synthesis and an alternative rooted and contextualized in the model of organizational research and diagnosis presented here. Proceeding from earlier discussions of psychoanalytic organizational theory and self and organizational identity, I describe the work of psychodynamically oriented coaching with executive leaders.

Chapter 10: Conclusions
This concluding chapter provides an overview of the theory and practice of discovering organizational identity. I describe it as a psychodynamic process of (1) disruption, (2) confrontation, (3) demystification, and (4) transparency. I define the aim of organizational research and consultation as developing participants' conscious and unconscious awareness of relational psychodynamics at work, assuming that if participants' and leaders' levels of awareness of self-other, subject-object, relations are enhanced, they might choose to promote a healthier and more humane work environment. I also summarize key concepts and ideas.

Appendix
Finally, in an appendix I include descriptions of and suggestions for interviewing and interview protocol, writing and analyzing field notes, participant observation, categories of psychoanalytic data, and research team processing.

Part One

THEORY

In this section I explain psychoanalytic organizational theory. I discuss its developmental roots in infant attachments and the tension between membership and separateness in the first chapter. With the establishment of a theoretical foundation, chapter 2 proceeds to considering organizational identity and the meaning of organizational membership. Next, in chapter 3, I discuss the intersubjective dimension of organizational identity in the context of group dynamics. Various types of work-group dynamics take shape out of compromise formations between conflicting work-group cultures. In particular, I explore the prevalence of psychological regression in groups as a collective, defensive response to anxiety and uncertainty.

CHAPTER 1

Psychoanalytic Organizational Theory

The concept of self draws attention to the establishment of identity and its maintenance as a basic biological principle that defines a person's development. . . . A sense of identity may be inborn, but the identity structure itself—its contents—is not inborn; it is an artifact, a creation which emerges.
Loss of identity is a specifically human danger; maintenance of identity is a specifically human necessity. (Klein, 1976, p. 177)

IDENTITY IS ROOTED in our biology and in our self-construction. It is innate and psychosocial. Identity gives us coherence in what otherwise is a nonsensical universe. Identity is our barometer for assessing, consciously and unconsciously, the personal costs and demands of organizational membership. It is this balancing act that is at the thematic center of this book.

In this chapter, I explain contemporary psychoanalytic organizational theory and present it as a psychosocial organizational analysis assembled around the idea of identity. The concept of identity transcends self while defining self in a relational and intersubjective context. It assumes that at the human core of organizations is a collective sense of self residing in a *potential space*.[1] This potential space takes the form of a psychological and imagined space (some might say a psycho-geographical space) located in the mind at the boundary of self and others. Individual *introjections* and *projections*[2] of self and others (external objects) shape how individual members come to *identify themselves as belonging* to a communal group or organization. This shared identity influences members' perceptions and narratives of work and organization.

My exploration begins with Sigmund Freud's writing as the foundation for psychoanalytic theory. This school of thought has evolved among competing paradigms over the last hundred years—a point of historical fact and epistemological development often underappreciated and overlooked by organization theorists, academic psychologists, and social scientists. In that spirit,

I articulate the presence of a historical shift in psychoanalytic theory from classical psychoanalysis and ego psychology to object relational theory. There is a shift to a model of the mind, meaning, and self-concept where perception and narrative are shaped principally by internalized relational experiences beginning in infancy and early childhood.[3] While the remnants of our Freudian past persist in contemporary psychoanalytic relational, feminist, constructivist, and postmodernist theories of the twenty-first century, we find a school of thought at present that is more psychosocial than psychosexual and that is amenable to theoretical application to groups and organizations. This paradigmatic shift to object relations theory and relational psychoanalysis requires an understanding of Freud's model of mind as the historical and intellectual context and footing for contemporary thinking.

Freud's Model of Mind

In *The New Introductory Lectures on Psychoanalysis* (1933), Freud amply illustrates his model of the mind:

> The ego's relation to the id might be compared with that of the rider to his horse. The horse supplies the locomotive energy, while the rider has the privilege of deciding on the goal and of guiding the powerful animal's movement. But only too often there arises between the ego and the id the not precisely ideal situation of the rider being obliged to guide the horse along the path by which itself wants to go. (pp. 68–69)

The ego in Freud's model of mind has the most difficult of tasks. The ego (otherwise known as "I") must manage the libidinal and emotive energy of the id (known as "it") against the societal and collective conscience and guilt associated with the rules and norms of the superego (known as "I-above"). Freud's metaphor of the tension between the instinctive and powerful horse and the rational and less powerful human rider characterizes his psychodynamic view of the psyche in perpetual conflict and his notion of ego (I) as struggling to manage the instinctual and impulsive desires of the id (it) against the contextual and repressive, legal and moral, requirements of society and civilization (I-above).

In the early twentieth century, before the advances in developmental and experimental psychology, infant research and attachment theory, and brain research and neuroscience, Freud, the neurologist, understood that humans are driven by *unconscious* (repressed and beyond awareness) impulses and motivations.[4] Freud's conception of a paternal superego as a countervailing force represented society and civilization as repressive and at times punitive. These higher-order psychosocial processes come into conflict with the primitive human impulses and desires of the primordial id.

This reality presented the individual ego with the challenge of locating a state of stable equilibrium or peaceful coexistence between opposing forces of id and superego. In *Civilization and Its Discontents* (1930), Freud posits "the three sources from which our suffering comes: the superior power of nature, the feebleness of our own bodies and the inadequacy of the regulations which adjust the mutual relationships of human beings in the family, the state and society" (p. 33).

Realizing that humans must have a mechanism to relieve physical and psychological suffering, to manage conflict and the harsh demands of internal psychic and external social forces, Freud introduced the construct of the mediating ego. In his view, the ego carries a significant function, one that requires a *compromise formation,* an act in which neurotic symptoms, such as dreams, fantasies, and psychological defenses, become products of conflict. These products or outcomes of conflict signify both parties (the repressed impulse and the repressing agency) to the conflict. In *The Language of Psycho-Analysis* (1973), Laplanche and Pontalis note that Freud underlines the fact that neurotic symptoms "are the outcome of a conflict. . . . The forces which have fallen out meet once again in the symptom and are reconciled, as it were, by compromise of the symptom that has been constructed. It is for that reason, too, that the symptom is so resistant: it is supported from both sides" (p. 76).

Freud's view of ego function within the psyche is one of compromise internally and externally, and of reflexively managing (via the ego) a dilemma between opposing forces of love and hate, separateness and membership. This is the paradox of identity, and for Freud, identity itself is reflected in the symptom and is constructed by the ego/self. Similarly, the Neo-Freudian Karen Horney (1945) calls the ego's functions "neurotic solutions" to anxiety, where the ego, or self, works out a compromise or reconciliation between contrary forces from within (as in drives and desires) and without (as in societal institutions and organizations).

The threads of a paradigmatic shift from a one-person to a two-person, and relational, psychodynamic theory are sewn into the fabric of Freud's writing and theorizing, particularly in his later works. In *Group Psychology and the Analysis of the Ego* (1921), he famously states, "In the individual's mental life someone else is invariably involved, as a model, as an object, as a helper, as an opponent; and so from the very first, individual psychology, in this extended but entirely justifiable sense of the words, is at the same time social psychology as well" (p. 1). Thus, object relations and attachment theory are discernible in Freud's later writings.

Klein and Object Relations Theory

The emergence of Kleinian and post-Kleinian object relations theory (Fairbairn, 1952; Greenberg & Mitchell, 1983; Ogden, 1989, 1994; Winnicott, 1965, 1971), infant research and observation (Mahler, Pine, & Bergman, 1975; Stern, 1985), psychoanalysis and attachment theory (Fonagy, 2001), and self psychology (Atwood & Stolorow, 1984; Kohut, 1977, 1984) fashioned a change in psychoanalytic theorizing from highlighting the oedipal stage, from two and a half to six years, to illuminating the pre-oedipal stage, particularly the first eighteen months, of infant attachments, and from the biological drive and instinct model to the relational model of human encounters. Consequently, psychoanalysis, as Modell (1984) indicates, evolved from a one-person to a two-person psychology. Thus, the guiding theories for insight and change moved from predominantly individual drives and instincts to the intra- and interpersonal and intersubjective dimensions of self and the external world of objects (Fairfield, Layton, & Stack, 2002; Gedo, 1999; Mitchell & Aron, 1999). As Moore and Fine (1990) describe it, object relations theory is "a system of psychological explanation based on the premise that the mind is comprised of elements taken in from outside, primarily aspects of the functioning of other persons. This occurs by means of the process of internalization. This model of the mind explains mental functions in terms of relations between the various elements internalized" (p. 31).

The psychosocial world of object relations theory is one of *projections* and *introjections* of self and other. Through introjections we internalize and define the experience of the other; then, in response, we externalize our attribution of the other, labeling them as good or bad, accepting or rejecting. Also, the theory of object relations links the idea of *repression,* defined as the exclusion of thoughts, feelings, and events from consciousness, with nascent cognitive and emotional (infantile) defensive actions such as *psychological splitting* and *projection,* which are featured in the work of Melanie Klein and the British school of object relations theory (Bion, 1962, 1965, 1967; Fairbairn, 1952; Guntrip, 1969; Winnicott, 1965, 1971). *Psychological splitting* refers to the infant's response to the threat of anxiety and insecurity by dividing contrary emotional experiences (good vs. bad) of the other (or primary caregiver) followed by projecting onto the other absolute categories of either good or bad, loving or rejecting. Psychological splitting and projection are defensive actions that enable the self to, for example, retain a positive self-image while externalizing a bad image onto the other.

A critical feature of this theory is the assumption that the quality (secure vs. insecure) of infantile attachments carries a profound effect on the adult personality. The effects of a secure, "good enough," as opposed to an insecure and "not good enough," attachment during infancy and childhood are critical to successful maturation. One's sense of self and identity and one's capacity for intimacy are an outcome. Winnicott (1965) refers to the developmentally crucial attachment phase as the "facilitating environment."

Object relations theorists describe an internal, infantile, narcissistic world. This nascent realm of objects is composed of an emerging self and caregiving others. Cognitively and emotionally, it is described as an internal world of fragments and bits and pieces of part-objects, good and bad, loving and hating, accepting and rejecting, satisfying and depriving, which reside side by side. These irreconcilable infantile internalized processes of experience, often called "introjects," are bifurcated and split apart, with one part denied, rejected, and located via projection onto the caregiving other. Klein refers to this period of infancy and cognitive-emotional development as the "paranoid-schizoid position." Derived from her observations of children and adult patients, she described a mode of early pre-oedipal, or occurring during the first eighteen months, past experience as largely unconscious, that is, segregated from consciousness, and shaped by anxiety and defensive psychological splitting and projection.

In *Mourning and Melancholia* (2006a), Freud develops the idea that "melancholia" is associated with grief and object loss (loss, rejection, or absence of a loved one or caregiver). Influenced by Freud's paper, Klein writes of a secondary position beyond the developmentally earlier paranoid-schizoid position. She calls this second mode the "depressive position," which is understood as a representation of the child's painful nonetheless successful experience of separation as part of the developmental process of moving toward relative independence. Thus the depressive position contributes to maturation via emotional loss and the ability to mourn. Conceding the paradoxes of human development and what future psychoanalytic and developmental theorists would describe as phases of attachment, separation, and loss, Klein and later Bowlby acknowledged grief and mourning as central to the depressive experience.

On the positive flank, assuming secure attachment, at this time the young child begins to experience subjective and relatively separate objects, particularly caregiving others, as more integrated and multidimensional, both good and bad, accepting and rejecting, nurturing and depriving. In contrast with the paranoid-schizoid position, in the depressive position what earlier reflected primitive defensive processes of psychological splitting and projection, and an emotional blindness to the reality that one and the same person might be experienced as both accepting and rejecting, now appears more nuanced, integrative, and whole. In *A Dictionary of Kleinian Thought* (1991), Hinshelwood explains:

> This capacity to stand aside and observe a relationship between two objects [mother and father, for instance] requires the ability to sustain feeling left out and therefore the full impact of the oedipal pain. It is this moment, in which the capacity for love and hate is joined by the capacity to observe and know, which is one of the great characteristics of the depressive position. Thus the depressive position is more than the attaining of the Oedipus complex. It involves the capacity to begin a better knowledge of the internal and external worlds . . . (p. 64)

The application of (Kleinian and post-Kleinian) psychoanalytic object relations theory to groups and organizations highlights experiences of participants under stress and the likely defensive response of psychological regression and retreat into paranoid-schizoid and depressive positions. These defensive and psychologically regressive actions include denial, splitting, and projection. They frequently occur along horizontal and vertical organizational boundaries.[5] Object relational theorists often observe fragmentation between functional specializations, subsystems, subcultures, and professions under stress and anxiety-producing dysfunction and conflict (Diamond & Allcorn, 2003; Diamond, Allcorn, & Stein, 2004).

Klein's theory of object relations underscores our *past* infantile roots in *present moment* adulthood and ways in which these internalized past experiences surface and affect present perceptions and emotional responses to others, particularly under the influence of fear and anxiety. Whether anyone can fully know the internal world and psychological processes of infancy, a time before language, is debatable. However, Klein's observations of adult patients' relapsing into primeval and nascent thinking, fantasizing, and acting—the paranoid-schizoid position—are tangible and observable outside the privacy of the clinic and consulting room and in a global world filled with hatred and violence between ethnic, religious, and cultural large-group identities.[6] Similarly, these psychodynamics surface between managers and workers, divisions, formal and informal groups, and individuals in dysfunctional and conflict-ridden organizations. These tensions and conflicts often make up the intersubjective structure of organizational identity.

Winnicott, Object Relations, and Holding Environments

Following Klein, D. W. Winnicott's object relations theory markedly advances the primacy of the mother-and-baby milieu as a metaphor for exploring and better understanding human relations inside groups and organizations. Mitchell (1988) compares Winnicott to Freud:

> Freud measured mental health in terms of the capacity to love and work; Winnicott envisions health as the capacity for play, as freedom to move back and forth between the harsh light of objective reality and the soothing ambiguities of lofty self-absorption and grandeur in subjective omnipotence. In fact, Winnicott regards the reimmersion into subjective omnipotence as the ground of creativity, in which one totally disregards external reality and develops one's illusions to the fullest. (p. 188)

Winnicott's object relations theory stresses the crucial attachment phase and the associated *holding* relationship between mothers and babies during the first eighteen months of life.[7] Winnicott, a pediatrician and psychoanalyst, viewed maturation as a dynamic and paradoxical relationship between the emerging sense of self (self-identity) and parental caregivers in what he calls the "holding environment" (Winnicott, 1971). He discusses the holding (or facilitating) environment in terms of the quality of caregiving and secure attachment between mother (caregiver) and infant. All the details of maternal care just before birth and for the first eighteen months after birth go toward making up the holding environment. This includes the mother's primary maternal preoccupation, which enables her to provide the infant with the necessary ego support. The psychological and physical holding an infant needs throughout his development continues to be important, and the holding environment never loses its importance throughout life. The idea of "holding" is meant as physical as well as figurative. *Good enough* holding and parenting are developmental antecedents to the individual capacity for critical and reflective engagement in roles of adulthood and work organizations (see Harlow, 1958). *Good enough mothering* is Winnicott's term for the parent's capacity to provide sufficient nurturing, reliable caretaking, safety, and security, which minimize anxiety (persecutory or paranoid) and distress in the baby's experience.

For Winnicottian object relations theory and attachment theorists (see Bowlby, 1969, 1973, 1980; Fonagy, 2001; Karen, 1998), maturation and development operate along a continuum between dependency (attachment, symbiosis, and dedifferentiation) and relative independence and autonomy (separation and loss, self and other differentiation). The psychodynamics of attachment, separation, and loss are central to the emerging sense of self and thus to identity and, consequently, the meaning of internalized experiences that are commonly repressed or dissociated from consciousness. Thus, the quality of attachment plays a major role in shaping identity and self-concept in addition to affecting the individual's eventual capacity to generate a sustainable safe and secure holding environment for herself and others, a finding that has withstood the test of time (see Leffert, 2010; Jurist, Slade, & Bergner, 2008).

For Winnicott, *potential space* is located in shared experience and imagination between self and other, mother and child, family and child. Rooted in infancy and early childhood, potential space signifies the play of imagination (in mind), where curiosity, creativity, learning, culture, music, art, science, and politics take shape. Potential space is the area (psychologically speaking) between reality and fantasy, presence and absence, subjectivity and objectivity, and self and other.[8] It is the metaphoric site of self-consciousness and the so-called intersubjective third.[9]

Ogden, Post-Kleinian Object Relations, and the Dialectical Modes of Experience

Thomas Ogden's (1989) interpretation and extension of Klein's idea of the "infantile roots of adulthood" (1959) and Winnicott's concepts of potential space and the holding environment (1971) inform the theory of organizations, organizing, and organizational identity presented in this book. Ogden suggests three, rather than Klein's two, dialectical modes of experience, which shape individual perception and sense of self. He departs from some followers of Klein in conceptualizing modes of psychological organization not as structures or developmental phases, but as processes through which perceptions are imbued with meaning. These psychodynamic processes articulated by Ogden are representations of levels of consciousness, from primitive and preverbal to fragmented and parceled to complex and dialectical.

Ogden's model of consciousness and modes of organized experience begins with recognition of the depressive and paranoid-schizoid positions and describes them in terms of five interdependent dimensions, including the primary anxiety dimension and the associated defense(s), the quality of object relatedness, the degree of subjectivity, and the form of symbolization. Descriptions of these modes of relational and subjective experience and their dimensions follow.

The Depressive Mode of Experience

The *depressive mode* of experience represents the mind's capacity to contain, process, and digest emotions. Central to this task is the capability for "symbol formation proper" (Segal, 1957), in which an interpreting subject represents the object as symbol and experiences the symbolized object as other, separate and distinct from self. This mode signifies a noteworthy advance from the position of merger, symbiosis, and total dependency. In the other orientation of the depressive mode, a self-interpreting subject is able to generate revelatory space between the symbol and that which it denotes. The self is experienced as a person who thinks his or her own thoughts, and feels and assumes responsibility for them.

To the degree that one experiences oneself as a subject it is also possible to understand other people as subjects in their own right rather than as depersonalized objects. Others are seen as capable of their own thoughts, feelings, and actions. They are seen as remaining the same people over time despite momentary shifts in how one feels toward them—the essence of identity. Along with the separateness associated with holistic object relations, this continuity of experience of self and other reflects the capacity to have experience situated in time—a presence of historicity in contrast with the ahistoricity of the paranoid-schizoid position. This mode of subjectivity is also a source of anxiety. One anticipates and fears the loss of the loved one (object), who acts independently. A defensive stance characterized by denial and suppression of one's need for others sometimes provides momentary security, or the illusion of security, against separation anxiety.

The Paranoid-Schizoid Mode of Experience

In contrast, the *paranoid-schizoid mode* is characterized by one's effort to manage and evacuate, to undo and disavow cognitive and emotional pain. In so doing, psychological regression and splitting and projection of the external world into all–or-nothing categories are manifested by perceptions and experiences of partial object relations. This means that others are experienced as fragmented objects who possess different qualities at different times. The primary dilemma for the paranoid-schizoid position is managing the intolerable anxiety related to loving and hating the same person. The resulting anxiety is managed through psychological splitting and projection, where the subject separates the loving and hating aspects of oneself from the loving and hating aspects of the loved object in order to prevent the bad and endangering from destroying the good and endangered.

For example, consider the primitive fears of contamination and hatred between embattled ethnic groups as exemplifying all-or-nothing psychodynamics. Object relatedness is accomplished through splitting, projection, and *projective identification*. A facet of one-self, either the endangered or the endangering, is symbolically placed into another person or group through the process of projection and then controlled within the recipient through identification. Here one observes the psychodynamics of projection and introjection at work. The subject projects the bad and contaminated association onto "the other," and the other then internalizes and responds to the projected shadowy image by identification with it and subsequently reaction to it.

In the paranoid-schizoid mode, immediate experience eclipses both past history and the future, thereby creating an eternal, ahistorical present. There is no interpretive, potential space for reflectivity and imagination that enables the subject to differentiate the symbol from that which is symbolized or the past from the present moment. Consequently, experience is two-dimensional. The world is concrete. Everything is and can only be the single thing that it is. Nuance, degree, gradation of self-other experience are inconceivable and outside the realm of awareness, unconscious. Identity is severely threatened and fragmented by the delusion of a colorless (black or white) world lacking in nuance.

The Autistic-Contiguous Mode of Experience

In addition to the depressive and paranoid-schizoid positions described by Klein, Ogden (1989) posits a third mode of experience called the "autistic-contiguous." Ogden suggests that it is in the autistic-contiguous mode that the most elemental forms of human experience and physicality are generated. It is a pre-symbolic, sensory mode in which sensations of rhythm and "surface contiguity" (p. 32) form the core of a person's first relationships with the external object world.

The sense of touch between mother and baby characterizes this infantile position where human experience is generated by the sensation of two surfaces coming together. There is a fundamental difference between this form of relatedness and the subject-to-subject relatedness of the depressive mode and the object-to-object relatedness of the paranoid-schizoid mode. What is important about this mode of experience is that it represents the physicality of attachment and bonding manifested by the sense of "pattern, boundedness, shape, rhythm, texture, hardness, softness, warmth, coldness, and so on" (Ogden, 1989, p. 33). The primary anxiety of this mode resides in the terror generated by the disruption of the continuity of sensory experience. Ogden refers to this as "formless dread." When separated from the mother, a baby directs defensive efforts toward reestablishing a feeling of continuity and integrity of his or her surface.

Upon initial consideration, it might appear that the depressive and autistic-contiguous modes of experiencing differ in terms of degree of psychological sophistication and achievement. Yet, they are similar in that both modes of coping with primary anxiety depend upon integrative and containing processes. In the case of the autistic-contiguous mode, continuity is sensation-based, while in the depressive mode, containment is accomplished through the psychological distance afforded by language and interpretation. In contrast, disintegration and fragmentation characterize the paranoid-schizoid mode.

Both disintegrative and integrative processes are part and parcel of a dialectical tension between the three positions. This has profound relevance for understanding behavior within work organizations and organizational identity. For example, under oppressive and unilateral organizational and managerial forms of hierarchic control and unnecessarily rigid and siloed divisional boundaries, reflective and participative processes are perverted by dominance and submission. Consequently, human relations in this situation tend to collapse into a paranoid-schizoid mode of relatedness, presenting multiple splits and fragments of a broken dialectic manifesting itself with an "us against them" social structure of allies and enemies, friends and foes, presenting the observer with a dysfunctional and suspicious organization. Mending the broken dialectic of dysfunctional and conflict-ridden organizations requires understanding participants' experience and the nature of the dialectical interplay.

Experience and the Dialectical Interplay

The notion of a dialectical interplay is critical to the psychodynamic conceptualization of organizational identity and well-being. Reflective and participative processes that contribute to productive organizations require a good enough holding environment for nondefensive communication between people. The good enough holding environment of organizations typically provided by leaders facilitates a safe and supportive psychosocial space where participants can embrace and constructively confront differences and tensions rather than denying and disavowing them through splitting and projection.

In this potential space, work looks and feels like play. Workers feel safe and secure in a good enough holding environment to play with a diversity of ideas and feelings. They feel supported and encouraged to invent and exper-iment with solutions to practical puzzles of task implementation, knowledge advancement, work, and organization. Reflective practices require workers to embrace complexity and creativity, which, from a psychodynamic perspective, occurs where and when anxiety about ambiguity, uncertainty, and loss relat-ed to change is adequately *contained* by leadership. In explaining his ideas of *container* and *contained,* Wilfred Bion (1962, 1967) describes how therapists, consultants, and particularly leaders assume the role of container and have the capacity to accept the other's rejected toxic emotions and thereby to process and reflect on the origins of these bad feelings without reacting so that even-tually they can offer and articulate such emotions in order that they might be heard and understood by the originating subject.[10]

Creativity emerges out of the ongoing interplay between destructive and creative forces, as Winnicott describes in his notion of potential space. Yet, organizational effectiveness and well-being are not reserved for nor specific to the depressive mode of experience. These organizational virtues and ethics also emerge out of the potential space generated in the dialectical tension and interplay between the three modes of experience and associated levels of con-sciousness. The collapse of the dialectic, in the direction of any one of the three modes, arrests the maturational capacity for effectiveness and well-being at work by interfering with reflective and open organizational processes. Psycho-logical regression and emotional underdevelopment in the individual, group, and organization is then a danger signal for the loss of reflective, open, and participative processes.

Ogden (1989) rejects the notion of the depressive mode as the developmen-tal pinnacle of psychological maturity. Rather, he suggests that the positions are "synchronic elements of experience" (p. 11). Consequently, he understands psychological change in terms of experiential shifts among the three modes of experience. Emotional well-being is characterized by an individual with flexible interplay across the multiple modes of relatedness. These three ways of organizing experience also do not exist as pure states: the characteristics of experience in each of the three types provide context for the others; they are inextricably interdependent. In dialectical fashion, Ogden stipulates, each simultaneously "creates, preserves, and negates the other" (p. 4). Ogden's dia-lectical interplay between the three means of organizing personal encounters highlights the relational thread behind reflective processes and organizational effectiveness as well as the potential for interference in, psychological regres-sion from, and fragmentation of human relations.

Accordingly, any potential collapse and disequilibrium of the dialectical tension can lead to relational breakdown. Potential space, which is at the intersubjective heart of organizational identity, symbolizes the dialectical nature of the depressive, paranoid-schizoid, and autistic-contiguous types of experience. These experiential and relational psychodynamics promote creativity and play in response to external challenges and threats. Collapse of the tension results in the loss of potential space. Its disintegration transforms interpersonal and organizational boundaries into fragments that disrupt surface containment and evoke primitive defenses such as psychological splitting, projection, and projective identification. According to Ogden (1989),

> Collapse toward the autistic-contiguous pole generates imprisonment in the machine-like tyranny of attempted sensory-based escape from the terror of the formless dread, by means of reliance on rigid autistic defenses. Collapse into the paranoid-schizoid pole is characterized by imprisonment in a non-subjective world of thoughts and feelings experienced in terms of frightening and protective things that simply happen, and that cannot be thought about or interpreted. Collapse in the direction of the depressive pole involves a form of isolation of oneself from one's bodily sensations, and from the immediacy of one's lived experience, leaving one devoid of spontaneity and aliveness. (p. 46)

Ogden's description of collapse emphasizes that the three modes of experience form a composite of being human.

Three Modes of Organizing:
Containment, Division, and Integration

The following section explains three modes of organizing through the psychoanalytic object relational lens. These modes are paradoxical and therefore require appreciation for the relational tensions inherent among them.

Organizations and the Depressive Mode:
Containment versus Control

The generative influences of the depressive mode are evidenced in a number of ways. The depressive mode assists the organization in maintaining a competitive edge by attending to loss and disappointment across the multiple domains. These include events such as unfavorable financial outcomes and market shifts, demographic and cultural changes, and interpersonal loss due to leadership transitions and departures. Managers and employees acknowledge history but do not consider it a future determinant or a deterrent. A sense of efficacy in organizational units and employees exists in the context of interdependent personal and organizational relationships that contribute to a coherence of organizational identity. There is balanced attention to brainstorming ideas and operating pragmatics. Conflicting ideas can exist without threat of compromising relationships. Members discuss and process strong feelings rather than hiding them or acting them out. People take responsibility for their actions.

When the leadership collapses in the direction of the depressive mode, the organization exhibits characteristics that Stacey (1992) refers to as organizational "ossification." Coherence gives way to rigidity. Communication structures become formalized. The cultural ambiance becomes one of stagnation and deadness. Power is concentrated at the top. Access to those in power is tightly controlled. Those who have responsibility may not be delegated appropriate and adequate authority. The leadership enforces cultural norms and values, stifling emergent creative change.

Unsuccessful containment by leadership of followers' toxic emotions and anxieties frequently results in leaders' perceived need for disproportionate control. Innovation and changes that are plausible with containment of members' toxic emotions and anxieties are replaced by social defenses and overdetermined bureaucratic controls. The leader's capacity to adjust and adapt by managing organizational processes and external pressure deteriorates. Morale, creativity, and effectiveness are compromised, and mistrust and suspicion surface among participants.

Organizations and the Paranoid-Schizoid Mode:
Division versus Fragmentation

On the positive and constructive side, the paranoid-schizoid mode, when counterbalanced with the depressive and autistic-contiguous, contributes to efficiency and productivity through division: differentiation and decentralization of tasks and functions (splitting up work and control). Ironically, diversification and innovation are promoted by questioning tradition and productive internal rivalries. The time between idea conception and product production is short, facilitated by energized informal lines of communication. Energy, intensity, spontaneity, and a sense of competing at the cutting edge characterize the ambiance.

However, when an organization and its leadership collapse in the direction of the paranoid-schizoid and an imbalance or disequilibrium results, idealization of the leadership, envy, and suspicion shape work relationships. Conflict and confrontation may be suppressed and replaced by acts of scapegoating and blaming. These psychodynamics typically promote toxic and uncontained emotions, and differences become polarized. Organizational dysfunction is likely, particularly where individual leaders and followers avoid personal responsibility. Employees defensively flee, the leadership makes mistakes, and people conceal errors. This makes it difficult for organizational members to learn from experience. The culture becomes one of mistrust, suspicion, and polarization.

Organizations and the Autistic-Contiguous Mode:
Integration versus Isolation

The primary contribution of the autistic-contiguous mode of experience on organizational functioning is maintenance of a sense of stability, cognitive and emotional integration, and grounding in the face of problems and change. One might say the feeling of a secure organizational attachment, an adhesive identification, is a critical element of the autistic-contiguous mode (Ogden, 1989, p. 71). Participants are able to enter the flow and natural rhythm of work. Tacit knowledge and reflective learning become more typical where people have a feeling for the work as well as for one another. The autistic-contiguous mode, when in harmony with the other two modes of experience, contributes to an organizational identity where work is experienced as creative and productive play.

Collapse into the autistic-contiguous produces separation anxieties among members resulting from the leadership's inability to provide a good enough holding environment that contains toxic emotions. Members feel an insecure attachment, a loss of structural and personal integration, and a sensation of falling with no net to catch and protect them. Organizational leaders and followers drift toward chaos and a sense of vulnerability from within and without. They may feel powerless and disconnected from their roles, work, each other, and their organizational identity.

Organizational leadership that collapses into the autistic-contiguous mode may use mimicry to make use of the surface identity of another object to replace its own identity. The leadership may resist mergers that are a violation of organizational boundaries with the external world regardless of rationale. The leadership may selectively maintain *pressure* to continually meet deadlines in the service of producing a self-defining surface to experience. Driven by organizational leaders, members may compulsively operate in crisis mode to create some sense, however false, of organizational identity.

In sum, the three dialectical modes of experience facilitate a deeper inspection of organizational leadership, dysfunction, and perversions of reflective and open systemic processes. When balanced, these three modes of experience support individual, interpersonal, group, and organizational potential space in which reality testing, creativity, trust, mutual respect, and fair play are cultural ideals. Breakdown among leaders and followers of this dialectical tension, in the form of polarized and fragmented object relations, perverts reflective and participative values and practices. Collapse, which is akin to psychological regression, into any one of the three modes of experience produces outcomes that can be reconciled by reflective and conscious leaders who understand the value of restoring and maintaining a good enough holding environment for members. Such reparative responses require leaders who contain (in Bion's sense of the word) participants' anxiety and thereby minimize psychological regression and disequilibrium. One might say the psychological capacity for holding and containment defines effective and humane leadership as a critical element of constructive organizational identity.

Next, this chapter concludes with a discussion of psychoanalytic data and the study of organizations.

The Application of Relational Psychoanalytic Theory and Data

The psychoanalytic study of organizations is frequently a historical and narrative depiction, formulated from months of fieldwork, data collection, and participant observation with organizational members and their leadership. Harry Levinson refers to this practice of storytelling as the product of organizational assessment—a participant-observational act of immersion and diagnosis (Diamond, 2003; Levinson, 1972, 2002).

In the present account of organizational diagnosis and assessment, I pay attention to the intersubjective structure or relational patterns of organizing. These are located at the symbolic hub of the multilayered model of organization (see figure 2 in chapter 2), which I discuss in chapter 2. The theory and method of organizational diagnosis that I describe throughout this book represents a shift from the practice of interpretation toward a focus on relational psychodynamics (Hoffman, 1998; Meissner, 1991; Summers, 2013). This shift highlights that the practice of interpretation requires a foundation and grounding in the context of intersubjective experience. Discovering organizational identity necessitates observation, participation, experience, and a reliance on the self (countertransference) as an instrument of organizational research. In sum, this perspective relies on observation and interpretation of intersubjectivity embedded in the experience of organizational membership.

At the heart of the relational approach to organization study is the practice of collecting psychoanalytic data. The distinction from nonpsychodynamic and behavioral theories and other methods of organizational research is that attention is paid to psychological (or psychic) reality and intersubjective experience. *Transference* and *countertransference* between action researchers and organizational participants is a focus of discovering organizational identity (Diamond & Allcorn, 2003, 2009; Hunt, 1989; Levinson, 1972, 2002).

Transference and countertransference psychodynamics signify the presence of shared emotions. *Transference* refers to an individual's unconscious displacement of emotions from childhood attachments in the past onto someone in the present, and *countertransference* refers to the other's unconscious experience and possible reaction to the individual's original transference of emotions, particularly when they are in unequal positions of power and authority. For instance, these concepts encourage researchers/consultants to ask: What emotions are participants projecting onto us in our roles as researchers and consultants? What emotions are we as researchers returning to the participants as a consequence of the role relationship? Do the participants see the consultants as spies or saviors? How are the consultants reacting to these attributions? Can the consultants understand why participants view them in one manner or another?

This methodological approach assists in answering the question "What is it like to work here?" Thus, in addition to environmental, structural, strategic, and cultural levels of organizational analysis (illustrated in figure 2), psychoanalytic data lead researchers into the core of organizational identity. These data include (1) historical (narrative) data, (2) observational data, (3) associative (intersubjective) data, (4) experiential (transference) data, and (5) empathic (countertransference) data (Kohut, 1984; Meissner, 1991; Ricoeur, 2012), which the reader may choose to remember by using the initialism HOAEE. These data and their collection are a significant point of distinction between this approach and the nonpsychoanalytic approaches found in the management and organization literature.

Historical data can tell us a lot about leadership and organizations. Organizational history covering critical incidents and transformations is frequently documented in news periodicals and other historical documents. There are typically historical records of critical events and relational dynamics surrounding the actions, decisions, policies, and strategies of past and present leaders. More significantly, there are the perceptions and experiences of these historical events narrated by organizational members—their memories, or reconstructions of the past in the present moment. These data are then shaped and interpreted by participant storytellers and documented by action researchers acting as empathic listeners and ethnographers. These narrative texts often convey more than a set of events that define a particular organization and its leaders. These texts can convey the reasons, meanings, motivations, and perceptions of organizational members as well. Organizational history as a form of story-telling, much like the essence of organizational identity itself, is located in the potential space between objective reality and fantasy, subject and object, self and other.

As personal history is retold in the analytic relationship, organizational history is reconstructed out of the relationship between two subjects, organizational researchers and members, and members and their leaders. These narratives are created in the potential space in the relational mind, where play and imagination reside. It is the experiential dimension where we live and work. While organizational history might capture certain facts and artifacts, it offers valuable perceptual and experiential insights as well. From a psychoanalytic perspective, these data contribute to our overall picture of psychological (psychic) reality, representing a fragment of the *actual* meaning and identity at work.

Observational data encompass a good portion of what is found. How one understands the meaning of these data is what actually matters. Understanding comes through articulation of observations, interpretations, and dialogue with organizational members, who are the ultimate arbiter of the meaning of observations and experiences. Interpretations must make sense to organizational participants. Observations beyond mere descriptions, while coming closest to the behaviorist's notion of facts, are given meaning by interpretation in the context of a relationship between researcher/consultant and research subject/client.

Psychoanalytic organizational researchers and consultants, immersed in organizations, listen deeply and observe, paying attention to their own reveries, "streams of consciousness," and "free associations." Of course this *associative data* is a tricky matter as organizational members must be sufficiently candid with researchers, who are typically experienced as "invited intruders."[11] Organizational members might respond defensively or suspiciously if asked by a researcher, "So, what comes to mind as you reflect on your work?" Associative, or intersubjective, data are valuable and ought to be considered in their representation of meaning and experience in any organizational setting. One might consider a psychoanalytic version of focus groups as a safe and nonthreatening potential space and holding environment in which researchers ask group members to free associate: "Tell us what comes to mind as you reflect on your work groups, formal roles, and organizational identities."

Experiential, or *transference, data* are also central to understanding how psychoanalytically oriented researchers and consultants work, and how they transcend the epistemological limitations of behaviorist and neo-positivist views that tend to objectify and quantify organizational phenomena. Talk is more than chatter. Being aware of researchers' own experiences as well as those of organizational members is critical for sorting out the relational psychodynamics and the ways in which organizational participants use researchers and consultants as objects of projection and projective identification.

Finally, *empathy, introspection,* and *countertransference data* are critical for organizational diagnosis as these data provide access to our own and to the participant's experience of organizational identity. Empathy involves forms of communication that enhance our capacity to more deeply understand and identify with the subjective experiences and perceptions of organizational members and their leaders. "For Freud, empathy was central to the interpretive process since it provided access of another's mental life that was different from one's own (Freud 1921)" (Meissner, 1991, p. 90). The use of empathy and countertransference data draws a vivid distinction between psychoanalytic and nonpsychoanalytic approaches.

Conclusion

The application of post-Kleinian relational psychoanalytic theory is the overarching framework for discovering organizational identity. Each case illustration offered in this book is considered in light of the object relational model and is intended to assist in illuminating the observations and experiences of working with organizations. The application of theory draws on psychoanalytic data and is considered in the context of the multilayered model of organization discussed in the following chapter. Articulating organizational identity as a representation of "we-ness" takes into consideration the dynamic and ever-changing psychological compromise faced by leaders and followers who attempt to balance demands for membership against separateness, and belonging against independence. In the next chapter, I examine the psychoanalytic concept of organizational identity and contextualize it in a multilayered model of organization.

CHAPTER 2

Self Identity and Organizational Identity

Identity must always be defined as having aspects of both separateness and membership in a more encompassing entity, and as developing functions that reflect one's role in and relationship to that larger entity.

This aspect of identity—we-ness—has its earliest prototype in the mother-child unit . . . from this symbiosis emerges a feeling of being part of a larger identity. (Klein, 1976, p. 179)

Humankind's archetype of personality and organization is embodied in the mother-child unit. One cannot begin to comprehend the paradox of human nature and contemporary organizational life without an appreciation of our socio-emotional roots in infantile attachment. It is humanity's collective home base, which signifies an extended period of profound dependency. Winnicott (1965) calls this symbiotic beginning "the facilitating environment."

Out of this deep relationship both the sense of self and the external object world are shaped and defined. The original tension between self and other, subject and object, transfers into the individual organizational member and the formal organization, where it is characterized in roles and relationships of power, authority, responsibility, leadership, and followership. These organizational dynamics are rooted in the Winnicottian "holding environment" and influence the inevitable tensions and paradoxes of membership and separateness, fit and misfit, cooperation and confrontation, learning and change against defensiveness and resistance to insight.

In this chapter, self and self-identity are explained and linked to organizational identity. The understanding of identity and its psychological roots is critical in the application of a contemporary relational psychoanalytic theory for understanding human groups and organizations. Following the discussion of self, self-identity, and organizational identity, this chapter concludes with a description of the multilayered model of organizations as an important context for the psychodynamic study of organizations.

Introduction to Self-Identity

For the most fundamental prerequisite of mental vitality, I have already nominated a *sense of basic trust,* which is a pervasive attitude toward oneself and the world derived from the experiences of the first year of life. By "trust" I mean an essential trustfulness of others as well as a fundamental sense of one's own trustworthiness. (Erikson, 1968, p. 96)

Best known for advancing the concept of identity and the life cycle as paradoxical in that every stage in the life cycle entails contradictory values and subjective experiences, which he views as developmental crises, Erik Erikson pioneered in his ego psychology the emphasis placed on secure attachment in the first year of life as critical to healthy development and maturation (Baum, 1987; Schwartz, 2005). For Erikson, identity is shaped by these developmental crises, beginning with trust versus mistrust. Each stage manifests a new and different thematic crisis requiring some degree of reconciliation. It is in the principal, early-attachment phase where a crisis between basic trust (secure attachment) and basic mistrust (insecure attachment) affects the nascent self and the emerging capacity to provide care for and to feel cared for by others. The sense of self is constructed in a relational world where maternal and parental sensitivity and emotional attunement are vital.

As noted above, this rudimentary attachment is central to what Winnicott (1971) calls the initial "holding environment," the original union between mother (parent) and child. Beginning with attachment and moving toward separation and relative autonomy, this symbiotic relationship establishes the cognitive and emotional structure and stage for maturation and the developing and evolving sense of self. If "good enough," this journey takes the child from a position of total dependency on caregivers to relative independency with a core sense of self or self-identity. This sense of self subsequently influences formal and informal roles and relationships in the workplace.

Identity is defined as the relatively enduring, "but not necessarily stable, experience of the self as a unique, coherent, entity over time. The *sense of identity,* a subjective experience, begins with the child's awareness that he or she exists as an individual in a world with similar outer objects, but that he has his own wishes, thoughts, memories, and appearance distinct from that of others"

(Moore & Fine, 1990, p. 92). This sense of identity is tested and compromised to varying degrees throughout the life cycle, as noted in Erikson's psychosocial stages of development. In adulthood, self-identity is uniquely challenged when individuals join groups, associations, and innumerable organizations. However, to say members' identities are compromised in the act of joining organizations requires further explanation.

The quality and integrity of the original attachment and psychosocial space signified by the relationship between child and mother is developmentally and characteristically momentous for the maturation of the individual and for the individual's sense of self. Thus, the quality of this bond is critical to the development of one's capacity to reconcile needs and demands for membership and affiliation against desires for separateness and individuality. In sum, maternal (and, more generally, parental) holding is the infantile developmental and relational precursor to joining, following, and leading in organizations.

From an applied psychoanalytic perspective, identity (and sense of self) is persistently engaged in the social realm of the other(s), what psychoanalysts call the object world, and so individuals are perpetually changing while retaining a sense of continuity (ego- or self-integrity). Put differently, the nature of this change is in the quality and character of the individual compromise between one's countervailing needs for independence and belonging, separateness and membership. The heuristic power of the concept of identity as it relates to our gaining a deeper understanding of individuals in the object world of groups and organizations is untold. While the notion of organizational identity is discussed and applied throughout this book, for now it is critical to convey its explanatory value as an organizing principle and construct, which is revealing when we are engaged in the study of organizations. I am following the lead of Freud and Bion in the next chapter, on group dynamics, when I state that when individuals join groups and organizations, some degree of psychological regression is inevitable. Self-identity is relatively steady while capable of compromising and adaptation.

From Self-Identity to Organizational Identity

"We" identities are also part of the "self." A sense of identity implies that one experiences an overall sameness and continuity extending from the personal past (now internalized in introjects and identifications) into a tangible future; and from the community's past (now existing in traditions and institutions sustaining a communal sense of identity) into foreseeable or

41

imaginable realities of work accomplishment and role satisfaction. (Erikson, 1964, p. 53)

The concepts of self-identity and organizational identity are, along with numerous other psychoanalytic ideas, relevant to a non-objectified study of organizations. What I refer to as a "non-objectified" study is intended to critique the positivist, rationalist, and behaviorist position and at the same time legitimize the study of subjectivity at the heart of organizational participants' experiences and perceptions that shape feelings and actions. These individual and collective experiences and perceptions, the relational psychodynamics of organizing, must be known and articulated in the discovery of organizational identity.

The concept of organizational identity is an idea critical to understanding the psychodynamics of organizations and the challenges of transformation and change in them. Decades ago, I started asking a question of doctoral students and fellow organizational researchers/consultants working in the field. This question, I believe, is key when doing fieldwork and immersed in organizational culture and engaged with organizational members: "What is it like to work here?" On the surface, this question is unremarkable, but it is central to locating the core of organizational identity. It is a query that psychoanalytic organizational consultants ought to silently reflect on as they observe, listen deeply, experience, free associate, identify, and empathize with organizational members, and as they try to understand the human subject at work and at play.

While interpretation is a component of studying organizations psychodynamically, as the reader will discover, the approach presented here is not interpretation-centric. Notwithstanding the use of relational psychoanalytic concepts and definitions, it should also become clear that as scholars we are in a perpetual search for language and for the best articulation of theory and process. From the perspective of qualitative organizational action research, the psychoanalytic study of organizations embraces empathy and identification, and pays attention to the knotted emotions of transference and countertransference dynamics.

Empathy, Identification, Transference, and Countertransference
The intent in asking the question "What is it like to work here?" is to understand the personal meaning and experience of joining and affiliating with a specific organization and of locating self, what Winnicott (1971) calls "true self" and "false self," within the context of an organization. *True self* refers to authenticity and relative autonomy of self, while *false self* refers to a compliant

self where excessive dependency of self on others or on objects, such as hierarchies and authorities, is predominant.

In claiming to have knowledge of an actual organization, one needs to know via psychological processes of *identification* how membership affects one's sense of self and how one's sense of self influences membership. Is one's sense of self enlarged and expanded, or is it diminished and suppressed? In the perspective put forth here, one of exploring organizational identity and fully and deeply interpreting visible organizational dynamics, organizational scholars aim to know how members *internalize* and *incorporate* relational and collective experience. What is the meaning of these internalizations and incorporations of organizational life?

Internalization and *incorporation* refer to the manner in which the self is organized around experiences, the process of taking in and making sense of experiences, feelings, and assumptions about others as subjects. In particular, early experiences shape our internal object world through psychological processes of internalization and incorporation of external object relationships. Ultimately, this line of inquiry has to facilitate the organizational analyst's reflective capacity for *empathy* and *identification* via countertransference with organizational participants.[1]

Behind this simple and yet complex question, "What is it like to work here?" is the supposition that organizational scholars value participants' experiences and perceptions within a context where they may feel unrecognized and not listened to. Thus, attending to this question assumes, if not demands, researcher sincerity and authenticity. It necessitates a healthy dose of naiveté and open-mindedness on behalf of researchers and consultants that is vital for self-consciousness and attention to transference and countertransference, as well as projection and introjection. This is essential for exploring human organizations and discovering organizational identity. It is also absent in most of the management- and organization-theory literature on organizational identity.

As noted in the previous chapter, transference and countertransference feelings are those everyday emotions and images projected on and triggered by relations with others. These projected and introjected emotions and images are shaped in part by past experience rooted in childhood and adolescence and then sparked by others in the present moment. Such memories are reconstructed in the present moment and come to shape how individuals think and feel about the *subjective* other. This application of psychoanalytic ideas demands consciousness of assumptions and beliefs, not for purposes of suppression, denial, and disavowal, defensive maneuvers that rendered them unconscious in the first place, but to assist consultants in making human contact and developing *empathy for* and *identification with* organizational members. Without doing so one cannot genuinely claim personal knowledge[2] and understanding of organizational membership, nor can one locate organizational identity.

Empathy and *identification* are used in combination here to describe psychological processes and relational dynamics that, when rendered conscious, enable psychoanalytically oriented action researchers to deeply understand and feel the position or predicament of the other. *Identification* refers to the psychosocial processes and relational dynamics of identifying with organizational leaders who represent the meaning of organizational membership (or followership). As noted above, the idea of organizational identity presented here differs from its application in most organization and management theory. The definition of *organizational identity* presented throughout this book is intended to indicate a deeper, more meaningful and substantial concept as it holds true to the original Eriksonian and psychoanalytic idea of identity and identification.

As illustrated previously, the relational psychoanalytic concept of organizational identity is derived from object relations theory and the emergence of self and self-identity out of the symbiotic relationship between mother and baby— what Erikson viewed as the original and profound tension between trust and mistrust, and what Winnicott describes as the facilitating environment. From a psychoanalytic framework, identity comprises a perpetual tension between self (as subject) and other (as object, such as the form and meaning of organizational membership). While resembling on the surface the social constructionist view of organizational identity as interactive and socially constructed, the psychoanalytic concept of organizational identity, in contrast, takes into account the unconscious processes of psychological regression, compromise formation, and intersubjectivity. Moreover, and critically, I see organizational identity as evolving out of the role and function of transference and countertransference psychodynamics between individual members, their organizations, and leaders.

It is also important to note that the definition of *organizational identity* proposed here is not only based on psychoanalytic concepts of mind and meaning but founded on psychoanalytic data (discussed later in this chapter), which include historical and narrative data, observational data, associational data, experiential data, and empathic and introspective data (HOAEE).

These data are derived by entering the field and immersing oneself into the organization—what is called "experience-near" as opposed to "experience-distant" methodology.

Organizational Identity and Management

Organizational identity is a concept in the management- and organization-theory literature discussed and applied from the vantage points of institutional theory and social constructionist theory. In the former, organizations are influenced by normative pressures arising from external sources as well as the organization itself. Organizational identity is described as something defined by the organization and tends to be a top-down, hierarchic structure of organizational identification (Ravasi & Schultz, 2006). In contrast, the social constructionist perspective assumes that organizational identity emerges out of the interactions between social actors and is constantly renegotiated (Scott & Lane, 2000).[3] For Humphreys and Brown (2002), efforts of senior managers to control processes of organizational-identity formation and participant identification are hegemonic acts of legitimation.[4] Many management and organization theorists assume that strategy, structure, leadership, and culture shape participants' identities. Marketing and branding to the environment along with internal strategies reinforce members' compliance and adaptation to the demands and expectations of leadership. Thus organizational identity comes to be viewed as a bridge joining organizational values and individual members (Brown, Dacin, Pratt, & Whetten, 2006; Hatch & Schultz, 2002; Ravasi & Schultz, 2006; Scott & Lane, 2000; Whetten, 2006).[5] For some management and organization theorists, organizational identity is an instrumental and manipulative tool for management coercion and control over subordinates.

Scott and Lane (2000) define organizational identity as "the set of beliefs shared between top managers . . . and stakeholders about the central, enduring and distinctive characteristics of an organization" (p. 44). Whetten (2006) describes it as "the central and enduring attributes of an organization that distinguish it from other organizations . . . signifying an organization's self-determined (and 'self'-defining) unique social space and reflected in its unique pattern of binding commitments" (p. 220). While these varied perspectives on organizational identity are descriptive, instructive, and credible in the study of organizational dynamics, they are similar to other scholars' applications of the concepts of organizational culture and socialization as encompassing values and underlying assumptions, or governing ideologies (Kunda, 1992; Schein, 1985).[6] I agree with most of their observations, with the caveat that highly significant psychodynamic factors intimately associated with self-identity and organizational identity are absent.

These versions of organizational identity do not sufficiently treat the organizational member as multidimensional with an internal world of psychological tensions and processes of self-organization. These tensions and processes shape the character of individual affiliation and social relations at work. Nor do these theories of organizational identity adequately acknowledge and embrace the contradictory and paradoxical nature of self and of the individual internal struggle between separation (independence) and membership (belonging). Conventional management and organization theories do not fully acknowledge the internal psychosocial world of individuals, which is problematic when using the concept of organizational identity.[7] Notions of embodied cognition and the like, such as that found in the work of Harquail and King (2010), who discuss emotions and embodied knowledge in their notion of the role of embodied cognition in organizational identity, do not quite capture the essence of organizational identity rooted in the unconscious emergence and evolution of the self.

Gioia, Schultz, and Corley (2000) argue that "the seeming durability of identity is actually contained in the stability of the labels used by organization members to express who or what they believe the organization to be, but the meaning associated with these labels changes so that identity actually is mutable" (p. 64). The authors offer one of the more interesting interpretations of organizational identity and the relationship between identity and image; however, this article displays a fundamental flaw in its conception of organizational identity. Behavioral and cognitive changes are insufficient and do not constitute identity change, they are merely evidence of defensive maneuvers and practices. These defensive acts may or may not serve organizational adaptation. This approach merely reinforces the emergence of a compliant false self among organizational participants. In addition, it exhibits organizational theories that inadequately distinguish between symbols (as things in themselves) and what they symbolize, such as labels and their signification of the ruling ideology or belief system rather than actual identity. These theories differ from the main idea of this book, that self-identity is rooted in attachment and intersubjectivity.

Self-identity originates in authenticity and spontaneity, what Winnicott (1971) calls the "true self" emerging out of the "good enough" holding environment. In adulthood and organizational membership, true self is typically repressed and unconscious. True self resides behind a fortress of defensive strategies and self-sealing processes, hidden underneath a compliant false self.

The false self is preoccupied with adaptation, interpersonal security, and minimization of anxiety. Gioia, Schultz, and Corley's notion of identity represents a falsification of true self-identity and of the perpetual tension between membership and separateness.

In addition, managements' interest in organizational identity as reported in some of the management and organization literature indicates a strategic, instrumental, and technical rational approach. Alvesson and Willmott (2002), who apply the concept of identity to explain organizational control and to theorize on methods of employees' liberation from these constraints, show how the regulation of identity becomes a framework for examining organizational control. The authors consider how employees are ordered to develop self-images and work orientations considered harmonious with managerially defined objectives.

This technical rational approach contradicts the Kantian moral philosophical tradition, which influenced Freud's original writings (Ricoeur, 2012; Summers, 2013; Tauber, 2013) and has shaped the moral and ethical sensitivities of many of his psychoanalytic associates. To paraphrase the second formulation of Kant's categorical imperative: individuals should not be encountered simply as a means to an end; rather, they should be treated as an end in and of themselves. It appears that not only the theorizing of Freud but also the ideas of Klein and neo-Kleinians such as Winnicott and Ogden are influenced by Kantian ethics. The Kantian categorical imperative, however limited by its admittedly unrealistic, exceedingly rational view of human nature, underscores the analyst's framing of the more mature and structurally integrated depressive position in object relations theory. Thus the depressive mode of mature experience is akin to Winnicott's idea of a true self. In this state, individuals maintain the capacity for genuineness and authenticity and, critically, they perceive the other as subject in her own right rather than simply as an objectified and externalized other.

Self-awareness shaped by the Kleinian depressive position fosters acknowledgment of a commingling of good and evil, love and hate, acceptance and rejection, presence and absence. With self-consciousness and reflectivity, empathy and identification are plausible in the depressive mode. Compare this to the less mature, psychologically regressive and defensive paranoid-schizoid position, with its more primitive object-to-object relationships characterized by a Manichean and Machiavellian world of manipulation and instrumental regard. This state of affairs might be anticipated and developmentally appropriate during childhood and adolescence, but it is problematic, destructive, and cognitively and emotionally narrow and immature in adulthood. Ironically, such amoral strategic and tactical instrumental relations are a cornerstone of twenty-first-century American politics and the power structures inside and outside of many public and private organizations.

From a critical[8] psychoanalytic perspective, one observes that the idea of organizational identity is frequently used by management for potentially coercive and manipulative reasons, which buttress what Winnicott (1971) calls a "compliant false self" among subordinate organizational participants and an unnecessarily divisive and exceedingly oppressive and defensive organization. From this critical perspective, organizational identity is observed to be used as a managerial tool of dominance over workers, where a false sense of interpersonal security and minimal anxiety cost workers' self-integrity and morale. It is precisely these dominant-submissive, oppressive hierarchic organizational dynamics that a contemporary psychoanalytic critique exposes in the interests of restoring respectful and humane relations at work.

From this psychoanalytic perspective, the definition and understanding of organizational identity transcends what at times is a one-dimensional, superficial, and instrumental treatment of workers, one that proffers no deeper explanation or understanding than an accounting of personnel, salary, budget, structure, policies, and strategic plans. Other approaches offer more promise in paying attention to organizational language and images, which leads to interesting descriptions and explanations of subordinate behavior. However, their analyses, for the most part, are not sufficiently rooted in the psychosocial concept of identity. Consequently, they rarely, if ever, address the actual relational, experiential, perceptual, and psychological reality of organizational members. It is the members' feelings and actions that affect, often deeply, fellow workers, and that subsequently impact the external environment of clients, customers, constituents, institutions, and democratic societies.

In contrast to what at times seems like a one-dimensional and Machiavellian view taken by management and organization theorists, when framed psychodynamically, organizational identity focuses on the inherent relational structure of intersubjectivity that shapes and defines members' experience and meaning of organizational affiliation and selfhood. The model put forth in this book describes a psychodynamic relationship rooted in meaning and memory, and comprising tension and conflict surrounding membership and separateness, belonging and independence. These pressures provide insights into organizational identity and the query "What is it like to work here?"

The Case for a Contemporary Relational Psychoanalytic Perspective

Why employ a contemporary relational psychoanalytic vision of organizations?[9] Simply put, *to know* organizations below their surfaces, deeply and at different levels of consciousness. Accordingly, and in contrast, by means of *empathy* and *identification,* one experiences, listens to, and observes participants inside of and interacting through their organizational roles. To understand organizations by paying attention to experience, listening deeply (Stein, 1994), and observing, one must immerse oneself in organizational dynamics. In the process, psychoanalytic organizational theorists articulate in field notes and recordings their own experiences of organizational entry (boundary maintenance), participation, and observation as a vehicle for learning about and publicly testing assumptions of the meaning of organizational members' lives and experiences at work. Organizational researchers then translate and depict via their observations, associations, and experiences of members, the structure of intersubjectivity at the heart of organizational identity. This hermeneutic, ethnographic, psychodynamic method of immersion and participant observation for studying organizations is simultaneously complex and concrete.

This book offers a perspective well grounded in clinical theory and drawn from over three decades of psychoanalytic research, writing, case studies, teaching, and consultation with work groups and organizations. It illustrates the relational psychoanalytic theory's depth and complexity in illuminating organizational culture and politics. Psychoanalytic organizational theory and practice is essentially the exploration and articulation of human experience and relational psychodynamics in an organizational context.

Thus, this theoretical framework for studying organizations demands larger context and a conceptual appreciation of systemic complexity. Holding in mind the multiple levels of analysis in which organizations are placed is critical and needs to be addressed before going any further. This transition is clarified by the multilayered model.

Organizational Analysis and the Multilayered Model

A twenty-first-century psychoanalytic approach offers organizational scholars an alternative to neo-positivist, nomothetic, quantitative, objectified, and physically and emotionally distant treatments of organizations and their presumedly one-dimensional members. Through the lens of the psychoanalytic concept of organizational identity, scholars are encouraged to apply an idiographic, qualitative, and psychodynamic approach to living, breathing, paradoxical human beings in organizations. Rather than representing a retreat from the human sciences and moving away from human subjectivity and turning a blind eye to the beating heart of human experience, the application of relational psychoanalytic theory signifies an engagement with and a moving toward the organization as an organizing, partially conscious and partially unconscious, collective human subject in action.[10]

What is needed for understanding organizations in depth is a conceptual model that adequately represents and captures the complexity of organizations and organizational processes at multiple levels of analysis that may include psychosocial dimensions. The multilayered model shown in figure 2 illustrates how organizations can be conceptualized, from the psychosocial framework to the larger environmental and political complexity of institutions and human organizations in action. This model provides a comprehensive conceptual framework of the complex milieu of human organizational dynamics, a framework that I sometimes regard as incomplete in other scholars' conceptualizations.

FIGURE 2 Multilayered Model of Organization

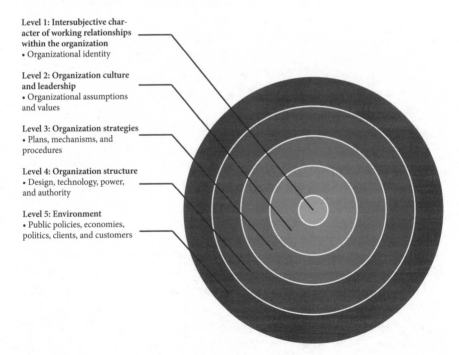

Level 1: Intersubjective character of working relationships within the organization
• Organizational identity

Level 2: Organization culture and leadership
• Organizational assumptions and values

Level 3: Organization strategies
• Plans, mechanisms, and procedures

Level 4: Organization structure
• Design, technology, power, and authority

Level 5: Environment
• Public policies, economies, politics, clients, and customers

At the core of the multilayered organization is the construct of organizational identity. This is where things relational and organizational are born and where things organizational and relational can go astray. The idea of organizational identity is at the heart and mind of organizations. It comprises a web of relational and intersubjective dynamics between participants who are engaged consciously and unconsciously in managing boundaries of self and other, leader and follower, and group and organization, as well as culture, strategy, structure, and environment. At the core, organizational identity is observed and experienced in participants' sense of "we-ness"—a collective sense of being a part of something simultaneously transcending oneself and confirming one's sense of self—a move from ego-ness to we-ness and object relatedness.

An Introduction to the Multilayered Model of Organization

A description of the multilayered organizational model starts at the external environment (level 5) and draws inward, toward the core of organizational identity (level 1). In the model, information and communication move across all five surfaces and boundaries of organization. Often called the "task environment," the external environment (level 5) of the organization is located at the boundary's edge, where the organization and its leaders engage markets, economies, public policies, strategic partners, competitors, clients, citizens, and customers. This is often where leaders assess complexity and strategize effective adaptive tactics to manage constant change and to sustain organizational power with respect to key actors in the environment. Thus, the next two layers of organizational action, structure and strategies, are critical to success and are intimately linked one to the other.

Structure (level 4) comprises the organizational design and technology that function as a vehicle for effectively or ineffectively delivering and implementing goals (level 3) manifested in strategic plans and procedures. In best-case scenarios, strategies (level 3) shape and reshape structures of organization (level 4). However, one frequently finds that organizational structures and hierarchies are antiquated and unnecessarily bureaucratized and rigidified, rendering strategizing for constant change unimaginative, inflexible, insufficiently reflective, and compulsively repetitive. People often take organizational structures (level 4) for granted and are resistant to changing them. Leadership's use of strategies and structures too often reinforces inordinate power and authority at the top of the hierarchic structure. This results in inadequate distribution of power and authority to competently trained and educated workers, which negatively affects service delivery and operations.

Strategy and structure (levels 3 and 4) are artifacts of leadership (level 2). At level 2, organizational culture, the collective and taken-for-granted espoused values and assumptions of the organization and its leadership are located. Organizational culture evolves from the ideology of its historical founders and is carried forward by current leadership. At the boundaries of organizational culture (level 2) one frequently observes the contradictions and inconsistencies between what members (particularly managers and executives) say and what they do in practice. The differences between the espoused theories of action and the actual theories in use are visible when one attends to the contrasts and contradictions in the language of espoused practices and beliefs against the actual practices and actions taken by organizational leaders and members.

It is critical to understand the belief systems of organizations and the nature of professionalization, socialization, and acculturation (level 2) that are part and parcel of what it means to be a member of the organization. This represents mainstream conceptualizations of organizational identity. Organizations are unique despite sharing common missions and goals. They often comprise subcultures (level 2) with different technical and disciplinary languages as well as different epistemological and professional assumptions about knowledge, power, and truth. Assumptions, values, and artifacts often reflect the character of leadership and leader-follower relations. Expansive and narcissistic leaders, for example, have their strengths and weaknesses, and the degree to which these leaders are self-conscious and self-aware may make a difference in their capacity to interrupt potentially destructive and harmful patterns of behavior.

From Organizational Culture to Organizational Identity

Understanding and assessing organizations requires a psychodynamic framework akin to that found in Nancy Chodorow's feminist psychoanalytic theorizing. In *The Power of Feelings* (1999), Chodorow comments,

> Contemporary psychodynamic ethnographers rely on traditional psycho-dynamic and emotional categories and are less exclusively interested in language than are the anthropologists of self and feeling. They are certainly a step ahead of thinkers who hold that only the social and cultural side of life matters and who ignore the personal, emotional realm. (p. 186)

From the framework of the multilayered model, organizational identity (level 1) consists of unconscious relational patterns discovered by way of historical, observational, associative (intersubjective), experiential (transference), and empathic (countertransference) data. Our capacity to articulate the meanings and motivations behind organizational members' actions and feelings is derived out of researchers' awareness of these psychosocial dynamics between action researchers and organizational participants, leaders and followers, and managers and workers. As noted above, organizational identity itself is a product of a compromise formation between members' conflicted needs for belongingness and independence, membership and separateness.

During feedback sessions, action researchers share their findings in the form of an organizational narrative or story (organizational diagnosis). Once shared with the group of participants, researchers ask for confirmation or rejection. The organizational narrative as verbalized by researchers and consensually validated by participants during feedback sessions ought to represent, if not emotionally resonate with, the character and psychological reality of organizational identity. Participants' feelings of identification with the organizational depiction give researchers confidence that they have captured the essence of organizational identity. Yet, as with any revealing and interpretive intervention, insight does not always result in positive change. There is often no speedy relief from previously unconscious destructive and repetitive behavior (see chapter 5).

Conclusion

Discovering organizational identity relies on a research process and methodology of participation and cooperation between researchers and organizational members—a research process and methodology that opens up what Winnicott calls "potential and transitional space" for mutual exploration and reflectivity. Such a psychological space must be experienced by workers as safe and secure enough to collaboratively explore the relational and intersubjective dynamics, meanings, and motives of the shared experiences between colleagues in the workplace.

The insipidness of organizational life and its intersubjective structures and psychodynamic patterns of relationships, conscious and unconscious, as signified by level 1, must be open to reflective inquiry if organizational identity is to be understood. A part of this work is to understand the degree to which the leader's ability to lead and manage is embedded in the character of emotional attachments. In particular I see from a psychoanalytic perspective the leader's ability to provide sufficient holding and containment[11] for organizational members as a critical function, which may well distinguish organizational well-being from organizational pathology (dis-ease, dis-stress, and dis-organization).

Having more fully articulated the idea of self-identity and organizational identity within the context of a multilayered organizational model, I introduce in the next chapter the phenomena of formal and informal group dynamics as a microcosm of organizational identity.

CHAPTER 3

Group Dynamics

In groups the most contradictory ideas can exist side by side and tolerate each other, without any conflict arising from the logical contradiction between them. But this is also the case in the unconscious mental life of individuals, of children and of neurotics, as psycho-analysis has long pointed out. (Freud, 1921, pp. 10–11)

FREUD (1921) AND Bion (1959b) observe that as individuals join groups and organizations, they exhibit *psychological regression*. This means they experience a metaphorical return to infancy and childhood. This linkage between psychological regression in groups and organizational identity is missing in the management and organization literature. It is the topic of this chapter.

The intersubjective experience of shared emotions between group members and leaders, known as *transference* and *countertransference dynamics*,[1] is a crucial feature of organizational identity. Groups are a microcosm of organizational identity. Divisions, units, and subcultures within larger organizations tend to echo the distinctive character and psychological structure of their company or public agency. Observing and experiencing work groups is a key step toward understanding organizational identity.

In this chapter, starting with Freud's and Bion's observations, I examine work groups from the vantage point of individual and group regression as a central feature of organizational identity. In doing so, I address why people in work groups behave regressively, the factors that cause the apparent reductions of intelligence and foresight among participants that are characteristic of psychological regression, the forms these regressive tendencies take in groups, and the nature of the ideal alternative: nonregressive, resilient work groups (Diamond, 1993; Diamond & Allcorn, 1987).

Our deliberations begin with a look at a psychological paradox of group and organizational membership, the psychodynamic conflict between opposing human needs for membership (identification and affiliation) and separateness (differentiation and independence) that provokes individual regression in groups. I then describe three types of regressive and defensive work groups: (1) the homogenized work group, with pre-oedipal, undifferentiated, and symbiotic features; (2) the institutionalized work group, with entrenched, defensive, and bureaucratic features; and (3) the autocratic work group, with oedipal, dictatorial, and oppressive features.

Subsequently, I describe a fourth work group, the resilient work group, as the ideal type with buoyant and reflective features. Suffice it to point out here that the resilient work group includes all the regressive potentials of the other three groups but is oriented toward task by keeping these three potential problems in mind and in balance. This chapter concludes by explaining the psychodynamic processes that promote regressive as well as progressive shifts in work-group dynamics.

Group Membership

The concept of psychological regression is critical to understanding organizational identity. The central dilemma for individuals in work groups, as in organizations at large, is to avoid becoming overly distressed by maintaining a satisfactory equilibrium and compromise between their individual needs for separateness (individuality, independence) and for group membership (affiliation, dependence). Establishing one's identity in groups is essential to functioning in role. This psychological process typically happens outside of awareness. Effective leadership must facilitate work environments that embrace diversity of people, skills, competencies, and modes of adaptation to hierarchic structures and norms. Human desire requires human contact where needs for companionship support one's sense of self. Leaders and followers, superordinates and subordinates, require varying degrees of identification, acceptance, self-assertion, and recognition.

When psychological regression is triggered by anxiety and feelings of vulnerability among group members, one often observes enhanced individual demands for group affiliation and recognition. One may also detect individuals' moving toward a position of *merger* (fusion, unification) in relation to idealized and powerful leaders and "superiors." Merger and the associated diminishment of self-other boundaries is a defensive reaction to fear and uncertainty where workers momentarily protect themselves from a loss of self-identity by way of group rejection. The participants' compulsive yearning to belong is heightened and their need for acceptance on behalf of alienated and disenfranchised fellow workers becomes overdetermined.

Customarily, group membership provides for infantile-like feelings of omnipotence through the experience of being part of a like-minded gathering. In the midst of such group-related experiences and perceptions, individuals feel as if they have transcended ordinariness for something grander, possibly a flawless, ideal, or seemingly omnipotent leader or group. Group membership often fulfills the expansive demands of the *ego ideal*, that near-perfect, aspirational sense of self at one's future best. However, participants may go to extraordinary lengths to maintain and enhance their identification with the group through a primitive form of merger with leaders. This symbiotic form of membership can produce sadistic and destructive actions by the group. Under the influence of psychological regression, participants act in a manner inconceivable outside the boundaries of group membership. For some participants, merely the act of joining a group provokes anxieties of anticipated rejection and abandonment, thus triggering psychological defenses and various forms of repression.[2]

Anxieties of separation and rejection from fellow group members and their leaders may also be present. Depending on the degree of overvaluation and overdetermined individual needs for membership and acceptance, some experience rejection by the group as akin to the self-annihilation or loss of self that is at the root of separation anxiety. Tragically, such individuals do whatever is required to remain part of the group and to keep the metaphorical oxygen flowing.

Organizational Context

In addition to the matter of members' regressive actions in response to anxieties about group membership, participants also feel anxious about the burden of overt events such as cutbacks and retrenchment, work-project overload, or system intervention. Regressive and defensive group dynamics are frequently provoked by stressors outside the control of workers. Group regression and its associated defensive actions are mostly counterproductive and rarely effective responses to threats to group and organizational identity. The psychology of regression in groups is a complex matter that can be better understood by reviewing some of the psychoanalytic, group, and organizational literature.

Organizations are a context in which individuals defensively respond to stress and anxiety. Typically, we observe individuals engaging a variety of defensive reactions with the intent of denying, disavowing, and suppressing the sources of their insecurities. Defensive reactions to weak, unrepresentative, or distant and resigned leaders, or to the uncertainties of politics and markets, are commonplace. Defenses can span the spectrum of emotional maturity, with humor and rationalization at the higher end and emotional immaturity with splitting, projection, and regression at the lower end. When working with a group under stress and anxiety, I have frequently observed and experienced psychological regression. Defining individual regression, Rycroft (1968) explains:

> The theory of regression presupposes that, except in ideal cases, infantile stages of development are not entirely outgrown, so that the earlier patterns of behavior remain available as alternative modes of functioning. It is, however, not maintained that regression is often a viable or efficient defensive process; on the contrary, it is usually a question of out of the frying-pan into the fire, since regression compels the individual to re-experience anxiety appropriate to the stage to which he had regressed. (p. 139)

Where and when participants experience vulnerability and danger from an unstable, unpredictable, insecure, and hostile environment (fantasied or actual), they retreat behind a fortress of primitive and infantile psychological defenses. In the case of groups or divisions within larger organizations (such as bureaucracies), one frequently finds conflict that is mismanaged or avoided by leaders and administrators. It is this lack of meaningful containment by leaders that takes participants "out of the frying pan and into the fire" of psychological regression.

As noted earlier, Winnicott (1971), with his concept of the holding environment, teaches us that the mother-infant unit is the most significant developmental relationship. This holding environment is our metaphoric home and the mental space to which we psychologically return under duress. Whether the relationship is between the individual and the family, the individual and the work group, or the individual and the organization, the mother-infant unit symbolizes the primary task of holding and containing, providing safety and security in the face of toxic emotions and anxieties. Where the holding environment fails and is not "good enough," psychological regression, the flight from reality into illusion and fantasy, results.

Self-Identity and Group Membership

Participants may enter the work group (and organization) with narcissistic needs for belonging and attachment that include excessive demands for self-aggrandizement, mirroring, and idealization. Members unconsciously expect to fulfill these needs with a substitute, good enough holding environment.

However, many newcomers are disappointed, and subsequently self-identity is threatened. Kernberg (1980) writes,

> Group processes pose a basic threat to personal identity, linked to a proclivity in group situations for activation of primitive object relations, primitive defensive operations, and primitive aggression with predominantly pregenital features. These processes, particularly the activation of primitive aggression, are dangerous to the survival of the individual in the group as well as to any task the group needs to perform. (p. 217)

Exposed to an unpredictable climate of constant change and uncertainty within groups and organizations, the critical balance between separateness (self-identity) and membership is often on shaky ground. Group members frequently and unconsciously engage in primitive psychological defenses such as *psychological splitting, projection of aggression,* and *projective identification.* These defenses protect the self from the anxiety of uncertainty and from losses of autonomy and separation.

Psychological splitting is characterized by a return to the fragmented relational world of infancy, in which self-other relations are categorized into absolutes of good or bad, all or nothing, accepting or rejecting, loving or hating. These are the "activat[ed] primitive object relations" Kernberg refers to. *Projections of aggression* are intended to discard and expel typically bad or persecutory images onto others as external objects while one retains good and secure images internally for oneself. *Projective identifications* arise in response to these initial projections, enabling the self to experience the rejected image vicariously through identification with the other as external object.

Psychological regression, with its associated defensive actions of splitting, projection, and projective identification, is intended to protect and preserve the self from perceived annihilation. Another defensive strategy is that of withdrawal and retreat into an imagined psychologically safe and secure internal psychic space. Klein describes this state of regressed withdrawal as signifying the need to save the ego (self) by internal object relations, to withdraw "inside" and out of the external world (Guntrip, 1969). For example, individuals may physically and emotionally isolate themselves from society to avoid an external world filled with persecution and disappointment.[3]

Unconscious fears of self-disintegration are a motivating factor in group affiliation born out of infancy and the desire for primary attachments. Individuals regress to protect themselves from separation and annihilation anxieties.

These anxieties are provoked by non-empathic and narcissistic leaders who tend first and foremost to themselves, securing their professional image and career. In the final analysis, psychological regression in groups stems from the failure of leaders to be present and adequately hold and contain participants' fears and anxieties. Ineffective and oblivious group and organizational leadership threaten the balance of self-identity and group membership.

A Typology of Regressive and Defensive Work Groups

The psychodynamics of individual and group regression are better understood when placed within an operational model. The development of the following types of work groups illuminates the impact of regressive and primitive defensive actions on work groups and the consequences for organizational identity.

Based on observations from decades of organizational fieldwork and consultations, I devised the typology of work groups presented here. It is by no means exhaustive. The application of relational psychoanalytic theory to groups in organizations assists in the interpretation of group and organizational dynamics (Bion, 1959b; Diamond, 1993; Freud, 1921; Kernberg, 1998; Klein, 1959; Kohut, 1984; Ogden, 1989; Winnicott, 1971). I contextualize this group typology by organizational culture and politics along with the multilayered model presented in the previous chapter (see figure 2). This typology reflects an effort to better articulate varied modes of experience and consciousness among group members as they cope with membership and separation anxieties. Each work group represents a predominant mode of coping with potential rejection, separation, and loss of affiliation. I present three regressive and defensive work groups, along with their associated conflicts and modes of experience: the homogenized work group, the institutionalized work group, and the autocratic work group. I also present a fourth, nonregressive and nondefensive group, the resilient work group (Diamond, 1993).

The Homogenized Work Group

The homogenized group is the most primitive and regressive; it conducts a collective flight from separation anxiety. This group is characterized by a lack of self-other discrepancy and is a psychosocial forerunner to the separation-individuation phase of infantile attachment (Bowlby, 1969, 1973, 1980; Fonagy, 2001; Frosch, 1983; Kernberg, 1980; Mahler, Pine, & Bergman, 1975; Stern, 1985). Individuation is minimal to absent. As the infant is attached to and totally dependent on the caregiving parent, homogenized-group members are fearful of and simultaneously merged to their leader. As group members they act as one, indistinguishable and undifferentiated (Diamond, 1993;

Turquet, 1975).[4] Thus, for the most part, they do not discriminate between self and others. More worrisome, they isolate themselves from outsiders, becoming detached and withdrawn from the external object world. The dangers of losing touch with reality, group isolation, and cultlike behavior are organized around the personality of the leader.

An unconscious, collective wish to return to the safety of the imagined maternal cocoon produces an avenue of flight from the perception of a hostile environment. Psychic safety is realized, if only momentarily, by group members within a delusional group culture, a culture of sameness in which members experience similar feelings and act uniformly. But the safety is short-lived; withdrawal from an external world of perceived persecution and annihilation results in a group capable of social denial and self-inflicted harm. Primitively regressed group members unconsciously operate in an internalized world of bad objects that threaten to devour the group identity.

From the group members' tortured perspective, separateness and independence of self from others is something to be feared as it represents an apparent (if not actual) threat to the group as a whole. Thus, the drive to conformity inhibits any inkling of deviance or what might be considered abnormal individual behavior. Fear and a sense of panic about the possible loss of control over group members exaggerates participants' separation anxieties. Consequently, group members fear both separation and hostility from the group and its members. In the homogenized group mind, public expressions of independence and autonomy in opposition to the status quo are viewed as highly dangerous.

Under these circumstances potential loss of shared identity for some is defended against by splitting categories of self and others into all-good (accepting) and all-bad (rejecting) part-objects. This phenomenon signifies a social structure of enemies and allies and of "us against them." Homogenized-group members internalize good self-representations while projecting bad and evil representations onto outsiders, such as external groups and organizations. Intergroup and organizational polarization and fragmentation result, serving as social defenses. To assure the illusion of safety and security, the group heightens uniformity and intense emotional investment in the identity of the home group.

Thus, the homogenized work group exhibits the symptoms of the schizoid problem described by psychoanalyst Harry Guntrip and the British object relations school. Individual members of the homogenized group collectively experience primitive aggression, which Guntrip (1969) defines as "an oral sadistic and incorporative hunger for objects [that] sets up intolerable anxiety about their safety" (p. 30). This "hunger for objects" is believed to take the form of a fantasy or delusion in which the subject desires to devour others perceived as threatening and hostile.

In *Group Psychology and the Analysis of the Ego* (1921), Freud argues that emotional ties join group members to one another by means of identification with a common ego ideal represented by their leader, who ultimately gives the group identity and a sense of belonging and commonality. In the homogenized group, members have affectionate needs for other(s), but they experience these needs as dangerous and potentially harmful. They perceive love itself as destructive (Guntrip, 1969). Group members fear that which they desire, the affectionate bond with an adoring other, signifying the absence of a good enough attachment to an all-loving, nurturing maternal object. In their search for the "good lost object," group members are confronted by anxieties of separateness, and they fear loss of identity. Homogenized-group members unconsciously identify with each other's feelings of self-annihilation and persecution. They have no authentic leadership to hold and contain their toxic emotions, so these fears and anxieties go unprocessed and undigested, which renders them more potent and unconscious.

Thus, homogenized-group members engage in a persecutory and paranoid transference of shared emotions. The subjects of persecutory transference experience others as out to destroy them. Persecutory transference reactions encourage cognitive and emotional splitting among group members, who define human relations as comprising "us against them," "good versus evil" absolute categories. Homogenized-group members see themselves as all-good and others (located in *other* divisions or departmental offices) as the all-bad other.

In sum, the homogenized work group is in large part a consequence of failed group leadership. Leaders of these groups have provided no holding or containment of workers' emotions under threatening and stressful conditions. Homogenized work groups develop in cases where leadership is weak, ineffectual, absent, ambivalent, and resigned. Homogenized-group members do not acknowledge individual differences among themselves, whether categories of race, gender, class, perceptions and emotions, or talents and skills. Their aggressive feelings toward each other and their associated anxieties prohibit individuality and independence as much as they inhibit the emergence of a successful leader.

Under these primitive relational psychodynamics, group members seem incapable of accomplishing collaborative work in which sharing different ideas and analyzing problems require open-mindedness and minimal defensiveness.

The primary unacknowledged task of this work group is individual and group survival. The suppressed and resigned qualities of homogenized work groups produce a form of group paralysis in which members find themselves on the horns of a dilemma. They experience themselves as neither in nor out, neither willing to commit themselves to group participation nor willing to commit themselves to a separateness from the dangers of group identity. Guntrip's (1969) description of the schizoid retreat, which he calls the "'in and out' programme," illustrates the paradox of the homogenized work group: "This 'in and out' programme, always breaking away from what one is at the same time holding on to, is perhaps the most characteristic behavioural expression of the schizoid conflict" (p. 36).

Ironically, the homogenized work group emerges in response to a lack of organizational leadership, recognition, and commitment. The absence of recognition and commitment may take the form of diminishing allocations of financial and human resources, perhaps the result of an ambiguous and temporary authority structure in which leaders are discouraged from assuming authority and leading. This type of situation results in uncertainty, distress, poor morale, persecutory anxieties, and aggression among group members. Ultimately, homogenized-group members are driven by anxiety and the unconscious desire to protect themselves from the consequences of their destructive feelings.

Case Example: Schizoid Withdrawal at a University Department
A university department that found itself operating in a hostile environment exhibited this schizoid withdrawal into homogenized subcultures. As a consequence of scant and indecisive leadership, direction, and financial support by the dean of the school, department members withdrew into a schizoid-like psychological retreat and survivalist mode. The dean had appointed a nontenured assistant professor to chair the department as it was assumed to be impossible to recruit a more senior chair because of the department's poor fiscal state of affairs. Department members viewed the dean's decision as evidence of the school's lack of support for the departmental mission and goals, and they considered the individual appointed chair unacceptable; consequently, the new chair was ineffectual. Department members were leaderless and felt persecuted. Their sense of organizational identity as a whole department became fragile, and many internal conflicts festered and went unresolved. Splitting occurred in response to members' anger and powerlessness.

The combination of positive and negative emotions and thoughts absent holding and containment by leadership reached a point where they could no longer be tolerated. Faculty required a relatively safe externalized target for their collective hostility. Instead of targeting the dean, whom they perceived as a dangerous target, they directed their bad feelings and aggression at one another. These actions resulted in departmental fragmentation into two antagonistic subgroups tied together by similar credentials and a common defense mechanism for coping with their rage and hostility. Each camp viewed the other as all-bad and at fault for their current predicament. Two homogenized subcultures had emerged within the department and paralyzed the whole group's ability to deal effectively with the absence of legitimate leadership.

Central to the homogenized work group is a regressive retreat from the outer reality into an internal world of illusion and lack of differentiation—an infantile state of oneness. In contrast, the institutionalized work group has what Max Weber called charismatic leadership and the capacity for self-other differentiation and discernment. However, it is vulnerable to the regressive effects of hierarchy and bureaucracy, where individuals collapse into paranoid-schizoid modes of action characterized by fragmentation, fight or flight defenses, and a social structure of "us against them."

The Institutionalized Work Group

The threat to group membership inside the homogenized group is rooted in infantile defensive withdrawal from the exterior and into the interior psychological reality. Participants deny and destroy individuality. They come to project aggression and hostility and withdraw into an undifferentiated symbiotic state. Institutionalized work groups manage stress and separation anxiety differently. They slip into paranoid and schizoid social defenses that foster psychological splitting and submission to formal top-down, hierarchic, over-rationalized, and depersonalized bureaucratic authority. Thus, institutionalized work groups attempt to contain anxiety by splitting and projection of their ideal and relatively independent self. They do so by submitting personal authority to impersonal and distant official leaders and by capitulating to the ritualistic and hierarchic social defenses and controlling social structures of bureaucratic institutions (Diamond, 1984; Jaques, 1955; Kernberg, 1980; Menzies, 1960). Kernberg (1980) writes,

> The study of large-group processes highlights the threat to individual identity under social conditions in which ordinary role functions are suspended and various projective mechanisms are no longer effective (because of the loss of face-to-face contact and personal feedback). Obviously, large group processes can be obscured or controlled by rigid social structuring.

Bureaucratization, ritualization, and well-organized task performance are different methods with similar immediate effects. (p. 218)

One underlying reason for constructing rigid bureaucratic social structures is to create a social defense against separation anxiety and as a reaction-formation against the perception of the "overwhelming nature of human aggression in unstructured group situations" (p. 218). In the previously described homogenized work group, a social defense of retreat into a symbiotic state materializes against the fear and anxiety of separation, which as a neurotic solution to anxiety merely perpetuates the threat to group membership.

In contrast, leaders of institutionalized work groups promote social defenses of control and fantasized, depersonalized containment of emotions. Bureaucratization and ritualization are institutionalized forms of control that promote dependency on rigid and routinized impersonal norms and social structures. Otherwise normal dependency needs of group members are manipulated and treated instrumentally, controlling and nullifying identity, separateness, and autonomy. Leaders of institutionalized work groups are obsessed with control and efficiency. They rarely delegate and typically micromanage workers, accelerating dependency needs and promoting psychological regression.

A special instance of projective identification is operating in the institutionalized group when public criticism, dysfunctions and inefficiencies, or demands for change arise. Members react defensively by splitting their perceptions of self and others into good and bad categories, and identifying a bad person or subgroup within the group self. Scapegoating is commonplace. Leaders' obsessive-compulsive preoccupation with control is aggravated by a paranoia and suspicion with respect to group members' actions. Not surprisingly, persecutory transference dominates the character of relationships in the institutionalized work group, particularly the leader-follower dynamics.

In contrast to the homogenized work group, the institutionalized work group encourages submission to oligarchic and hierarchic authority. Although self-other boundaries are frequently confused, they are not seemingly obliterated, as in the case of the homogenized work group. Self-identity exists but must submit to authority to maintain attachment and one's job. Anxiety and aggression are contained by leadership's practice of institutionalized repression fueled by generalized fear and paranoia. Kernberg (1980) notes of aggression,

An important part of nonintegrated and unsublimated aggression is expressed in various ways throughout group and organizational processes.

When relatively well-structured group processes evolve in a task-oriented organization, aggression is channeled toward the decision-making process, particularly by evoking primitive-leadership characteristics in people in positions of authority. Similarly, the exercise of power in organizational and institutional life constitutes an important channel for the expression of aggression in group processes that would ordinarily be under control in dyadic or triadic relations. Aggression emerges more directly and much more intensely when group processes are relatively unstructured. (p. 218)

In summary, institutionalized work groups and their leaders rely on structure and process to control aggression and their attachment and separation anxieties. Rigid routines and impersonal norms and authority perpetuate an illusion of stability, equality, and dependability—a social defense system. Participant dependence on rules, regulations, and procedures, and reliance on hierarchic impersonal authority, evoke "disclaimed action" (Schafer, 1976, 1983) and lack of personal responsibility (Diamond, 1985; Diamond & Allcorn, 1985). Institutionalization also results in a rigid structuring of boundaries, an insistence on loyalty and role conformity, and a general obsession on behalf of leadership with control of subordinate behavior. These are indicative of a paranoid regressive trend and persecutory transference of emotions underlying the group's actions and its structuring of itself and its organizational identity.

On the surface this group accomplishes work in a routine and rational fashion. Procedures, rules, regulations, and quantification take priority over quality of work, substance of product and service, and overall meaning and purpose of task accomplishment. Intra- and inter-organizational boundaries are rigid and relatively inflexible. Bureaucratic administration replaces charismatic leadership. An emphasis on micromanagement and the control of subordinate behavior renders delegation of authority unlikely. Paradoxically, the tendency of institutionalized work groups to operate as practically closed systems fosters perpetual insecurity and paranoia and an obsession with protection from external aggression. Frequently, politically unpopular governmental agencies operate under these regressive and defensive measures due to the politics of overzealous subcommittee interference or vociferous careerist political appointees.

Case Example: Social Defenses at a Public Agency
One public agency was organized and divided into professions and highly specialized divisions. It no longer effectively coordinated work processes and operations into accomplishing primary tasks. It was nearly dysfunctional and

highly ineffective. In response to persistent legislative criticisms and investigations, the division's leadership produced an institutionalized group of micromanagers (an inner managerial circle of power and authority) to more tightly control workers and services in an effort to prevent more public criticism. Not surprisingly, the resulting institutionalized culture of micromanagement made the coordination of tasks and communications exceedingly cumbersome and inefficient. Withholding of information and resistance to greater supervision and control among workers accelerated in response to reactionary organizational leadership and management obsessed with control of subordinate behavior. Workers had to negotiate layered and complex hierarchic channels of communication for minor authorizations and approvals. These demands of excessive and obsessive accountability paralyzed otherwise competent professionals, who felt powerless, mistrusted, disrespected, and angry with leadership and management.

Defensive strategies and rigid hierarchic structures fortified by micromanagement along with excessive control on behalf of leadership signified unconscious and counterproductive reactions. Management blamed and scapegoated workers for the dysfunctions rather than seeing them as the potential solution to the ineffectiveness and lack of coordination.

In sum, organizational leaders and managers of the institutionalized group were closed to new ideas and innovations. They suppressed worker participation and delegation while stressing obedience to authority. Insight and change were in a frozen state. At the surface the institutionalized work group differs sharply from the less structured, more informal and personal autocratic work group, which controls subordinate behavior and manages anxieties through patriarchic and charismatic leadership and authority.

The Autocratic Work Group

The autocratic work group does share with the institutionalized work group the circumstance in which participants forfeit their independence and separate identity for membership and group identity. In contrast to homogenized and institutionalized work groups, autocratic-group members identify with their charismatic and frequently narcissistic leader, from whom they derive omnipotent control over their aggression and separation anxiety. Guilt and shame arising from feelings of ambivalence and hostility toward the idealized leader are common. While the institutionalized work group is characterized by too much organization and distant and impersonal leadership, the autocratic group is described by personal authority and the personality of the leader, sometimes the patriarch of the figurative or literal "family business." In the process of joining and becoming group members, follow-ers, as Freud (1921) describes, exchange their ego ideals and internal author-ity for identification with the authority and ego ideal of the group leader (father), who then, wittingly or unwittingly, comes to dominate the group conscience.

The autocratic work group is constructed on the relational foundation of mirroring and idealizing transference.[5] Members grow to feel guilty about their vacillation between feelings of affection and aggression toward their idealized, admired, and often loved and feared leader. The autocratic work group is similar to Freud's portrayal in *Group Psychology and the Analysis of the Ego* (1921):

> Human groups exhibit once again the familiar picture of an individual of superior strength among a troop of equal companions, a picture which is also contained in our idea of the primal horde. The psychology of such a group, as we know it for the descriptions to which we have so often referred—the dwindling of the conscious, individual personality, the fo-cusing of thoughts and feelings into a common direction, the predomi-nance of the affective side by the mind and of unconscious psychical life, the tendency to the immediate carrying out of intentions as they emerge—all corresponds to a state of regression to a primitive mental activity, of just such a sort as we should be inclined to ascribe to the primal horde. (p. 54)

Autocratic-group members endow their leader with primitive, sadistic, and omnipotent qualities. Group members are guilt-ridden and submissive. They either turn their anger and aggression against themselves, evoking a depressive and ambivalent quality to the group experience, or project aggression outside group boundaries. Reminiscent of the depressive position described by Klein and her followers, the autocratic group offers members a prototype of infantile feelings of guilt, atonement, and forgiveness.

> Guilt derives from the ambivalence and hostility toward the object, with its possible destruction. Atonement is achieved by the ego taking itself as a weak, hateful object, and placing the superego in the role of parents whose forgiveness has to be sought by abject behavior. We find here a dou-ble identification: the ego as bad parent and the superego as the good one. Ultimately forgiveness may be achieved through fusion with the superego. (Frosch, 1983, p. 184)

Inevitably autocratic-group members become disappointed with their idealized leader, who cannot possibly meet their fantasied expectations nor successfully contain their hatred, aggression, and separation anxiety. The primitive crime of the primal horde's symbolic murder of the father-leader is reenacted. The leader is replaced and each reenactment of the crime is followed by a period of remorse and mourning. Members who sense their capacity to love and hate the same object are confronted with ambivalent feelings, which require their attention and acknowledgment if the group is to progress toward a resilient work-group identity.

In contrast to the primitive aggressive defenses of homogenized groups and the rationalized defenses of institutionalized groups, autocratic groups rely on the defensive strategy of "identification with the aggressor" (A. Freud, 1966). Identification with the aggressor is a common oedipal defense against the anxiety of external threatening objects associated with superego development during puberty. In further contrast, institutionalized groups and their leaders represent a manner of containing the anxious, violent, and explicitly sadistic social organization of the primal horde, and homogenized groups offer a solution to separation anxiety and aggression by schizoid withdrawal, where thoughts and feelings are severed indefinitely and language and communication are lost.

Finally, autocratic work groups are not dysfunctional; they are capable of carrying out tasks and meeting goals. The presence of stable, identifiable leaders serves to direct and coordinate the work and to hold and contain, if only for a period of time, toxic emotions of group members. A utopian myth is created when group members come to identify with the leader and his character and ideals. Their inevitable fear and disappointment with the idealized leader and their unconscious wish to replace him produces guilt and shameful anxiety. As a result, the group's work is affected by shifts from a utopian elation to a demystified, depressed position filled with mourning and guilt.

Although most common in family-owned businesses characterized by the norms and authority of a patriarchal system[6] ruled by the "law of the father," the autocratic group also appears in the traditionally conservative and patriarchal culture of many public agencies under the domination of career bureau chiefs in government. For example, units or offices within a complex public organization may operate as (semiautonomous) kingdoms where subordinates come to idealize their autocratic boss, and in which intergroup (interoffice) boundary disputes over jurisdictional authority, status, and prestige of each unit relative to the others are commonplace, while loyalty and deference to authority are strongly encouraged among members within these units.

Case Example: Identification with the Aggressor, Idealization,
and Disappointment at Public Agencies

Agencies within one governmental department were managed by bureau chiefs who had fifteen to twenty or more years of experience. Subordinates publicly expressed their loyalty, admiration, and idealization of bureau chiefs. Their obedience to authority and the high level of social cohesion were observable traits of the agency units. In private meetings among staff when bureau chiefs were absent, however, negative feelings and otherwise undiscussed problems could be acknowledged. In the presence of bureau chiefs, staff consistently deferred to their bosses' authority, suppressing thoughts, feelings, and ideas. "Identification with the aggressor" (the dominant bureau chief) was a predominant regressive and defensive group strategy. Agency membership and a sense of belonging took precedence for workers over separateness and independence.

Analysis of Regressive Work Groups

The three work groups, homogenized, institutionalized, and autocratic, exhibit regressive and defensive solutions to separation anxiety and fears of aggression. The institutionalized and autocratic groups, however, represent alternatives to the more primitive defensive solutions of the homogenized group. That is, the institutionalized and autocratic work groups are compromise formations against the regressive schizoid withdrawal of the homogenized group, which is a collapse into an autistic-contiguous[7] mode of experience. Members of homogenized work groups retreat into a nearly undifferentiated state of being, where self-other boundaries and individuality are absent. The institutionalized group culture, with its underlying paranoia, and the autocratic group culture, with its charismatic leader and underlying depressive position, are psychosocial constructions derived from less primitive psychologically regressive interpersonal relationships. Regardless of how disturbed and distorted interpersonal relationships in work groups become, empathy, identification, reparation, and consensual validation are plausible where symmetry and relative equilibrium between homogenized, institutionalized, and autocratic work groups are reestablished.

The autocratic work group offers members the opportunity to repair self-other relations that are split apart, thereby promoting more holistic and reality-based work bonds. However, in both institutionalized and autocratic groups, separateness and independence are subordinated to membership and belonging. Nevertheless self-identity and independence have greater potential to emerge in these work groups, in contrast with the more primitive and schizoid homogenized group.

The primary motives of group behavior are consistent, while the regressive and defensive actions differ. The interpretive value of the work-group typology rests on the underlying developmental characteristics of self-other relations, which are observable in work-group responses to organizational and environmental pressures. Contrary to common wisdom, psychoanalytic interpretations of group dynamics in organizational settings are not entirely negative and pessimistic. In fact, an understanding of the regressive qualities of group dynamics in organizations provides us with a more holistic and balanced view of effective work groups, one that is more complex and multifaceted, and one that is signified by psychodynamic tensions between all three work groups.

The Resilient Work Group

The resilient work group incorporates all the regressive potentials of the homogenized, institutional, and autocratic subcultures. The difference is that leadership is capable of recognizing, holding, and containing the insecure feelings and anxieties among workers that promote defensive and regressive actions.

In contrast with the previous three defensive work groups, in which mostly unconscious and regressive actions and covert goals are dominant, the resilient work group is first and foremost a task-oriented work group. The resilient group is distinguished by a reflective process that promotes members' awareness of fantasies, regression, and covert actions.[8] Participants, particularly leaders, realize the necessity of insight as a learning skill that supports the emotional well-being and competence of group members. Twinship, which signifies relational patterns of essential sameness and alikeness (see self psychology and the work of Kohut), seems to play a prominent role in the psychodynamics of the resilient work group. The twinship transference signifies an emotional bond between people that is based upon their need to be seen and understood by others who are essentially like them.

In the homogenized work group, one finds a high level of cohesiveness and absolute ideological loyalty to the organizational leadership and culture. The homogenized work group promotes idealizing transference of followers onto leaders with an emphasis on membership over separateness. In contrast, empathy and mutual understanding, which are essential ingredients in collaboration and cooperation, stem from the inherent values of the twinship transference. For example, the psychodynamics of twinship promote the practice of mentoring and the development and strengthening of talents and skills that enhance self-competence and self-esteem among group members. This can, in effect, reduce the narcissistic proclivity for grandiosity and idealization among members and, thereby, minimize mirroring and idealizing transference dynamics. It can also limit persecutory and paranoid transference dynamics as a consequence of members' commitment to taking responsibility for their actions. This means that one worker's feeling victimized will lead to some acknowledgment by other workers of their role in the victimization process rather than an impulsive and projective turning to scapegoating behavior. On the negative side, the twinship transference may produce work groups of individuals who merge (overvalue identification) with each other and their leader(s). This can create problems and an emotional pull toward the homogenized work-group formation. If unacknowledged and uninterrupted, the twinship transference between leaders and followers may deny them their individuality and differentiation. This may, in turn, encourage regressive psychodynamics of a homogenized-group nature.

The resilient work group is, therefore, not a utopia. It is capable of all the regressive and defensive actions that characterize the other three work groups. Members may resort to regressive and primitive defensive actions in response to perceived danger and separation anxiety. In fact, as noted, transference dynamics are not absent: they are simply more cognitively and consciously accessible to members and thus potentially less counterproductive. Resilient-group members recognize that progress and change are unlikely without psychological regression and collapse into the defensive patterns characteristic of the previous three types of work groups. They also acknowledge that change without individual and group resistance to that change is unlikely. The compulsion to repeat, observed particularly in transference dynamics between individuals, is characteristic of everyone to differing degrees. This phenomenon of repetition will be discussed further in chapter 5. Resilient workers are, therefore, sensitive to and conscious of acts of resistance and defense as opportunities for learning and developmental change rather than suppression. They endeavor to learn from experience and are capable of recognizing defensive regressive actions. To reiterate, resilient workers are simply more conscious of and attentive to their personal and collective regressive actions.

The dynamics of the resilient work group differ from traditional humanistic views of sophisticated collaborative human relations. In contrast, resilience emphasizes the need to pay attention to participants' inevitable regressive and defensive tendencies under stressful circumstances. This shift in conscious-ness can be facilitated by insightful leaders and psychodynamically oriented consultants and researchers. Psychological defenses and regressive actions lie behind all group and organization dynamics. The character of the resilient work group represents a qualitative difference from more traditional prescrip-tions for collaborative work groups in that it emphasizes the necessity for more deeply understanding cognitive and affective work-group processes in order to achieve work-group effectiveness and intentionality.

In sum, resilient work groups emerge from organizational interventions that focus on learning from experience by attending to unconscious group pro-cesses. Enhanced awareness and normalizing of leader-follower transference dynamics and regressive and defensive group actions is instructive. Resilient-group dynamics are more readily available when leaders promote safe holding environments and containment of toxic emotions. They are also more frequent when leaders genuinely value collaboration and participation among mem-bers and when socio-technical and political factors do not function as serious constraints on lifting oppressive managerial practices.

Case Example: Transitioning from Negative to Positive
Transferences in a Public Bureaucracy
One relatively autonomous unit in a public bureaucracy learned with the help of consultants to identify transference dynamics between supervisor and staff. After a lengthy exploration into how the group reacted to environmental cir-cumstances, such as expanded work roles due to cutbacks, the group members improved their ability to process the emotional nature and stress of their work relationships so they could minimize counterproductive behavior. This in-volved clarifying and then redefining the interdependent nature of their roles as required to complete shared tasks. Once the unit members associated their thoughts and feelings with observable group tendencies under stress, they real-ized the need to explore their reactions to constant change in the environment recurrently. That realization altered their work-group culture and facilitated the emergence of a more reflective and consciously aware group process.

The members' heightened awareness of collective transference tendencies enabled them to work more effectively in a setting that demanded innovation and creativity. The driving force behind their ability to overcome excessive dependency on the consultant, a mere reflection of their dependency on the supervisor, was their desire for mutual understanding and validation of their frustrations. Finding that which they had in common with each other helped them to better appreciate and empathize with one another. Becoming aware of their idealization of the supervisor and assuming responsibility for counterproductive actions helped them to be a more collaborative group and to be more respectful of each other's individual talents and skills. The idealizing transference gave way to a more constructive and productive twinship transference among the staff and with their supervisor.

The Psychodynamics of Group Transition

Striking a balance between membership and separateness is the central dilemma of group and organizational identity. Each of the four work groups represents one possible solution to the problem of anxiety and aggression produced by the central dilemma inherent to all groups. However, the three regressive work groups solve the problem of separation anxiety by overemphasizing group membership and underemphasizing separateness, self-identity, individuality, and (as in the example above) recognition. Any of the four work groups can, at least momentarily, resolve anxiety and manage aggression.

However, these groups are not static (see figure 3), nor do they fit into rigid categories that exclude the potential for change. Much like Ogden's (1989) modes of experience (discussed in chapter 1), the regressive work groups are joined dialectically. In that linkage they confirm, negate, and reconfirm one another. Group transition from one position to another occurs regularly and unwittingly. Work-group transitions occur as leader-follower psychodynamics change. The nature of self-object transference and countertransference dynamics between leaders and followers, supervisors and subordinates, must be altered for a shift in work-group identity to occur.

For example, the homogenized work group is relatively leaderless as its members see the promotion of separateness and individuation as antagonistic. Leaders require minimal acknowledgment of differentiation between themselves and their followers. The unconscious fantasy of group members assumes it is too dangerous to be different. Some combination of power, authority, personality, and risk taking would be necessary to move the homogenized group from a state of schizoid withdrawal toward a more progressive state of object (self-other) relatedness, which requires differentiation.

Group and organizational leadership is a reciprocal process. It requires followers. Followers, wittingly or unwittingly, empower leaders. To a significant degree, leadership rests upon unconscious assumptions, expectations, and processes. Leaders persist as long as the emotional and ideological leanings of followers support the legitimacy of leaders' power and authority. In the homogenized case, the "best-suited" person may be the most schizoid in

FIGURE 3 Group Transitions

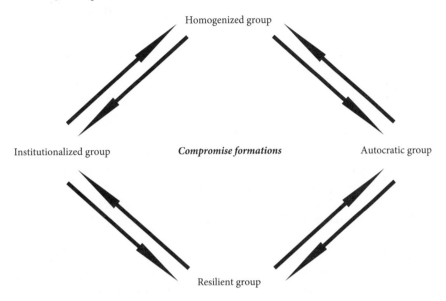

character, someone whose inclination is to retreat and move away from others. Out of this vacuum the nascent and emerging leader influences followers first by gaining their attention and then by manufacturing an alternate defensive and seductively attractive fantasy.

Transference phenomena capture the underlying psychodynamics of group transitions. Awareness of transference dynamics helps researchers and consultants illuminate subtle shifts in leader-follower interactions that promote change in organizational subcultures. Every transition signifies a new compromise formation in the group's search for a collective defense against separation anxiety. The work-group typology helps to identify different levels of consciousness and maturity in object (self-other) relationships.

For the homogenized work group, for example, to leave the comfort and protection its members find in schizoid withdrawal and isolation requires aggressive and fight-oriented leadership and redirection of its energy toward an object (someone or something), an identifiable target external to the perceived group boundary. A move from the homogenized subculture to the institutionalized work group would not require a change in the persecutory transference as much as a perceived new solution to anxiety, an unconscious mission for dealing with separation anxiety and feelings of victimization. Members would turn from resignation to overt aggression, targeting specific individuals or groups to blame as the source of their problems and anxieties. These defensive actions on behalf of the group would produce an "us against them" mentality, which would further enable group members to depersonalize and dehumanize chosen others.

Once a leader who has the necessary agenda (an unconscious fit between leader and follower), whether impersonal or charismatic in nature, is identified, group members unify and then follow either in retreat from their current predicament or in search of a common enemy. The emergence of a shift in transference dynamics signals a readiness to accept a new work-group identity. The new work group emerges (either institutionalized or autocratic) out of a compromise formation produced by changing transferences and emotional attachments between leaders and followers.

The collective escape from the most primitively regressive homogenized work group begins with the often unconscious establishment of a leader-follower tie. The homogenized work group, it should be stressed, represents an unconscious fear of group rejection and loss of group membership. Its hostility toward independence and autonomy demonstrates the likelihood of its members' vulnerability to schizoid withdrawal. Both institutionalized and autocratic work groups are capable of regressive action in the direction of homogenization, on the one hand, and more progressive action in the form of resilience, on the other. Group and organizational actions are dynamic and in constant motion. At any point in time and space, groups are located somewhere along this continuum between regressive homogenized-group dynamics and progressive resilient–group dynamics. The institutionalized and autocratic work groups are closer to the midpoint on a continuum between regressive and progressive actions.

Summary of the Four Group Types

Below I provide a brief overview of the previously discussed regressive and defensive work groups as well as a description of the resilient work group. These psychosocial states are not mutually exclusive; rather they are complementary and symmetric, comprising four relational modes in group dynamics.

First, in the homogenized work group, one finds profound psychological regression represented in the autistic-contiguous state in which self-other relations are undifferentiated and symbiotic, and where a loss of self-consciousness combines with the inability to verbalize one's experience and perception.

Second, the institutionalized work group is characterized by a paranoid-schizoid mind-set, where expelling bad internal objects and protecting and retaining good internal objects are predominant. Also, the inability to reflect on the self and the incapacity to assume responsibility for one's actions are typical. Finally, scapegoating and blaming and a preoccupation with defending boundaries and borders are emblematic.

Third, members of the autocratic work group have a depressive mind-set. In this group, one witnesses retreat into sadomasochism, relations of submission and dominance, patriarchic and hierarchic norms, defense of the status quo, and sycophantic followership.

Fourth and finally, the resilient work group acknowledges the presence of all three defensive and regressive work-group dynamics. Members and leaders know that work groups and organizations inevitably exhibit these defensive and regressive proclivities at different points in time. It is human nature. Leaders of resilient work groups hold the figurative center (as in potential space) and contain the toxic emotions inherent to group and organizational membership.

Conclusion

An understanding of regression in work groups enhances reflectivity and self-awareness among group members and thus increases the group's opportunity for learning, effectiveness, and change. More importantly, the resilient leader and work group that value analysis of group process are capable of intervening in and turning around, if only momentarily, regressive and destructive group patterns. Finally, the resilient work group does not perceive itself as superior but as human and psychodynamic. Its commitment to analysis of the group self (and organizational identity) does not obliterate regressive action but, rather, produces leadership and group awareness through a reflective process that creates the opportunity for change and development.

This fluid, dynamic, and dialectic model of group dynamics is not a case of the ego's taking the place of the id, as in Freud's (1933) rational-drive model for managing instinct. Instead, it is a case of attending to unconscious processes and establishing what Winnicott (1971) calls "potential space" (discussed in the subsequent chapter).

As shown in this chapter, group features, regressive and progressive, are organized around patterned relational dynamics between members and their leaders, and between members themselves—the essence of organizational identity. These patterned relationships serve as psychological defenses against anxieties over loss, separation, and change. I next explore the key idea of intersubjectivity and potential space as the location of organizational identity.

Part Two

KEY CONCEPTS AND APPLICATION

In this section, I apply psychoanalytic concepts to develop and expand our understanding of organizational identity. The section begins with the ideas of intersubjectivity and potential space, followed by the psychodynamics of repetition and the compulsion to repeat, then metaphors and metaphoric processes, and finally the concept of the unthought known. Each chapter in part 2 represents one more dimension in the study of organizational psychodynamics linked to organizational identity. Discovering organizational identity requires the opening up of potential space between organizational researchers and participants. These unique and characteristic relational patterns of intersubjectivity and transference and countertransference dynamics are revealed by way of experience-near research and immersion in the organizational field. Organizational identity is not adequately captured and cannot be fully understood by assuming an experience-distant "objectivist" position. It requires an idiographic, case-by-case, psychodynamic approach to fieldwork and intervention. At the center of the contemporary relational psychoanalytic method of studying organizations is the critical association of intersubjectivity and potential space, discussed next.

CHAPTER 4

Intersubjectivity and Potential Space

I suggest that the time has come for psychoanalytic theory to pay tribute to this *third area,* that of cultural experience which is a derivative of play. Psychotics insist on our knowing about it, and it is of great importance in our assessment of the lives rather than the health of human beings. The other two areas are inner or personal psychic reality and the actual world with the individual living in it. (Winnicott, 1971, p. 102)

T HE THEORY AND practice of psychoanalytically informed organization studies require key concepts that enunciate the dialectical, experiential, relational, and perceptual nature of organizational psychodynamics. Intersubjectivity and potential space[1] are two critical ideas in this discussion as they direct attention to the relational dimension of the researcher's frame of reference as a participant-observer of organizations.

The so-called intersubjective third[2] embodies creativity, play, and imagination, which emerge out of the relational and cooperative dynamics between two or more persons. For Winnicott, potential space,[3] located in the third area, is where humanity lives, experientially, the creative and imaginative mental space between illusion and reality, self and other, and the location of play. It is also the location, psycho-geographically, of organizational identity.

Intersubjectivity and Potential Space in
Psychoanalytic Theory and Organizations
Insight, learning, and change in individuals and groups, as in psychoanalysis, emerge out of reflective inquiry into psychological and relational processes at work. These interactive dynamics comprise creative and destructive, progressive and regressive, forces. The social and psychological structures are conscious and unconscious, fantasied and reality-based. The psychosocial tensions occur across boundaries between leaders and followers, researchers/

consultants and organizational participants, self and others. At the boundaries of these paradoxical and intermediate organizational psychodynamics are cognitive and emotional forces of human nature, which are patterned relational systems that Winnicott aptly labels "potential space."

Regardless of whether we call these forces of human nature dialectical, paradoxical, split and fragmented objects, or simply conflicts, psychoanalytic organizational researchers and consultants observe the emergence of an *intersubjective dimension* at work. It is in this intermediate and *transitional* area that meaningful relationships evolve. It is within this mental space of what Ogden (1994) calls the analytic third that the psychoanalytic work of organizational research and consultation is conceived. In this chapter, I examine the relational structure of intersubjectivity and the development of potential space (see Benjamin, 2004; Britton, 2004; Cavell, 1998; Gerson, 2004; Green, 2004; Lacan, 1991; Minolli and Tricoli, 2004; Mitchell and Aron, 1999; Ogden, 1994, 2004; Winnicott, 1971; Zweibel, 2004).

The concept of an intersubjective structure between self and other, subject and object, is a focal point for studying organizational psychodynamics. This intersubjective dimension is the location for witnessing, experiencing, and interpreting compulsive, rigid, and frequently destructive and dysfunctional individual and group processes. In this chapter the "triangular space" of intersubjectivity is seen as the frame of reference, the position of the analytic third, where psychodynamically oriented organizational researchers observe, analyze, and provide consultation (figure 4). This third area is the location of Winnicott's (1971) potential space, where the culture of openness and discovery, imagination and creativity, is possible when organizational researchers assume the position of the analytic and intersubjective third.

In the next section, I discuss the concept of intersubjectivity in psychoanalysis, crucial to organizational identity, along with how one further conceptualizes the intersubjective in a psychoanalytic approach to organizational research and consultation. I provide a case example to better articulate the nature of intersubjectivity in the process of participating and observing, analyzing, and intervening in organizations.

The Concept of Intersubjectivity in Psychoanalysis

The idea of intersubjectivity in psychoanalysis stems from an acknowledgment of the reparative significance of empathy and identification, reflective action[4] and participant observation. An intersubjective framework acknowledges the narcissistic nature of human relations and interactions. Analyzing human

FIGURE 4 Visualization of Intersubjectivity and Potential Space

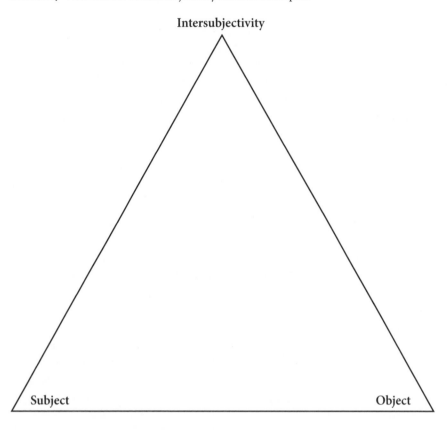

interactions for the purpose of improving organizational well-being places importance on the shared emotions of transference and countertransference. The necessity of self-consciousness in the observer and her capacity to use herself as an instrument for "experience-near" research is a critical part of the theory and application. The introduction of the concept of intersubjectivity represents a shift in the psychoanalytic paradigm from one- to two-person psychology. In fact, this emphasis on the intersubjective dimension might be considered a three-person psychology if one takes into account the Winnicottian notion of a third area of potential space.

The intersubjective realm is where the insightful and productive work of repairing and integrating otherwise fragmented and broken human systems occurs. Organizations are, or so it is assumed, cooperative human systems. The phenomenon of intersubjectivity is highlighted as it occurs at the psychological, relational, and structural boundaries between people, divisional units, and organizations.

In the history of psychoanalysis, this notion of the production of a third subject surfaces most prominently with the paradigmatic shift from the classical drive model to the contemporary relational model—a transition from focusing on instincts to focusing on relationships. As noted in earlier chapters, the former is more preoccupied with intra-psychic structure and the psychodynamics of tension reduction, while the latter is more encompassing of intersubjectivity and object relational motivations. Intersubjectivity is recognizable in shared emotions of transference and countertransference dynamics and the associated act of projective identification. This refers to the emotional bonds of the past being displaced onto the present and unconsciously binding one person to another.[5]

Figure 4 illustrates intersubjectivity as a frame of reference and position taken up by organizational researchers. This theoretical and analytic position is the location of potential space, from which reflective individual and group processes are observed, witnessed, analyzed, and consulted. Thus, the intersubjective perspective is located at the apex of the triangular space. From this perch, consultants experience, observe, and interpret the collision of psychological forces at the boundary between subjects and objects (self and other) at work. That is, by positioning our attention at the boundary of subject-object, self-other, we observe, experience, and better understand relational dynamics. Potential space is the location of betweenness where we examine the quality of intersubjectivity and relational attachments that shape the character of organizational identity.

Thus, application of the intersubjective frame of reference facilitates our capacity as organizational researchers/consultants to simultaneously participate in and observe potentially collusive and destructive organizational psychodynamics. As noted, consciousness of intersubjectivity enables us to attend to the emotional whirlwind of positive and negative transference and countertransference dynamics—the shared emotions of individuals and their mutual subjectivities.

In this regard, it is worth noting that Bion's (1962, 1967) concept of *containment* is operational in the consultant-participant encounter: the intersubjectivity signifies the psychodynamic processes in which the recipient (consultant) of frequently toxic emotions eventually verbalizes and effectively communicates back to the projector (participant) his disavowed subjectivity, and does so in a form the projector can receive, reclaim, and find meaningful if not reparative. In the example of an "oppressive and sadistic boss," the presence of intersubjectivity as a focal point for insight and change is realized when the boss takes back and reclaims from the workers his previously persecuting and abusive projections and treatment of them. The boss takes responsibility for originating the hostilities surrounding hierarchical relations. How do we understand this turnaround, psychodynamically? From the reference point of intersubjectivity, at the outset the boss (projector) makes use of the recipients (workers) as a container for his own toxic emotions. Workers respond in kind to the hostile attacks via projective identification. In the reflective practice of psychoanalytic organizational research and consultation, potential space is discovered.

From the vantage point of this potential and transitional space, the leader gains perspective and psychological distance. He may hear the voices and legitimate complaints of his employees for the first time. This enables him to realize the psychodynamics between self and others, subjects and objects. He is then able to locate himself as the originator of these toxic emotions.

In the process of recovering split-off and evacuated bad parts of himself, the boss's self-integrity can be restored, along with a capacity to better distinguish sensations of "me versus not-me." Thus, a more unified and realistic sense of self internalized with good and bad objects exists in an expanding potential space.[6] This quality of consciousness and self-confidence is something we wish to recruit among future leaders and executives. It is simply an aspirational ideal.

Intersubjectivity and Potential Space as Emerging Organizational Identity

In table 2, I present the categories of my thinking on intersubjectivity as a framework in psychoanalytic organizational research and the discovery of organizational identity. Relational psychoanalytic organizational research and consultation is framed around dialectical tensions such as the opposing forces of group versus individual and social versus psychological structures. Intersubjectivity is a critical and unique dimension of psychoanalytic organizational research and consultation. From this reference point, researchers and participants perceive the system as a human relational network by way of reflective and transitional processes focused on psychological boundaries of self and other, leader and follower, individual member and organization.

Intersubjectivity in psychoanalytic organizational research and consultation is illuminated by the potential space in which depressive and reparative processes related to insight and change such as grief and mourning are triggered. That

TABLE 2 Intersubjectivity and Organizational Identity

Reflective inquiry about

Dialectical tensions	• Social versus psychological structures
	• Group versus individual
	• Fragmentation versus integration
	• Dominance versus submission in role
	• Change versus resistance to insight and change
Intersubjectivity and potential space as location of organizational identity	• Organizational culture and identity (developmental, relational, and intersubjective processes)
	• Psychological reality (experience, transference and countertransference, and splitting and projective identification)
	• From paranoid-schizoid toward depressive modes of experience
	• From fragmenting toward integrative processes
	• Change as emotional loss (grief and mourning as reparative processes)

is, participants' feelings of object loss provoked by change permeate the potential and transitional space (see Diamond, Allcorn, & Stein, 2004). While depressive, these psychological processes signify a positive shift from a suspicious and manipulative, and paranoid and schizoid, mind-set that engages in psychological splitting and projective identification to one of grief and mourning. This is the depressive mind-set of humility, mutual recognition, and reparation.

In the case example to follow, the intersubjective dimension signifies an awareness among participants of this emerging triangular space and organizational identity. This results in part from the consultant's presentation of the organizational narrative and the simultaneous containment of the members' toxic emotional dynamics—a good enough holding environment. The consequence of listening deeply (Stein, 1994), having empathy, and identifying is the production of a good enough holding environment and potential space for exploration, experimentation, public testing, and reconsideration of individual assumptions. The presence of a holding environment provides participants with a space for reflective thinking and interpretation, and an emotional container by way of the consultants for unconscious and previously unarticulated feelings and anxieties.

As we engage organizational participants in this process of reflective inquiry, organizational identity emerges as an intersubjective structure transcending the subject-object duality. This intersubjectivity signifies participants' capacity to occupy the potential space of observation, reflectivity, and double-loop learning (discussed in chapter 5). Entering this mental space enables research subjects and participants to produce alternative relational and narrative organizational structures, creating the possibilities of change. Consequently, working and playing in potential and transitional space facilitates more meaningful, productive, and humane communicating and organizing. The intersubjective frame of reference empowers participants in the discovery of their shared and collective organizational identity.

In sum, during the course of psychoanalytic organizational interventions, researchers and consultants reflect back to participants the character of intersubjectivity and organizational identity. Members link "here-and-now" interactions with the organization and its historical narrative and collective past. The intersubjective framework is fostered by researchers' efforts to enhance the members' capacity for reflective action and insight for change. Gathering the fruits of these efforts requires intervention in the psychodynamic processes of human relations at work. Consequently, these interpretive and experiential endeavors establish a more enduring potential space for playful and reflective intersubjectivity within the organization.

Organizational Identity, Change, and Intersubjectivity

As discussed above, insight for change occurs when consciousness of intersubjective and relational structures, at individual, group, and organizational levels, evolve. Locating and attending to the in-between area of relational and organizational boundaries is essential to repairing fragmented relationships and linkages. The psychoanalytically oriented organizational researcher and consultant promotes a dialogue at the moment participants appear open and minimally defensive. This enables participants to suspend long-held assumptions, ideologies, and beliefs about themselves and their organization. Typically this occurs following some exploration of resistance to insight and change, which is characterized by greater participant openness to learning and curiosity about each other's intentions and expectations (as illustrated in the case below).

In the following example of an intervention, intersubjective awareness emerges when participants are in contact with each other and their leaders in a reflective process. From the vantage point of intersubjective consciousness, it becomes plausible to acknowledge and reclaim projected emotions and attributions. It is also possible in the safety and security of potential space for participants to observe and experience their organizational identity.[7]

Case Example: Potential Space in a Department of Psychiatry

The chair and several senior faculty members of a university psychiatry department realized their department was riddled with deeply personal and frequently vicious interpersonal conflicts and had become dysfunctional, so they sought a comprehensive organizational consultation. They told the researchers that frequently, when the colleagues met as a group to discuss departmental business or to engage in intellectual, theoretical, and clinical discourse, which included case presentations, their differences and disagreements escalated into personal hostilities. The leadership and department membership were unable to tolerate or contain the discord. Consequently, meetings would frequently end with the members destructively personalizing their differences, attacking one another's character, and further fragmenting the department into ideological camps and unproductive divisions.

The frequent dysfunction and turmoil among members worried them greatly as they needed to engage the department in serious strategic and business planning to cope with a changing environment. Many knew it was time to reexamine their mission, goals, and strategies, in order to turn around decreasing student enrollments, diminishing patient populations for psychotherapy, and depleted institutional morale. Political and economic conditions in health care and the impact of managed care had made reimbursement more difficult and were discouraging many medical students from specializing in psychiatry. Those who did were discouraged from practicing psychotherapy for economic reasons as well. The department head and her executive team of administrators and clinicians felt something needed to be done; they needed more effective strategies to adapt to what they perceived as an unwelcoming community environment. Yet, they could not accomplish a shift in mission, goals, and strategies until conflicts from within were reconciled and until they had developed the capacity to work more effectively as a team and with a stronger sense of affiliation to the department.

The consultants provided this department of psychiatry with a structured method and process for organizational assessment, feedback, and interventions. Following on-site interviews and data collection, the organizational researchers presented the department with a depiction of their organization. It was during this time of telling the organizational story and offering it to the participants as a representation of their organizational identity that a glimmer of *intersubjective awareness* in the group emerged in a climate of otherwise injured narcissism, self-centeredness, and broken and distorted relationships.

The department members gathered to hear and view before them the narrative of their organization—the story derived from the factual, historical, and narrative data of the consultants' structured and semistructured interviews, observations, and participation in groups and committees. The consulting team presented the organizational assessment using a flip chart. With the goal of establishing a potential space, the organizational consultants essentially proclaimed to the participants, "Here it is. This is our best depiction of who you are as a group and organization derived from our experience, observations, interviews, and extemporaneous dialogue."

Sometimes at this point in the process, organizational researchers can sense the group shifting their attention away from themselves as individuals and toward a more systemic and collective image, an image that signifies the structure of intersubjectivity: "You are more than any one individual in this room, you are a group, an organization, yet all of you share responsibility for your organizational identity." With this in mind department members temporarily shifted their conceptual framework and expanded their perspectives beyond a preoccupation with internal fragmentation, angst, and interpersonal conflicts, and toward imagining themselves as an organization, not simply a collection of individual clinicians and administrators.

In this case, it was as if in the progression of dialogue and facilitation of transitional and potential space (moving into the intersubjective dimension), members momentarily transcended their narcissistic preoccupations and their proclivity to be entrapped in dyadic relations and thus moved beyond self-righteous obsessions about interpersonal conflicts and the associated "us and them" social structure. By refocusing on themselves as sharing an organizational identity, they could temporarily melt resistances that were previously barriers to reflective processes.

Psychoanalytic organizational research requires participant engagement with the processes of organizational diagnosis and the discovery of organizational identity. Resistance to insight and change—such as the belief of some that the researchers could not change anything, which was based on the assumption, stated by several participants early on, that "you [the consultants] cannot change personalities, therefore you cannot possibly change our department"—would have to become softer and allow for reflective learning.

The telling of the organizational story altered group members' mind-sets and associated defenses. Their attention moved from individualistic preoccupations with arguments and ideological differences and toward the collective good. They seemed to overcome their obsession with interpersonal conflicts and the associated psychological splitting of the group into enemies and allies. In their place, they started to see themselves from the vantage point of inter-subjectivity and potential space. They could see themselves as constituting a shared organizational identity. With a different mind-set and repeated group sessions, the participants moved away from fragmented and hostile relationships and toward more holistic and reparative ones. However short-lived it might have been, the capacity to acknowledge, tolerate, and value differences among members developed.

Finally, an incident of sabotage late in the consultation process depicted the value and function of the intersubjective dimension of potential space. Such an incident is not an unusual event in organizational assessment efforts. Late in the intervention, a protective and conflicted female member introduced a purloined letter to the group during a consultation session. The author of this letter was absent and it was obvious that the broadcaster lacked his permission and that he was unaware of her intent to make it public. The letter turned out to be an all-too-familiar vicious and personal attack on one of their colleagues, who was present at the session. In response to the letter, group members acted with anger, shame, and regression and retreated into their preexisting oppositional and ideological camps. Some defended the perceived and assumed victim of the attack, while others attacked the messenger for bringing the appropriated letter of hostile feelings out into the public, particularly without the author's permission or knowledge. The group collapsed into familiar paranoid and schizoid dynamics.

The consultants were struck by what they observed and experienced. The behavior felt and appeared very much the same as what they had seen when they arrived and began the organizational diagnosis and intervention. The consultants called for a ten-minute break (a needed "time-out") to assess and process what was going on. During the break several members in pairs aggressively lobbied the consultants as "judges" and defenders of some imagined paternal law, insisting that they "deal with" the incriminating letter and the "malicious and cruel individual who wrote it." It was as if members were demanding justice (in the author's absence) and the consultants were present to dispense justice and determine punishment (consultants are often viewed unconsciously, if not consciously, as judges). Primitive and regressive psychological processes of splitting and projected aggression provoked scapegoating and a retreat to fragmentation of the department in the present moment.

Upon reconvening, the group consultants reminded participants of their reparative task as a group. They pointed out that what was going on was indicative of the competing narrative patterns and themes inherent in the organization and consistent with the depiction of the department in the organizational study. The consultants had just witnessed an enactment, which confirmed in real time the defensive and counterproductive tendencies in the department that overvalued and overpersonalized minor differences of theory and practice.

The consultants continued the reflective process by suggesting that participants now had an opportunity to acknowledge this moment as a representation of their organizational identity. Here was an opportunity to assume collective responsibility for their actions. Once they could acknowledge these relational patterns as part of their collective past, they could move forward in a productive and progressive manner. Inevitably, there would be future opportunities to revisit this framework whenever they fell backward into the hostilities of the past.

Here the consultants were giving the group in the midst of sadomasochistic and paranoid-schizoid dynamics an opportunity to step back and, with some psychological distance and perspective (afforded by the holding environment and potential space), reflect on their actions as a group and a department. Upon entering the reflective and potential space, participants were able to see that the introduction of the letter and their reaction to it perpetuated fragmentation. The present experience of mutual aggression, they could see, was reminiscent of their propensity to act regressively and suspiciously. In the past this paranoid shift of mind-set had rendered them dysfunctional as a group and an organization. They could see how this present incident denoted their collective tendency to retreat into fragmented and broken relational states. Previously self-centered and emotionally blind to the business of the larger organization, they had gained perspective and an opportunity for self-correcting actions in the future as a consequence of learning from experience and developing an intersubjective frame of reference.

For the psychoanalytically oriented organizational researchers and consultants and for the participants, focus on intersubjectivity and relational dynamics implies, metaphorically, conscious movement into the third area of potential space, where researchers and participants engage in reflective inquiry. The depth of reflective practice enables participants to detect regressive group processes and their associated negative consequences on the organization. Seeing the patterns of intersubjectivity and transference dynamics unique to their group and organization enhances consciousness, insight, and potential change. Joining the researchers and consultants at the apex of the triangle (figure 4), figuratively speaking, participants generate opportunities for intervention and change. With greater awareness and a shared desire to move forward, members are able to acknowledge entrenched narcissistic injuries and destructive dynamics such as projective identifications, which may arrive in the form of a purloined letter along with unconscious intent.

The colleagues could now return to the task at hand. Discovering organizational identity by way of the potential space, they reminded themselves of their commitment to the therapeutic and educational aims of the department. Group members felt they were better equipped to identify defensive actions in themselves and in the group. Defenses such as psychological splitting and projective identification had interfered and derailed the quality of their collective actions. They came to "know" their organizational story, that is, "know" as in the *unthought known* (see chapter 7), and consequently they had a better grasp on organizational identity.

Narrative Processes, Intersubjectivity, and the Organizational Story

The case example illustrates a key element of psychoanalytically oriented organizational research and intervention: organizational diagnosis, once complete, is presented publicly to participants in the form of an organizational story. This narrative process represents the production of intersubjective awareness in the form of a story coproduced by participants and researchers. This organizational story is intended to capture the essence of organizational identity.

The organizational story is derived from organizational research that more generally includes participant observation, qualitative data collection, and the analysis of transference and countertransference dynamics (Diamond, 2003; Diamond & Allcorn, 2003). The organizational narrative emerges between researchers/consultants and organizational participants. Organizational researchers/consultants are responsible for the theory and method, while the participants with the promise of anonymity and confidentiality agree to share candidly their experiences and observations.

In contrast with mainstream consultants, participants are often surprised by the psychoanalytically oriented organizational consultants' narrative directness and absence of camouflage or euphemism during feedback sessions. The organizational story is stripped of defensiveness. It resonates with participants because it gives voice and authority to their stories. "I can hear myself," some attendees claim out loud.

With potential space, workers are able to understand and appreciate their ongoing dynamic relational system. The organizational story offers members an alternative relational perspective—a perspective, despite the jargon, that tends to treat workers respectfully as human subjects rather than as objects or instrumental parts of a larger impersonal system. The discovery of organizational identity transcends the level of the individual and shifts the mind-set toward the organization as a relational and experiential system. The discovery of organizational identity out of the reflective, transitional, and potential space enables organizational participants to reclaim their humanity, with all its flaws and greatness.

The intersubjective dimension is a critical element of the discovery of organizational identity and the process of intervention for change. This potential space is woven out of participants' threads and their confirmation of the collective narrative. Participant-validated organizational identity promotes reflective and facilitated processes for planning, restructuring, resolving conflicts, and problem setting and solving. These reflective processes and associated actions are authorized and supported by leaders through consultants, who support a good enough holding environment and containment of participants' anxieties about separation and loss.

Reflecting on Organizational Identity, Intersubjectivity, and Potential Space

Organizations are relational, experiential, perceptual, and intellectual systems with an espoused collective mission and task environment. Viewing organizations as identities, which are collectively produced by participants and their leaders, implies the assumption of responsibility and ownership on the part of individuals who perpetuate and reproduce these organizational cultures (relational systems) with their everyday, often automatic and unconscious, routines and actions. From a contemporary psychoanalytic and systems perspective, organizational cultures are the construction of conscious and unconscious dialectical (social and psychological) forces between participants and with other organizational entities. And, while one might argue that these systems evolve and emerge automatically, if not unconsciously, over time, the notion of organizations as social-psychological and dialectical constructions supports the value of participants' reclaiming them (as their own creation) by associating their conscious and unconscious actions with the production of manifest and latent dimensions of the organizational identity.

The capacity of members to make intellectual and emotional connections with their collective representation of organization (externalized self-system) is critical to meaningful and valuable organizational-change processes (Diamond, 1984, 1988). The intersubjective dimension of organizational change heightens consultants' and participants' awareness of the organization as a relational system and their part in its production, destruction, and reproduction. This self-consciousness and reflectivity enable attention to defensive resistances to insight and change while enhancing members' capacity to assume responsibility for productive and counterproductive relationships and elements of organization.

The idea of intersubjective awareness as developing among participants in potential space is central to relational psychoanalytic theories of organizational change. The notion of the more humane organization as a good enough holding environment for reflection and change encourages psychoanalytic organizational scholars to attend to the perceptual, intellectual, experiential, and emotional productions of organizational participants that stem from linkages, couplings, boundary crossings, and collisions between members.

With its emphasis on relational psychodynamics, the concept of intersubjectivity accentuates for researchers the often dysfunctional and toxic psychodynamics of splitting, polarization, fragmentation, projection, introjection, and projective identification among organizational members. Further, as a frame of reference it enables organizational participants, with the assistance of psychoanalytic organizational researchers and consultants, to attend to the concept of organizational identity (as intersubjective structure composed of psychoanalytic data). From the intersubjective perspective, organizational identity emerges out of mutual recognition between workers and along with their capacity to transcend the subject-object duality found in the "us and them" social structures that are characteristic of so many regressive groups and organizations.[8]

Conclusion

The notion of intersubjectivity in psychoanalysis acknowledges that human nature is object-seeking and relational and that human interactions are dialectical and triangulated, which is a critical theoretical matter for organizational scholars. Developing the intersubjective dimension and the level of consciousness inherent to it requires repetition and the capacity of psychodynamically oriented consultants to pay attention to transference and countertransference. However, intersubjective awareness does not guarantee the ability to resist psychological regression and the relational distortions characteristic of projective identification. Nor does it promise the capacity to resist the participants' unconscious proclivity to over-control and manipulate subordinates with unequal power and authority. It does, however, offer a frame of reference for acknowledging and consciously articulating many of the destructive and counterproductive everyday practices of organizations and their leaders.

Thus, the concept of intersubjectivity brackets and clarifies the psychoanalytic organizational consultants' placement of their attention in consultation with participants. The notion of intersubjectivity in contemporary psychoanalysis and in psychoanalytically informed organizational research and consultation locates the triangular space (transitional and potential) in which authentic change and reflectivity are possible. Thus, the role and function of participant observation and the use of *oneself* as a barometer of relational sentience is enhanced by our understanding of the critical concepts of intersubjectivity and potential space. The capacity to interpret and experience self-object relationships in the context of groups and organizations as good enough or not good enough holding environments is transformative.

Next, I discuss the human act of repetition, and the compulsion to repeat, as another key feature of organizational identity. I also explore transference and countertransference and change and resistance to learning and change in the recurrence of structurally patterned relationships.

CHAPTER 5

Repetition, Remembering, and Change

Remembering then is what has to replace repetition. The struggle against resistance—what Freud calls "working through" (Durcharbeiten)—has no other aim than to reopen the path of memory.

But what is it to remember? It is not just to recall certain isolated events, but to become capable of forming meaningful sequences and ordered connections. In short, it is to be able to constitute one's own existence in the form of history where a memory as such is only a fragment of the narrative. It is the narrative structure of such life histories that makes a case history. (Ricoeur, 2012, p. 21)

Human nature is undeniably repetitive. Repetition is a normal and inescapable human characteristic. In sport, art, poetry, music, and child play, individuals exercise repetition—often unbeknownst to them. While individuals tacitly and constructively employ repetition as in the reflective practice of professional experts,[1] they typically do so where learning and years of successful practice are internalized along with advanced skills and competencies. So-called experts do what they do well because they no longer feel insecure and self-conscious and thus do not think too much about nor obsessively overthink "it." The baseball pitcher, when asked how he pitched a perfect game, simply says he was "in the groove."

Nevertheless, workers, managers, and leaders also engage in compulsive, and sometimes counterproductive, defensive repetitions. These typically unconscious repetitive patterns shape organizational identity. In this chapter, I explore organizational identity, learning, and change through the lens of repetition and the compulsion to repeat. In doing so, I am linking psychoanalytic theory with organizational theory, systems learning, and change, to address the question, how is the natural proclivity for repetition, productive and unproductive, constructive and destructive, addressed in organizational-change processes? In other words, how does the compulsion to repeat block and suppress practices of feedback and learning?

Organizational Diagnosis and Feedback:
Confronting a Destructive Repetitive Cycle

The psychoanalytic method of organizational study and change, which informs the practice of organizational diagnosis and feedback, is similar to the practice reported throughout this book and elsewhere (Diamond, 1993; Diamond & Allcorn, 2009; Levinson, 1972, 2002). The organizational diagnosis shapes the organizational story, a narrative (or multiple competing narratives) describing thematic and repetitive relational organizational dynamics. Discovery of the essence of organizational identity is the intended result, and the identity is typically confirmed by participants through processes of empathy and identification.

The organizational diagnosis is typically presented in feedback sessions where researchers say, "So, here's what we observed, heard, thought, and experienced. Tell us if you recognize yourselves in this story. Does it resonate?" In other words, do the participants *identify* with the organization depicted in the narrative?

Case Example: Repetition at a Police Department

A veteran police chief of twenty-five years in a department was rather set in his ways. He was convinced that complaints by his officers in the field were unfounded and otherwise "typical of any police department." The chief and his management team of captains seldom went out on shifts with the patrol officers. The captains' job responsibilities as outlined by their chief did not require them to do so. The police chief and captains spent their working hours during the daytime behind their desks, relying on the sergeants for information about street-level policing. Consequently, one of the primary complaints of patrol officers and their sergeants was that the chief and his captains were out of touch with the "reality" of police work and furthermore that they did not understand the challenges of everyday policing faced by the officers on the downtown streets and in neighborhoods. The chief's routinely dismissive attitude about the complaints of his sergeants and patrol officers was mirrored in the defiance of his captains. Predictably, the patrol officers were resentful and angry, experiencing the chief and his captains as "unappreciative" and "remote, disapproving parents." Consequently, sabotage and inappropriate practices on behalf of the patrol officers (such as abusing police vehicles, not engaging in traffic stops, unnecessarily aggressive behavior) occurred with some frequency, reinforcing the captains' and chief's shared view of the patrol officers as "juveniles."

A repetitive cycle of negative attributions and self-sealing defensive processes had ensued between them, with no foreseeable end to the persistent conflict. Over time this culture of "us against them" was taken for granted despite the stress it placed on everyone. This daily automatic and unconscious collective compulsion to repeat relational patterns between the two groups was unproductive and destructive. The "dismissive" and "withholding" police chief and his captains were too anxious and defensive to investigate and address the concerns of the police officers, and the "angry and rejected" police officers were resistant to hearing the perspective of the chief and his group of compliant captains.

Polarization, fragmentation, and unresolved conflict between the groups were perpetuated. An unconscious compulsion to repeat these opposing relational dynamics reinforced a dysfunctional status quo within the police department. Participants appeared to passively accept and defensively give in to what they rationalized either was typical of other police departments or was simply irreconcilable differences between the groups.

As discussed in chapter 3, when people in groups feel vulnerable they behave regressively, adults in childlike roles, and in defending themselves they engage in psychological splitting, projection, and projective identification. In this case, there is a vicious circular and self-sealing phenomenon at work.

In the case of this anonymous police department, the organizational research team communicated the story of an organization in persistent structural and psychological fragmentation, a dysfunctional department. A group of some officers and their leaders engaged in a self-sealing defensive process manifesting a deeper collective "unthinking" compulsion to repeat. There were a number of questions considered among consultants after providing the narrative depiction and observing participants' (and consultants') responses and feelings: Does the membership recall and acknowledge the negative repetition that is causing conflict, dysfunction, unproductive blaming, and defensive reactions? Is this group ready to learn from insight and assume personal responsibility, thus breaking with defensive routines and the status quo? Do organizational participants identify with the stories (competing narratives)[2] of opposing groups and the consequences of dysfunctional communication and disorganization?[3]

Compulsions to Repeat and Learning for Insight and Change

The work of confronting unspeakable, automatic, and previously unconscious compulsions to repeat "us against them" social acts of disavowal and scapegoating begins with observations and above-the-surface manifestations of latent emotions (see figure 2, levels 2–5). These initial observations attend to cognitive-behavioral processes of organizational learning and action (Argyris & Schon, 1996).

The cognitive-behavioral perspective represents the way many organization scholar-practitioners think about the link between observable habitual repetition and what is called "single-loop" or "self-sealing processes," which result in limited learning and change. Systemic learning and change are inhibited by individual and relational compulsions to repeat. The motivations of conformity and compliance in hierarchic and paramilitary organizations frequently undermine the importance of challenging the status quo and acting autonomously.

Attending to self-sealing interpersonal and organizational processes, which reinforce the status quo with defensive reasoning, routines, and so-called undiscussables, is a necessary but ultimately unsatisfactory level of analysis and intervention. This above-the-surface approach to change proffers a description of organizations as systems of learning, which typically involves a reflective practice of illustrating or mapping out cognitive and behavioral processes at work. This can be insightful and constructive, but it does not get at the emotional roots of defensive practices and relational dynamics at the heart of organizational identity. Moving from the manifest to the latent content, shifting collective attention of participants from above the surface to deeper recollections and memories of relational, perceptual, and experiential processes, requires the application of a psychoanalytic framework. Repetition is not merely a surface phenomenon, it has deep roots in human nature.

Organizational learning, psychoanalytic theory, and the compulsion to repeat can be better understood through the concepts of transference, countertransference, grief, and mourning.[4] Unconscious and automatic processes such as these must be understood consciously and at a level of self-awareness that eventually transcends the passive repetition in personal and professional relationships. Cognitive and emotional awareness can lead to the ability to break away from destructive and unproductive self-and-other, "us against them" relationships. Such change in the status quo requires conscious processes of remembering and the depressive practice of working through the grief and mourning of changing a familiar and ritualistic everyday practice.[5]

The distinction drawn by Loewald (1971) between *passive reproductive* forms of repetition and *active re-creative* forms is illuminating for organizational identity and change. Discriminating between destructive and constructive repetition is an insightful framework for interpreting collective acts of repetition within organizations. Telling the story is a central component of organizational diagnosis and the psychoanalytic method. It is the "royal road" to remembering and capturing destructive repetition and ineffective learning in organizational culture and identity.

In the case of the police department in the example, routines and rituals making up organizational identity were taken for granted and repeated without thought or reflection. The purpose of any intervention is assisting participants in remembering and becoming more conscious of the repetitive nature in their work processes and dynamics. Successful interventions must confront compulsive and schizoid organizational identities with regard to participants' passive, destructive, and repetitive dynamics.

Defensive Organizational Identifications and Passive Repetitions

Bureaucracy and administration theorists (Argyris & Schon, 1974; Crozier, 1964; Diamond, 1985; Merton, 1963; Weber, 1947) in the past have asserted that routine and repetitive structures of authority and accountability ensure clarity of tasks, roles, and responsibility. Some psychoanalytic theorists in the object relations tradition who study groups and organizations, such as Kernberg, claim that bureaucratic structures can positively assist management in minimizing the human proclivity to engage in psychologically regressive, counterproductive, and at times destructive behavior in groups and organizations (Bion, 1959b; Freud, 1921; Kernberg, 1998).

Configurations of authority and interpersonal relations at work produce and perpetuate organizational identities and ideologies in the form of organizational cultures and subcultures (see the discussion of group dynamics in chapter 3). These institutional identities are shaped by repetitive thematic and patterned narratives signifying experientially shared organizational stories, metaphors, and histories. Due in part, however, to the institutionalization of repetition and routine in the service of production, organizational members become oblivious to their workplace identity and practices. The status quo of defensive routines becomes automatic and unconscious. Organizational identity becomes harder to consciously access and articulate.

These bureaucratically structured and mechanistic work environments are taken for granted and grow to be numbingly familiar, functioning largely out of immediate awareness. This was the case within the police department, where the chief and his captains settled into a daily office routine insulated from the police officers and the realities of their unpredictable, at times dangerous and hostile community environment. For both groups in relation to each other, repetition and acting out replaced remembering and conscious awareness of their respective roles in producing and reproducing conflict and dysfunction on a daily basis. This was not about to change given the passive and avoidant behavior of the chief and captains. So, in effect, leadership was passively condoning the conflict and dismissiveness between captains and officers (management and workers).

The familiarity and automaticity that comes from routinization may be experienced as satisfactory to some, if only because eventually the taken-for-granted practices and mind-set are rendered unconscious. Weberian bureaucratic structure, command and control, and paramilitary organizational cultures are commonplace among traditional policing agencies and might appear administratively rational and reasonable on the surface.[6] However, the individual and group participants (officers and workers) eventually come to experience the routinized and repetitive social structures as rigid, confining, habitual, and mindless. While the chief and his captains found such routines suitable in a defensive and rationalized manner,[7] police officers experienced their organizational leadership as inaccessible, uncaring, and dismissive and so found the same structures unsuitable. More importantly, officers experienced suffocating limits on their discretion and autonomy, which in the real world of policing is problematic at best and dangerous at worst.

The case example of the police department presented in this chapter might be described as manifesting a detached and schizoid organizational identity (see homogenized and institutionalized work-group dynamics in chapter 3). The schizoid organizational identity comprises disconnected and remote organizational leadership and concurrently angry and hostile followers. It is characterized by detachment and a fortress mentality, which is notable in the actions of the chief and his captains. Consequently, this department's leadership perpetuated a culture of mistrust and a department defensively structured by an "us against them," Manichean mentality. This schizoid mind-set was apparent in their respective attitudes to citizen groups in the community as well. Rather than identifying themselves as protectors of and partners in the public safety of the community, they tended to perceive themselves as working in opposition to various segments of the community. Thus, unresponsive leadership unable to provide holding and containment of officers' frustrations and anxieties produced the schizoid problem of organizational fragmentation and dysfunction. The schizoid organizational identity of the police department appeared insurmountable.

Organizational identity is repetitive and ritualistic, comprised of defensive patterns that regulate threats to personal security and self-esteem by structuring and defining organizational life (Diamond, 1993). Individual, group, and organizational transformation requires awareness of repetitive and fragmented psychological and social structures. Fragmented and schizoid psychological structures and social structures typically mirror each other. The interactive mirroring effect here is paradoxical. One group subculture defines and identifies itself by opposition to another group subculture and vice versa.

This paradox is illustrated by the case of the schizoid police department. The police officers' group defined the group composed of the police chief and his captains as parental, dismissive, and contemptuous. The police chief and his captains defined the police officers' group as juvenile and disrespectful. Categorical absolutes were contrived out of infantile defensive actions such as psychological splitting. A Manichean psychology of us against them, good versus bad, right versus wrong, and knowing versus ignorant came to define the organizational identity of the police department.

Repetition is reinforced by fragmented thinking and interpersonal dynamics. Repetition and the compulsion to repeat are signified by unconscious transference and countertransference psychodynamics between leaders and followers, management and workers, captains and officers, in which emotions from childhood attachments are displaced onto someone in the present and that person unconsciously experiences them and possibly reacts, as described in chapter 1. Regressive organizational and interpersonal interactions perpetuate conflict and produce polarizing and rigid relational patterns. Opposition and conflict appear unending, resistant, frozen, and irreconcilable.

Deep learning and change is akin to what the philosopher and psychoanalyst Jonathan Lear calls the "primordial struggle."[8] Potential or anticipated change is often met with defensive resistance and aggression rooted in anxieties over loss of identity. Anxieties around separation and loss are associated with attachments to objects such as leadership, role, and organization. *Objects* here refers to internal object relations, which tend to be associated with emotional attachments.

For many, the anticipation of profound change provokes an existential threat over the loss of the illusion of certainty and predictability. These anxieties are embedded in the developmental psychodynamics of attachment, separation, and loss. Systemic learning cannot occur in the presence of ineffective leaders who lack the capacity for containment and who do not provide adequate holding.

Next, I consider the concept of repetition in light of organizational learning and change. The idea of organizational learning is presented through the pioneering work of Argyris and Schon (1978, 1996) and Argyris, Putnam, and Smith (1985). Pertinent to this chapter are indications for the heuristic limitations of the cognitive-behavioral approach when it is lacking a contemporary relational psychoanalytic application.

Repetition and Limited Learning: A Critical Review of the Theory of Organizational Learning and Change

Argyris and Schon (1978, 1996) view unproductive repetition and self-sealing processes as a consequence of faulty defensive reasoning and limited learning. In general they view individuals as having a limited capacity to produce deep and profound change at the levels of psychological and social structure. Accordingly, limited learning is manifest in individual and organizational theories of action where vicious circles of self-sealing processes and ineffective relational and systemic feedback loops create poor outcomes.[9]

Single-loop learning (also known as *first-order processing*) refers to this limited and unreflective capacity for individual and systemic change (Argyris & Schon, 1978, 1996). Argyris, Putnam, and Smith (1985) argue that limited learning and resistance to real change are governed by individual needs to avoid embarrassment and exposure as "incompetent" executives, managers, and workers. Organizational participants who work at this level of defensiveness become, in effect, incapable of surfacing errors and publicly testing privately held assumptions and attributions that might make them anxious or threatened. Hence, the repetitive and self-sealing processes of single-loop learning and defensive behavior curtail participants' ability to address interpersonal and organizational dysfunctions.

With single-loop learning, individuals are able to shift behavior and strategies to solve problems, but they are not capable of questioning and altering values, norms, or what Argyris and Schon (1978, 1996) call their own "theories of action." Theories of action are the combination of individually espoused theories and theories in use: what people claim they would do, on the one hand, and what they actually do in practice, on the other.

Single-loop learning reinforces defensive routines that unilaterally protect individuals from embarrassment and thereby block their public testing of assumptions and attributions that they hold privately in their heads. Frequently, espoused theories and theories in use are in contradiction and intentions do not match outcomes, and individuals are unaware of this conflict. Moreover, discussion or dialogue around the presence of such contradictions is unmentionable and considered taboo.

Deep change relies upon minimal defensiveness, critical reflection in practice (which Argyris and Schon call "double-loop" or "second-order" learning processes), and the ability among organizational members to fully articulate problems. This hyperconsciousness involves surfacing and attending to governing values, norms, and theories of action, which often perpetuate deep and persistent problems and foster errors in the first place. Argyris and Schon define individuals' capability for changing the status quo as the "double loop" of reflective practice in which the individual can fully admit to and articulate errors and problems, and subsequently invent and test solutions to these well-articulated problems. Such actions, for Argyris, Putnam, and Smith (1985), include changes in which individuals are able not only to question their behavioral and strategic assumptions but also to question and alter their underlying norms, values, and theories of action.

When pressed to answer the riddle of what makes the difference between those who can and those who cannot double-loop learn, Argyris, Putnam, and Smith (1985) indicate that the difference rests with the degree to which individuals are motivated by competence and effectiveness. In addition, they indicate that double-loop learning does not come naturally to anyone and therefore it has to be learned and practiced, ironically, through repetition.

In sum, proponents of organizational learning view resistance to change as a vicious circle of self-sealing behavior (Argyris & Schon, 1978). One is reminded of the myth of Sisyphus and the meaningless and mindless task of pushing a rock up a mountainside (see Kets de Vries, 2007). Time has stalled. It is irrelevant or nonexistent, as in the atemporal state of unconsciousness and primary-process thinking in psychoanalytic theory. Fragmented and repetitive psychological structures block reflectivity. Such defensive actions produce agents who are not cognizant of time or history. In the compulsion to repeat, routine and rational human actions are rendered automatic, unconscious, and ritualistic (Diamond, 1985). The repetitive actions at the surface of organized performance in modern organizations frequently make up dysfunctional, inefficient, and maladaptive processes and structures. What I am calling the cognitive-behavioral approach to learning (individual and organizational) is halted at the edge of explanation by its acknowledgment that limited learning is rooted in faulty reasoning and rationalization (Argyris, 2004), while, in actuality, the psychological roots of repetitive, automatic, and defensive actions are infantile and emotional. As Argyris (2004) himself indicates, defensive routines reinforce the status quo, limit learning and change, and are derived from the individual's desire to avoid embarrassment.

Organizational researchers and consultants are well served by a theoretical framework and comprehensive theory of human personality that informs their understanding of the human compulsion to repeat and resist learning from experience. Such a theory should provide insight into the human tendency to engage in what appear at the surface to be worthless, futile, and self-defeating acts of repetition, acts that reinforce the status quo with maladaptive strategies and structures. These compulsive practices have been described from a cognitive and behavioral perspective as self-sealing processes of single-loop learning (Argyris & Schon, 1978; Argyris, 1983) and from a psychoanalytic framework as indicative of ritualistic defenses (Diamond, 1985, 1993). Both perspectives encourage the acknowledgment of these defensive and dysfunctional repetitive actions. Theorists of organizational learning and change generally agree that professionals and their organizations would benefit from learning how to engage in reflective practices, which can move them beyond the vicious circle of single-loop learning and the limitations of unproductive repetition. Therefore, it is insufficient to attend to these cognitive and behavioral processes without exploring the defensive psychological and emotional roots of the compulsion to repeat.

The Circularity of Compulsive Repetition: The Psychodynamics of Single- and Double-Loop Learning

What Argyris and Schon (1978) refer to as "single-loop learning" and "self-sealing practices," psychoanalytic theorists might interpret as "repetition compulsion," the phenomenon of automatically and unconsciously repeating actions, thoughts, and feelings. Freud (2006b) originally referred to this compulsion to repeat, among other things, as evidence of a death instinct, or destructive drive. Individuals blindly repeat actions that reproduce painful outcomes. It is as if masochism were at play in these thoughtless, repetitive acts—acts that are self-defeating, punitive, and potentially harmful to the individual, group, and organization. In Freud's metapsychological schema, one can imagine a punitive superego (conscience, "I-above") directing the individual ego ("I") in repetitive actions that evoke identical results. This defensive maneuver of repetition compulsion signifies an attempt on behalf of the individual (self/ego) to manage anxiety by repressing, forgetting, denying, and undoing the presence of the object that stirred the anxiety in the first place. According to Lear (2005), what Freud observes is compulsive repetitiveness: "Repetition is not the aim of the repetition, if there is an aim here it is to avoid facing up to the looming situation by inducing disruption and anxiety" (p. 160).

In other words, the compulsion to repeat is inherently about avoiding and undoing the problem at hand. This was particularly true in the case of the police chief and his captains. They preferred to perpetuate the fantasized rationalization as explanation for their broken department by stating how they were no different than any other police department, and that police officers are juveniles. This rationalization among leadership and management (chief and captains) not only reinforced the status quo and resistance to change, it also perpetuated juvenile and aggressive behavior among the officers on the city streets. Continuing on with their unaltered daily routines meant they could operate as if nothing were wrong. In reality, negative news reporting on the department and its officers transpired frequently. Consequently, city officials demanded change in officer morale and performance as well as improved relations with the community and citizens.

Evidence for compulsive repetitiveness is documented in the move from individual to work-group and organizational analysis. For example, Bion (1959b) depicts basic assumption groups of fight/flight, pairing, and dependency; Menzies's (1960) classic empirical study of a nursing service of a general hospital portrays social systems as a defense against anxiety; Kernberg (1998) explains bureaucratization as a defense against anxiety; and I describe facets of "bureaucracy as externalized self-system" in my article by that title (1984). While intending to merely illustrate behaviors and strategies governed by individual reasoning, Argyris and Schon in their model of single-loop learning, self-sealing processes, and defensive routines depict what psychoanalytic theorists call "repetition compulsion" (or the compulsion to repeat). Such actions are seemingly automatic and unconscious and, more pertinent to our discussion, shared among people in cooperative systems such as organizations.

The individual and group compulsion to repeat is innate to human nature. For individuals, groups, and organizations, repetitive actions are frequently unconscious and counterproductive. In the article "Between Memory and Destiny: Repetition" (2007), Marucco writes, "The analyst is then summoned to halt this circularity of repetition in which the subject loses himself" (p. 319). Transcending the vicious circle of self-reinforcing feedback loops described in the organizational learning literature requires meaningful and proactive change in the form of intervention and disruption of individuals, groups, and organizations that are operating automatically and unconsciously. In fact, individuals engaged in the compulsion to repeat lose self-consciousness and can even jeopardize their capacity as effective change agents. These repetitive cycles demand our attention in considering the psychodynamics of constructive organizational learning and change. Locating oneself and others behind the structure of repetition is a critical step in discovering organizational identity.

The Structure of Repetition

In the discussion that follows, I explore the structure of repetitive processes in individuals, groups, and organizations with the aim of better understanding the psychodynamic processes of meaningful organizational insight and change. Authentic and genuine change in organizations requires a conscious and persistent breaking-up and undoing of unconscious repetitive structures in individuals, groups, and organizations, which is precisely the function of organizational diagnosis as a precursor to intervention strategies and practices (Diamond & Allcorn, 2009; Levinson, 1972, 2002).

A paradigmatic shift drawing from contemporary infancy and clinical research, attachment theory, neuroscience, and object relations theory (as explained in earlier chapters) has occurred within contemporary psychoanalysis. This change describes the individual as "object-seeking," which in the contemporary psychoanalytic literature of object relations refers to the individual motivation to relate to and form attachments with others. Psychoanalysts now view the self (substituting for the concept of the ego) as organizing experience and shaping perceptions and thereby one's sense of self and other—a metaphorical self-organization. Memories and experiences of self are rooted in attachment and in earliest (infantile) internalizations of mothering and holding. Ultimately, internal (self and other) object relations, as represented by organized experiences with significant others, shape individual perceptions of others and influence the character of shared emotions in routine transferences and countertransferences between organizational members.

Contemporary psychoanalytic approaches define organizations as relational and experiential systems (Diamond & Allcorn, 2009). From this perspective, analysts view the organization as a collision between social and psychological defensive structures (Diamond & Allcorn, 2009). One cannot fully understand an organization without interpreting the meaning and quality of interpersonal relationships and experience within it—as in discovering organizational identity. Thus, the intersubjective dynamics of transference and countertransference between individual members, leaders and followers, of the organization are central to understanding the nature of repetition and repetition compulsion in organizations. Without the understanding derived from hours of interviewing individuals and groups, and as a result of observing and participating in everyday work routines and processes in the police department, the consultants could not have empathized simultaneously with the officers on the street and with the chief and captains in the main office. This empathic understanding of two groups with opposing narratives engaged in mutual self-destruction was critical to telling their story, establishing the potential space for breaking the compulsion to repeat, and promoting organizational change.

Repetition in Transference, Countertransference, Grief, and Mourning

Acknowledgment of the potency of feedback loops in organizational learning and change (Argyris, 1983) is fundamental in the role played by transference and countertransference dynamics. Proponents of organizational learning lack a concept of transference. Consequently they cannot fully understand the resistance and negative emotional reactions to exposing individual contradictions and to attempts at publicly testing fellow workers' privately held assumptions and attributions.

In the contemporary psychoanalytically oriented organizational theory and method presented in this book, I acknowledge that participants engage in transference and countertransference dynamics with colleagues, managers, and executives as well as with consultants. These transference and countertransference dynamics unconsciously influence and complicate relationships between supervisors and subordinates, between executives and staff, and between co-workers. It is worth repeating that *transference* in organizations describes the psychodynamic processes in which individuals compulsively and repeatedly project feelings rooted in childhood attachments and earlier relationships onto colleagues and supervisors in the present, and that *countertransference* describes the unconscious and automatic emotional responses of others to the experience of projected and displaced emotions directed onto them. Adult workers unwittingly engage in childlike roles and relationships, as in the case example of the police department. This is particularly evident in hierarchic arrangements between leaders and followers in contemporary organizations.

The consultants' telling of the organizational story is met with a sense of recognition, validation, and confirmation, on the one hand, and feelings of shame, exposure, and incompetence, on the other hand. Rather than simply confirming the consultants' perceptions of the organizational story, organizational members find themselves face to face with strange, repressed, denied, and split-off parts of themselves. Underneath superficial appearances, members often feel confronted by the combination of subjective and objective (internal and external) realities of past performances. Performances that are understood as forms of acting out repetitively and habitually, such as transference and countertransference patterns of interpersonal relations, are contrary to their emotional well-being and contrary to effective administration of organizational tasks, missions, and responsibilities (Diamond, 1985, 1993).

According to Freud (2006b),

> We soon realize that transference is itself merely an instance of repetition, and that this transference involves *repetition of the forgotten past* [emphasis added] not only onto the physician, but onto all other areas of the patient's current situation. We must therefore expect that the patient will yield to the compulsion to repeat—which now takes the place of the impulse to remember—not only in his personal relationship to the physician, but in all other activities and relationships taking place in his life at the same time; for example, if during the course of treatment he chooses a love-object, takes some task upon himself in a project of any sort. The greater the resistance, the more thoroughly remembering will be replaced by acting out (repetition). (p. 395)

For Freud, resistance to change is about acting out, and acting out takes on an automatic and unconscious repetitive form for the individual in that it shapes the character of transference and of primary relationships. Lear (2005) notes, "Transference, then, is a repetition that cannot (yet) be remembered in the right sort of way" (p. 136). Without cognizance of their history, the police officers in the case example and their superiors acted out toward each other in repetitive patterns that shaped and reinforced their regressive and childlike experiences of one another. Officers were perceived as disobedient children by leadership, while the chief and his captains were perceived as dismissive and uncaring parents by the officers. Competing narratives signified deeper meanings and motives that produced repetitive cycles of destructive interaction.

To break this vicious circle of destructive repetition and self-sealing behavior would require a transitional process in which participants claimed responsibility for the dueling narratives and subsequently acknowledged emotional loss and the need to mourn as the path to change. Profound change is a process of consciously letting go of old routines and repetitions and simultaneously internalizing new and alternative practices. In the case of the police department, this would require a narrative reconciliation of sorts across the organizational boundary between the two groups in the conflict. A third and alternative narrative would need to emerge from the acceptance and confirmation by the chief, captains, and officers of an organizational diagnosis that best depicted the story of a police department unwittingly stuck in unproductive repetition and the compulsion to repeat.

Thus far it has been argued that repetitions are inevitable in the emotional attachments of individual and organizational life, shaped by the emotional knot of transference and countertransference dynamics. It is incumbent upon us to sort out the nature of these repetitions. Transference dynamics are repetitive relational patterns, constructive and destructive. They are at the heart of organizational identity.

Reflective versus Unreflective Practice

In distinguishing repetition from repetition compulsion, Loewald (1971) maintains that there are two forms of repetition in human life: repeating by action, otherwise known as "acting out," and repeating in what he calls the "psychical field," otherwise known as the mind (cognitions and emotions). Loewald explains, "Acting out is a concept strictly related to the concept of reproduction in the psychical field; i.e. acting out is an alternative to remembering in the narrow sense" (p. 59). One might think of this as the process of undoing painful memories, as with trauma. When considering repetitive acts, Loewald provides a useful and insightful difference between passive and unconscious reproduction, and active and conscious re-creation. Paradoxically, for Loewald, reproduction and re-creation are not only oppositional forces, they are complementary actions. Thus, passive reproduction and active re-creation are two sides of the same phenomenon, parts of the whole gestalt. Passive reproduction is a defensive repetition, often manifest in a form of "acting out." It represents an unreflective practice, while active re-creation is a nondefensive repetition, a form of awareness and reflective practice.

Action in the outer world can be understood as acting out only insofar as it is seen as taking place *instead* of repetition in the psychic field. If such action occurs as *the external manifestation of or as the result of* psychic re-creation, then it is not acting out but re-creative repetition in the external arena. (Loewald, 1971, p. 60)

Lear (2007) describes passive repetition as "imagination trapped in unfreedom" (p. 304). As with the case of the police department, paranoid-schizoid[10] modes of experience, manifested by polarized and coercive relational dynamics of psychological splitting and projective identification, predominate (Ogden, 1989). As a schizoid organization, the police department was polarized and psychologically split into an "us and them" structure. Consequently, officers projected aggression onto the chief and his captains and vice-versa, resulting in both groups' identifying with the other's projection—"imagination trapped in unfreedom."

Table 3 clarifies the dissimilarity between passive and active repetition. It describes the unconscious, ahistorical characteristics of passive reproductive repetition as a self-sealing process. This self-sealing process reinforces paranoid and schizoid modes of experience, emotional and cognitive (ego or self) disorganization, and defensive and compulsive interpersonal and organizational dynamics. These psychodynamics are destructive and counterproductive, indicative of what Freud (1920) calls the death instinct.

In contrast, active and re-creative repetition signifies the capacity "to face the future" or "the possibility for new possibilities" (Lear, 2007). Active repetition requires historical awareness and self-consciousness. As with Klein's and Ogden's relational, integrative, and reparative description of the depressive mode of experience, actions are grounded in reality. The depressive mode is characterized by making contact with others, not splitting and fragmentation of self and other. Repetition in this mode is intentional and reflective, supportive of deeper learning and change.

As stated at the beginning of this chapter, repetition is a normal and inescapable social and psychological phenomenon. Beyond the so-called malady of repetition compulsion, repetition is essential to the development of ego mastery.[11] Active and re-creative repetition is a crucial ego function that supports the establishment of self-confidence and competence. It is an essential dimension behind reflective practice.

Active repetitive practice supports second-order, double-loop learning and reflective action. Organizationally, active repetition is central to building effective systems. It is essential to designing effective and efficient work flow, rational and reasonable divisions of labor, structures of accountability, task specialization, delegations of responsibility with authority, role clarity, and the

TABLE 3 Differences between Passive and Active Repetition

Passive Repetition	Active Repetition
Unconscious	Conscious
Ahistorical	Historical
Ego disorganization	Ego organization
Schizoid or fragmented psychic structure	Integrated psychic structure
Paranoid-schizoid mode of experience	Depressive mode of experience
Primitive defenses such as psychological splitting and projective identification	Mature defenses such as rationalization and humor
Unreflective practice	Intentional and reflective practice
Death drive	Eros and libidinal drive
Passive reproduction	Active re-creation

matching of intentions with outcomes. Of course, in many bureaucratic institutions, passive repetition produces structural and operational dysfunction, goal displacement, limited learning from experience, and minimal reflectivity in practice. This was certainly the case with the police department. Awareness of organizational identity and thematic repetitive patterns of managerial responses to critical incidents is essential to real change. Officers and superiors of the police department articulated numerous critical incidents, which were then presented in the narrative organizational diagnosis. With confirmation of the narrative and their organizational identity, the members of the department could coherently confront the defensive nature of their passive repetition.

Organizational Stories: Narrative
Themes and Repetitive Structures

Psychoanalytically oriented organizational research and consultation involve the construction of organizational stories (narratives) from repetitive patterns, themes, and points of urgency. These narratives, if shaped by empathy and identification, evidence "listening deeply" to groups and individuals (Stein,

1994) and, if woven out of repetitive themes, signify organizational identity (Diamond, 1993).

Rooted in organizational stories told by organizational analysts and shaped by transference and countertransference dynamics between key players, organizational interventions can expose these unthinking, ahistorical, nonreflective, and unconscious vicious circles of self-destructive repetition. The organizational story as told by the consultants often triggers the processes of emotional loss and mourning. Participants come face to face with the reality of inevitable change and the grief associated with the need to let go of familiar and comforting old attachments to rituals and routines, such as the emotional knots of transference and countertransference between leaders and followers. When confirmed by participants, the organizational story activates resonance and deeper understanding of the link between unconscious actions, repetition, and reinforcing the status quo. A sense of responsibility and ownership of the present dilemma is then possible, but it is not ever definite. Change occurs when memory and reflectivity replace unconscious repetitive actions.

Frequently the collective history and critical moments in the life of an organization and its members are suppressed and taken for granted. These memories are often displaced by a sense of the most immediate and concrete problems of the moment and thereby rendered unconscious. Routinely, organizational members rationalize their not wanting to reflect on the past, saying it is "a waste of time" and "irrelevant to the business at hand." These groups are stuck in regressive positions where primitive, first-order cognitive processing tends to be siloed, fragmented, and ahistorical. Thus, as noted above, the model, method, and process of organizational diagnosis is designed and intended to elicit historical and narrative data organized around crises and critical incidents of the past. Psychoanalytic organizational researchers and consultants expose the hidden relational dynamics behind the superficiality of everyday work life, resulting in an organizational narrative that is "telling them what they know," as in the unthought known (see chapter 7), or as Freud's patients are reported to have said in one form or another: "Oh, I knew that. I just hadn't thought of it."

Organizational Diagnosis, Repetition, and Change

In organizational diagnosis, researchers and consultants reach a critical phase in the processes of organizational change when they share feedback (organizational story) with participants. These participants often experience the telling of the organizational story with mixed and conflicting emotions (Diamond, 2008). By this point in organizational assessment, ideally, consultants have established good enough trust and empathy through positive transference and countertransference. Once the organizational story is shared with and confirmed by participants, consultants scrutinize participants' response to the narrative. The consultants indirectly ask participants to reflect on the cost of their suppression and denial, and the price of individual and collective pain and suffering resulting in a fragmented group and organization. It is also helpful to point toward the consequence of these defensive routines in producing antagonistic camps—dismissive parents versus resentful juveniles, as in the case of the police department. Psychoanalytically oriented organizational consultants can further ask participants to consider how their defensive resistance against this knowledge and self-awareness works for them and against them. The social and psychological benefit of constructive confrontation at this stage is intended to promote claimed actions and responsibility among participants. Since change cannot be immediate and takes time and active repetition, researchers and consultants have to follow up with participants. On-site follow-up interventions enable consultants to illustrate defenses in real time and in participants' routine daily operations, asking, "There it is. Do you see it? Can you claim it?" In his book *Freud* (2005), Lear describes it,

> Psychoanalysis itself is a building up of a practical-cognitive skill of recognizing the fractal nature of one's unconscious conflicts as they are unfolding in the here and now—and of intervening in ways that make a satisfying difference. (p. 52)

Conscious and external acknowledgment by participants is an important step in the process of change, but it does not necessarily reflect deeper understanding of patterns and shapes of organized experience that are rendered unconscious and part and parcel of the intersubjective life of organizational identity.

The psychoanalytically oriented consultant is forever skeptical of the depth of insight and change. This skepticism is based on her awareness of unconscious processes and the ritualistic nature of repetition compulsion and psychological regression. Despite the participants' agreement with the narrative content of the organizational story, without the capacity to reflect on their actions and practices over time and in the moment, change may be limited and short-lived. Without the capacity to observe and experience these patterns and repetitions in the moment, participants will not come to understand their collective past and its impact on the present moment at work. As Freud (2006b) puts it,

> It is now quite plain to us that the start of a patient's analysis does not mean the end of his illness, and that we need to treat the illness not as a matter belonging to the past but as a force operating in the present. (p. 396)

Process Consultation Psychodynamics:
Interrupting the Compulsion to Repeat

Similarly, unconscious defensive and repetitive patterns of organizational identity are dynamic. While organizational diagnosis includes historical and narrative data, *interventions open up systems to themselves, enabling the possibility of learning from reflection.* For example, in process consultation (Schein, 1999), consultants attend to the organizational dynamics in the here and now in ways that expose historical patterns and institutionalized defensive routines for organizational participants. Psychodynamic interventions such as process consultation are intended to raise the level of awareness in individuals, groups, and organizations about defensive routines stemming from transference dynamics that inhibit participants' capacity to learn and make effective changes. Even the most successful of consultations do not leave the organization radically transformed from dysfunctional to functional or from failing to succeeding. Rather, more often such interventions help organizational members learn to detect, intervene, and interrupt the repetitive and self-sealing processes in their organizations before they get completely out of hand.

Ultimately, it is the degree of enhanced awareness, and consciousness, and the capacity to change and to intervene based on what participants know from their emotional attachments, collective history, and culture that makes a difference. Awareness of the passive repetition is possible as participants become more attuned to the signals of defensive and unconscious processes steering the management of the organization. Nevertheless, the human nature of repetition compulsion does not disappear, it is rather better known, thought of, and periodically worked through. As Lear (2007) describes it,

> If we think of the concept of working through in its broadest context, it seems to me to be nothing other than the process in which the human psyche is reoriented towards, habituated into, happiness and freedom. I do not

mean any particular moment of joy, but the conditions in which a human can flourish. When in analysis we see an analysand locked in repetition, we thereby see an imagination trapped in unfreedom. Working through is precisely the process by which the analysand's imagination is opened up for new possibilities. This possibility for new possibilities is precisely what it is to face the future creatively. (p. 304)

In the case of the police department, officers and their superiors felt stuck and could not imagine their way out. Psychoanalytic organizational research and consultation uncovers the compulsion to repeat embedded within transference relations between participants. Cognizance of transference patterns is crucial to the capacity to melt away the routinized and repetitive cycle of self-sealing behavior. Psychoanalytic organizational diagnoses tell the story of repetitive themes and passive reproductive repetitions at work. If masked by defensive rationalizations, whole policies and administrative programs may be produced by professionals and policy analysts without reflectivity.

Conclusion

Real organizational change requires working through and breaking away from compulsive and repetitive cycles. These *passive repetitions* are defensive and unconsciously relied on by participants to abate their anxieties. Planned organizational change requires participants' self-awareness and organizational empowerment. It requires a hold on repetition in the form of *active re-creations*. This means that participants can identify patterns of compulsive repetitions and self-sealing processes that limit organizational learning and effectiveness. Having this awareness and competency translates into participants' ability to confront and potentially reverse resistance to change. When deeper and more profound change is desired, psychoanalytic organizational research and consultation and the discovery of organizational identity are beneficial. Insight precedes change. Consultants and participants need a psychodynamic framework that views organizations as experiential and relational. Genuine change requires analysis of intersubjective structures, active repetition, and working relationships.

In this chapter I located a central feature of resistance to organizational learning and change in passive repetitions and the compulsion to repeat. Profound change necessitates a confrontation with psychological and organizational compulsion to repeat. This confrontation is one of substituting nonthinking for thinking, unconscious processes for conscious ones.

Chapter 6 continues this exploration of organizational insight and change with the analytic and linguistic application of metaphors and metaphoric processes. It explores how these metaphoric processes and organizational images shape organizational identity.

CHAPTER 6

Metaphor and Metaphoric Processes

Metaphor is pervasive in everyday life, not just in language but in thought and action. Our ordinary conceptual system in terms of which we both think and act is fundamentally metaphorical in nature. . . . But our conceptual system is not something we are normally aware of. (Lakoff and Johnson, 1980, p. 3)

In the previous chapter, I explained the human act of repetition as both constructive and destructive, and as both facilitating and restricting the potential space of learning and change. In this chapter, I explain metaphor and metaphoric processes, which are also both constructive and destructive. In particular, I contrast the phenomenon of frozen metaphor with its fluid counterpart. In *Images of Organization* (2006), Morgan distinguishes among multiple images of organizations. These include organizations as machines, organisms, brains, cultures, political systems, psychic prisons, instruments of domination, and more. Each image shapes differently and rather significantly how organizational theorists frame and subsequently analyze organizational dynamics.

Metaphor and Change

Passive repetitions, discussed in the previous chapter, entrap forgetful minds inside perpetual emotional knots and vicious circles of unconscious transference and countertransference. Frozen metaphors and metaphoric processes similarly obstruct insight and change, while fluid metaphors and images ignite creativity and imagination essential to change in the status quo. It should be noted that each image and metaphor has its strengths and weaknesses, its emphasis and de-emphasis of particular variables and levels of analysis.

Metaphor is often understood as a figure of speech, or the act of seeing something in terms of something else, as in a symbol or implicit comparison.

But it is much more than that. Metaphor is an imaginative and unconscious process of mind central to the possibility of constructing meaningful, relational, and collective exchange. It is at the heart of our mind's conceptual systems.

Metaphor transcends words. It makes connections. It bridges diverse people, groups, and organizations. Metaphor is shaped by emotional and unconscious processes. It is formulated out of creativity and the play of imagination. It emerges out of the capacity to construct transitional and potential space.

Metaphor is therefore rooted in the human facility to communicate experience and emotion, to make human contact. With metaphor, individuals have the potential to experience resonance with (alien) others, across borders and boundaries (self and others, subject and objects) and amid diverse groups.

In this chapter I explore the unconscious imagination and its metaphoric processes, out of which meaningful human experience, mutual understanding, consensual validation, and organizational identity originate. From a psychoanalytic perspective, the *fluidity* and openness of metaphoric processes are seen as critical to group and organizational insight and change. Consequently, awareness and understanding of *frozen* and closed, or fixed, metaphoric processes that block the potential for positive transformation and change are also important. Change can be understood as group processes of movement from freezing to unfreezing to refreezing, or from binding to unbinding to rebinding. A brief case example of frozen metaphor, intended to illuminate the discussion of metaphoric processes, imagination, and change, follows.

Case Example: Frozen Metaphors at a Public Works Department
Many years ago a public works department requested an organizational study. The presenting problem articulated by a newly appointed director described an agency threatened with legislative defunding due to its persistently going over budget and not meeting scheduled timetables for work completion on construction projects. In fact, the agency had gained a poor reputation for having workers who stood by equipment at construction sites awaiting authorization for change orders and requisitions. The new director felt as if he had inherited a dysfunctional agency.

In the process of organizational assessment of this department,[1] including interviews, observations, and factual and historical data collection, the participants often referred to themselves as "working in silos." Narrative data from interviews of architects, engineers, accountants, lawyers, administrators, and construction managers, as well as observational and conversational data collected over the course of six months, revealed a frequency among workers to use the metaphor of silos in describing their organization, as workers in many other organizations do.

Ultimately, the consultants came to understand that workers were describing frozen rather than fluid processes. They experienced themselves as working inside rigid disciplinary and specialized silos. The concept of silos as frozen metaphor described participants' work relationships and experiences, and their incapacity to exchange viewpoints, ideas, technical knowledge, perspectives, and frustrations. "Working in silos" meant they were trapped within their professional and divisional fortresses. Thus, they felt unable to work across boundaries and between professional subcultures, despite the fact that collectively they shared responsibility for the completion of agency construction projects. From interviews and observations of organizational participants, it became clear to the consultants that the frozen metaphor of the silo embodied as-yet-unarticulated feelings. Organizational participants frequently referred to silos as descriptive of their jobs, as being within silos, and of their organizational dysfunction.

Participants described their experiences of lateral relations as being within hard surfaces, using descriptive words such as *suffocation, stifling of ideas and emotions, excessively limited mobility,* and *entrapment.* "Working in silos" meant they felt stuck inside their functional specialization, without the power and authority to effectively communicate with colleagues across professional divisions and units. They felt trapped within their respective professional roles.

Frozen metaphoric processes were characterized by structurally enforced closed-mindedness and limited lateral mobility among these agency workers. In contrast, fluid metaphoric processes and open-mindedness are embodied in an ability to cross boundaries, creating interdisciplinary collaboration. Participants working in these conditions feel less encumbered personally, interpersonally, and with respect to their superiors. They tend to be less debilitated by anxiety and more capable of sharing their diverse and distinct experiences with colleagues. In the case of the public works agency, fluid metaphoric processes were unrealized and to participants seemed *unimaginable.*

While there is more detail to this case study than is presented here, the point of offering this illustration is to provide the reader with a point of reference for understanding metaphoric processes.

Psychological Origins of Metaphoric Processes

Metaphor is rooted in the unconscious imagination. It is a linguistic and psychological vehicle for articulating experience without which we might not fully understand the meaning of and motivation for organizational membership and affiliation. Freud's *Group Psychology and the Analysis of the Ego* (1921) is an example of imagination and metaphor at work. Freud interprets the nature of affiliation through processes of individual *identification* with the ego ideal of the group leader, and these processes are essential to understanding group cohesion. He offers a deeper understanding of the group mind by analyzing leader-follower (self and other) object relations—a context shaped by suggestion, contagion, and empathic mirroring. Group members unconsciously *transfer*[2] and thereby forfeit their individual and separate ego ideals, their autonomy, over to the seductively narcissistic self-image of the leader. In essence, group members *transfer* their personal autonomy over to the authority of the group leader. Dependency is substituted for independence, membership takes the place of separateness and differentiation. According to Freud and Bion (1959b), this happens as a consequence of the entrants' experience of anxiety and regression as characteristic features of joining a group (see chapter 3). Entrants feel threatened and insecure. They react to these anxieties by splitting good and bad self-images and consequently projecting idealized images onto the omnipotent figure of the organizational leader with whom they come to identify.

This metaphoric act of transfer involves a linguistic and psychological shift. This shift signifies a transition away from passive, repetitive, compulsive, frozen, and unconscious metaphoric processes, such as the case example of silos, and toward more proactive, fluid, and consciously open linguistic processes. As in the case example, the silo metaphor can be seen as representing organizational members' feelings of entrapment, ineffectiveness, and powerlessness. Thus, in the public works agency, transition required acknowledgment of the historical and psychological effects of oppressive and authoritarian hierarchic leadership, which restricted workers from leaving their silos and better coordinating tasks and projects. Workers were unconsciously operating on the basis of past assumptions held by previous leaders and organizational cultures. Progress meant that they had to engage their professional colleagues by crossing previously forbidden disciplinary boundaries.

Metaphor as a creative and imaginative psychological process produces the capacity to mend and repair dysfunctional organizational boundaries and relationships. A deeper understanding of metaphor (fluid or frozen) augments our collective understanding of organizational identity. The human proclivity at the public works agency to defend borders and boundaries (intra- and extra-organizational) against perceived threats—which resulted in the silo metaphor—was instituted from the top down, or imposed on workers. Imagination and creativity, which are critical to insight, restoration, and change, are unavailable to groups stuck in frozen metaphoric processes such as the silos. Change is dubious and organizations are frozen in time and space. Workers stuck in frozen metaphors and metaphoric processes cannot imagine a different reality than that of fragmented and conflicted organizational membership.

In this chapter, change for individuals, groups, and organizations refers to constructive and reparative transformation. It represents a restoration of more satisfying and productive human relations (peaceful coexistence and mutually beneficial and healthful exchanges) across interpersonal, geographical, group, and organizational borders and boundaries. I view progressive change as an open, fluid, and generative metaphoric process. Progressive change stands in opposition to frozen metaphoric processes, which are involuntary, automatic, unconscious, and repressed. Frozen metaphoric processes are examples of repetition and the compulsion to repeat discussed in the previous chapter. These apparently frozen and repetitive unconscious relational dynamics were prominent in the public works agency. As consultants listened, empathized, and identified, participants became more engaged in a reflective and conscious process of discovery and change.

In the following sections, I present a fuller understanding of metaphor and metaphoric processes and discuss their application to organizations and organizational change.

Metaphor as Process

The word metaphor comes from two Greek words meaning "to carry over," and refers to a set of linguistic processes whereby aspects of one object are carried over or transferred to another object so that the second object is spoken of as if it were the first. (Arlow, 1979, p. 367)

In the case example of the public works agency, the participants did not initially see the concept "we work in silos" as idiosyncratic. Rather, the workers saw it as typical of any public agency. During the course of the organizational diagnosis, agency workers simply took the silo mentality for granted. Taking it for granted, of course, meant that it was rendered unconscious until the study resurfaced it as a meaningful metaphor, after which its significance seemed to resonate with the participants.

Transference as Metaphoric Process

Metaphor, as previously noted, is frequently defined as seeing something in terms of something else. For instance, in the case example, workers saw the new director as the old director. In many instances, organizational members see incoming consultants as spies or saviors. In the case of the police department discussed earlier, the captains viewed the officers as juveniles and the officers viewed the captains as dismissive parents. Psychoanalytic organizational researchers and consultants might interpret the present as signifying the past and the past as suggestive of the present. Past and present are related metaphorically and paradoxically. This implies, as in the sharing and displacing of human emotions known as *transference,* that from the perspective of both metaphorical domains, past and present have an effect on each other. One understands the present in view of the past, and the past in view of the present. Memory is *recontextualized* and linked to unconscious metaphoric process (Modell, 2006, pp. 35–38).

Since humans are meaning-generating creatures, when we make contact with one another, the process entails transferring, consciously and unconsciously, our psychological reality and individual modes of organizing experience, developed in the past, onto the present. According to Moore and Fine (1990), transference is "the displacement of patterns of feelings, thoughts, and behavior, originally experienced in relation to significant figures during childhood, onto a person involved in a current interpersonal relationship" (p. 196). This process is largely unconscious and therefore outside the awareness of the subject. Transference occurs as a result of the nature of the here-and-now object relations between self and other triggering familiar assumptions and archaic feelings rooted in previous attachments.

This viewpoint broadens the notion of metaphor toward a supralinguistic and psychoanalytic perspective. As Richards (1955) puts it, "Words do not mean, we mean by words. The total fabric of our meanings which constitute the world as we know it, consists not of actual or inherited experience, each attached to an appropriate word or set of words, but linguistic and psychological laws regarding recurrent likenesses of behavior in our mind and in the world to which words are variously adapted by us" (p. 12). In the case example, the metaphor of silos was meaningless without consideration of what it meant to the many workers who used the metaphor to describe their experience of the public works agency. Hawkes (1972), more broadly, claims:

> Language is an organic, self-contained, autonomous system which divides and classifies experience in its own terms and along its own lines. In the course of the process, it imposes its own particular shape on the world of those who speak it. . . . a language creates reality in its own image. To use language thus essentially involves getting at one kind of reality through another. This process is fundamentally one of transference, i.e., a metaphorical apprehension of the world and its realities. From this point of view, all language, by the nature of its transferring "relation to reality", is fundamentally metaphorical. (p. 59)

The notion of "getting at one kind of reality through another" poignantly defines the metaphorical act of transference of emotions among workers. Articulating the meaning of the silo metaphor and connecting that meaning to frozen metaphoric processes led consultants to discover organizational identity as a shared social defense.

Within formal organizations, structural hierarchy and roles of power and authority frequently provide a context for transference and countertransference (between super- and subordinates) reminiscent of childhood experiences of power relations. Participants bring these past experiences and associations to present relationships and interactions in the form of transference and countertransference dynamics. The present is a metaphor for the past as the past is a metaphor for the present. The displacement of patterns of thinking, feeling, and action from the past onto the present occurs in everyday life and is expected to be especially prevalent in organizations where issues of power and authority are present and memories are recontextualized. Members of the public works agency learned to adapt over time to a psychologically regressive organizational identity that limited their discretion to a degree reminiscent of that in childhood. Silos were partly created by psychological splitting and projection, where those inside the silo were good and those outside were bad. According to management, for example, all the workers were bad (incompetent) and needed to be controlled and held accountable by the chain of command. The image of them working inside silos helped to establish the managers' control over presumably irresponsible workers. The managers were not only in silos as well as the subordinates, their hierarchic control and domination of subordinates were reinforcing the silo mentality throughout the organization, fostering distrust and uncooperativeness among managers and subordinates, vertically and horizontally.

Countertransference: The Researcher/Consultant's Experience

Countertransference works much the same as transference. It arises in response to organizational members' transference of emotions onto consultants, which triggers emotional reactions from the consultants' inner object worlds and personal biographies. Emotions are then unconsciously displaced onto organizational members, which in turn influences researchers' perceptions. Countertransference is the consultants' own unconscious responses to organizational members. Unprocessed countertransference dynamics between consultants and participants can be problematic.

Psychoanalytically oriented organizational researchers and consultants, however, are more likely to pay attention to these cognitive and emotional reactions and to think of them as psychoanalytic data. These data are in fact critical to empathy and identification with the predicament of organizational members. Acknowledgment of countertransference dynamics places emotional pressure on researchers such that working with others as a team of consultants in the field becomes advantageous to their processing their individual reactions and to constructive utilization of countertransference data.

Countertransference is always present in participant observation in the workplace. Some organizational theorists include under the general concept of countertransference all of the consultant's emotional reactions to the organizational participants, conscious and unconscious. This broader definition can be viewed as a counterreaction, as compared with the more narrow definition of countertransference. In the case example above, the consultants processed experiences and reactions to participants following daily engagements.

Finally, the theoretical implications of using transference and countertransference as metaphor to better understand the psychological reality of organizations and organizational identities requires elaboration.

The Metaphoric Nature of Transference and Countertransference in Organizational Identity

Organizational life is rich with transference dynamics between participants as well as between individuals and their image of organization reflected in the organizational identity and the psychodynamics between leaders and followers, consultants and organizational participants, and members themselves. Individual executives may evoke positive transference from some employees and negative transference[3] from others, depending upon the quality and vicissitudes of internalized authority relations and childhood experiences. Employees may evoke positive or negative transference on the part of executives depending on, for example, how responsive they are to receiving direction. The perception of resistance may be unconsciously associated with a memory of a past relationship with a parent who stubbornly resisted the efforts of the child to affect the parent. Moreover, groups and divisions within organizations transfer their collective experiences and perceptions onto other groups and divisions within the organization.

These same processes of transference are frequently evoked among participants relative to consultants, who are often viewed as intruders and outsiders. In this regard, the analysis of transference and countertransference dynamics offers insight into the relationship between consultants and organizational members, and into the aims and fantasies of organizational members regarding their relations with each other and their experience of power and authority. These psychodynamics, as signified by the many dimensions of subject-to-subject relations, are components of organizational identity. Attention to these relational dynamics frequently reveals the unique character of group and organizational identity. As with the case example, observation of typically frozen and closed-minded, defensive and fixed, metaphoric processes in the present moment belong to and are shaped by the past. Psychoanalytically oriented researchers and consultants therefore view them as unconscious acts of psychological regression.

Transference as Shaped by Psychological Regression

As illustrated in chapter 3, on group dynamics, psychological regression[4] represents an unknowing effort among organization members to manage their anxieties about uncertainty and loss of control. Regression is defined as a metaphoric but consequential return to earlier modes of object relations when conflicts emerge. To put it simply, adults come to rely on familiar, yet unconscious, childhood defenses to combat anxieties at work. Regression is most often accompanied by the interplay of transference, projection, and splitting. Psychological regression signifies the meaning and interpretation of adult behavior as a metaphor for past experience in childhood.

Group and organizational membership necessitates an intrapersonal compromise between individual demands for dependency and autonomy, membership and separateness. These are dilemmas of human development rooted in the psychodynamics of separation and individuation. The mere presence of a group, Bion (1959b) observes, presumes a defensive state of psychological regression among all the participants. Referencing Freud (1921), Bion explains, "Substance is given to the phantasy that the group exists by the fact that the regression involves the individual in a loss of his 'individual distinctiveness' (1921: 9). . . . It follows that if the observer judges a group to be in existence the individuals composing it must have experienced this regression" (1959b, p. 142). For Freud and Bion, psychological regression coincides with group and institutional membership. Certainly this is illustrated by the case example of the public works agency through the frozen metaphor of silos.

Conclusion

The example of organizational silos in the case of the public works agency represents a return to our original primitive world of touch and surfaces, the autistic-contiguous mode of preverbal and embodied experience. Thus, silos and the silo mentality are a manifestation of psychological regression (Diamond, Allcorn, & Stein, 2004; Diamond, Stein, & Allcorn, 2002) and a collective image shared by organizational members. Silos illustrated frozen metaphoric processes located in transferences and projections of organizational members. Silos also represented their loss of freedom and relative autonomy as workers in a bureaucratic organization. In addition, silos signified a psychological time and space in which the desire for safety and security was dominant. The intervention, as an avenue to opening up the (potential space) system of organization to itself, raised the awareness of organizational members about how they created and maintained the silos that isolated them from one another. The researchers opened and maintained a potential space where the silo metaphor could be examined and reimagined as a feature of organizational identity. In doing so, organizational members moved from frozen metaphoric processes that limited creativity and progress to fluid processes that enabled them to view structural boundaries and borders as healthy containers that are permeable and welcoming structures rather than forbidding and isolating barriers.

As knowledge of metaphor is embodied and experienced, the unthought known is a deep embodied and experiential knowledge. In the next chapter, I consider the idea of the unthought known and its function in feedback sessions with organizational participants.

CHAPTER 7

The Unthought Known

We could say that personal idiom is known but has not yet been thought and that it is part of the unthought known. So one of the features of a psychoanalysis is to think the unthought known, which is part of the core of the individual, and to do so through object usage and the drive to unfold the self through time and space. (Bollas, 1989, pp. 40–41)

In this chapter, I apply the psychoanalytic concept of the *unthought known*[1] to the process of discovering organizational identity. In particular, the concept of the unthought known is helpful in understanding the nature of defensive resistance and in telling the organizational story in feedback sessions with organizational participants. Organizational participants, or clients, frequently respond to narrative feedback[2] that action researchers gather in a manner that suggests that organizational identity is known but has not yet been thought. Thus, it is critical to help participants unpack what they know so they can better articulate organizational identity in a meaningful, conscious, reflective manner. While organizational researchers' and consultants' narrative descriptions of patterned intersubjective dynamics and organizational culture might be consistent with participants' actual observations and experiences, they often have not been thought of, or have not been thought of in productive ways that might positively influence effectiveness and change. On the one hand, organizational identity is unconscious and outside of awareness (Diamond, 1993), while on the other hand, it is a form of collective knowledge that as yet is unthought (Bollas, 1989; Diamond, 2008). I provide a case example.

This chapter explores and advances our understanding of the psychosocial dynamics associated with feedback sessions designed to provide a narrative of organizational identity that resonates with employees, and with the context of transference and countertransference between organizational consultants and employees. In the context of larger organizational diagnosis and intervention, a shared, collective understanding of the challenges is a necessary prerequisite for learning and change efforts. Individuals and groups are frequently convinced that their perspective of what is "really wrong" is accurate. Similarly, others are fixed to their opposing viewpoints. The challenge for consultants is to formulate a collective depiction that truly reflects the points of view of *all* participants, and then to offer this depiction in a group setting for validation and confirmation (Diamond, 1993; Diamond & Allcorn, 2003; Kets de Vries, 2001; Levinson, 2002).

Feedback sessions are typically filled with anxiety and tension, and one never knows exactly what to expect. In the interests of further exploring the experiences of participants in this and related cases, I delve into several psychoanalytic ideas that bridge Freudian psychoanalysis and more contemporary psychoanalytic self psychology (Atwood & Stolorow, 1984) and object relations theory (Bollas, 1987; Winnicott, 1971). These particular concepts illuminate the psychodynamics of feedback sessions and the nature of transference-countertransference interactions. I explore the interpretive and process significance of consultants' empathy for and identification with participants. These psychoanalytic concepts highlight the emotional (perceptual, experiential, and relational) dimensions of organizational diagnosis and change.[3] Foremost among these concepts is the *unthought known*.

Transference and Feedback Sessions and the Concept of the Unthought Known

As members of a cooperative system, individuals and groups are linked together, emotionally and cognitively. The concepts of transference and countertransference capture these emotional bonds through the unconscious structure and patterns of working relationships known as the organizational identity. The commitment to interpreting the context of transference and countertransference dynamics between organizational participants and consultants is critical (Diamond & Allcorn, 2003).

In particular, the concept of the unthought known to a degree refers to primitive, preverbal and infantile, modes of experience. Adapting Bollas's (1987) idea of the unthought known to feedback sessions, it describes organizational participants who cannot as yet express their conflict in words, so the full articulation of preverbal transference evolves in the consultant's countertransference.

Case Example: Feedback and the Unthought Known at a Police Department
The meetings were thick with anxiety, anticipation, and restrained aggression. The officers in a police department (also discussed in chapter 5) anticipated a presentation that might validate their anger and hostility toward their captains and police chief. Feelings of frustration and vulnerability were palpable. Officers were anxious about how much of their story the consultants would actually share in feedback sessions with the entire staff. The consultants too were anxious about how the feedback might be received by the stressed police officers, captains, and chief.

In preparing their organizational diagnosis, the consultants had collected data over several months and formulated an organizational story. The narrative and presentation were based on and included an image of a dysfunctional and fragmented organization as perceived by officers, civilian staff, stakeholders, and leadership. Drawing from the psychoanalytic data,[4] the findings described what had been communicated scores of times during the individual and group interviews. Officers and other staff perceived the captains as "dismissive and out of touch," and the leadership perceived the officers as "acting like unruly children." Each group treated the other in a manner consistent with these expectations. There were competing narratives.

Following the presentation of the organizational diagnosis and assessment,[5] the captains and chief were uncomfortable and initially defensive, indicating that in their minds this described many police departments and was nothing new. The officers and staff confirmed the findings of their collective perceptions and experiences as depicted, commenting, "You nailed it," implying that the interpretation resonated with their own experiences. They indicated that they felt validated and understood. However, this corroboration led one agitated sergeant to say, "Yeah, but we knew this already!" Another added, "Nothing is going to change."

How do we understand these comments? Do we take them at face value and assume that nothing has been accomplished by openly articulating problems and issues in a coherent and confirmable manner?

These comments represented participants' cynicism about change given their experiences, to say nothing of their cynicism about consultants. This in part related to the fact that public agencies are notorious for their periodic reorganizations, in which they raise expectations and ultimately leave employees feeling disappointed and angry when the change efforts do not meet them. These emotional reactions among officers and staff might be expected.

It is the role of psychoanalytically oriented organizational researchers and consultants to interpret and articulate participants' unacknowledged and un-articulated feelings. In this context, to say something is an unthought known refers to the absence of conscious thought and reflectivity about, for instance, the intergroup conflict, which is known at a deep, preverbal, embodied, and unconscious level of a participant's consciousness. Feelings, frustrations, and memories are frequently embodied, unprocessed, and unspoken; this is the psychodynamic nature of organizational identity—it is known but not as yet thought. In the present case, the police officers felt empathy and identification with the consultants' observations and experiences of the police department and its members. Officers responded with confirmation: "Yeah, but we knew that already!" The organizational story is understood and felt as true by the participants with the assistance of consultants as the observing and partici-pating others. The unthought known turns into a thought known by way of confirmation and validation of the shared organizational narrative. The orga-nizational story and the language articulating it are claimed and emotionally processed by department members. The consultant's self in countertransfer-ence becomes an instrument of research and consultation. This is the essence of psychoanalytically informed, experience-near consultation.

From a theoretical perspective, individual acknowledgment of "not know-ing" requires consultants' and participants' open-mindedness and the capaci-ty for reflectivity in practice. Organizational psychologists Chris Argyris and Donald Schon (1996) might in contrast see limited reflectivity and faulty rea-soning at work. These are characteristic of what they call "model 1 theories of action" and the defensive routines of "single-loop learning." However, there is more going on. Discussing the "undiscussable" requires overcoming uncon-scious resistance to emotionally fraught and disorganizing issues or problems. To do so demands that individuals confront their anxieties and associated de-fenses, which reinforce such undiscussables.[6]

One forgets or no longer attends to experiences associated with unaccept-able, unpleasant, traumatic experience. Attention and memory become se-lective. For Freud (1938) and Klein (1946), unconscious processes involve psychological splitting of the ego. This splitting into part-object relations, according to Klein (1959), originates in infancy as a defense against perse-cutory anxieties. Splitting of the ego means that whole-objects (others) be-come part-objects, dividing and discriminating self and object into good or bad, all or nothing, nurturing or rejecting, loving or hating. People experience anxiety about change and the loss and uncertainty associated with it. These psychodynamics provoke regression (adults to childlike roles) and psychological splitting manifested in the "us against them" mentality. This phenomenon is on display in the case example of the embattled police department.

Psychoanalytically oriented organizational theorists and consultants assume that contemplation of such unconscious dynamics among individuals, groups, and organizations is critical to insightful organizational diagnosis and assessment. A primary goal of organizational diagnosis presented here is the articulation of organizational identity. Ideally, the organizational narrative is viewed as constructed, perpetuated, and owned by organizational members transforming the unthought known into conscious and articulated organizational identity. This approach to organizational diagnosis requires that consultants and organizational participants attend to the psychological dynamics and underlying assumptions, experiences, and perceptions shaped by the members' collective history of organizational culture and leadership. In other words, in the context of transference and countertransference, the discovery of organizational identity demands the consultant's use of self as an instrument of observation and reflection.

Feedback to Organizational Members in a School of Medicine

Sometimes during presentation of an organizational diagnosis, consultants are confronted by groups that respond oddly, such as one group of physicians and medical staff who responded with silence. In this instance, the consultants felt the need to let the silence settle into their skin and bones, if you will, into the experience of everyone present. It seemed important to surrender to the silence and the inevitable anxieties associated with it and to allow the weighty affect to become embodied in the group. So the consultants simply did not say anything for approximately five very long, agonizing minutes. At the end of this period of silence, the lead consultant looked at the consulting team seated by his side in the front of the auditorium and said, "Okay, I guess we missed it, let's go." Then the lead consultant closed his folder of papers and signaled to the team that it was time to leave, and they turned toward the door. At this moment a senior physician in the back of the room of sixty or so medical doctors and staff stood up and proclaimed, "No, you got it right! It's time we dealt with it!" It was as if the group felt frozen, confronted, and rather shocked by the cold, wet reality of the narrative truth of their organizational identity. It was as if this more senior physician was unconsciously authorized by the group to speak on their behalf. Once this symbolic leader had acknowledged the "unthought known," other participants followed with vocalized confirmation.

This reverberation among participants and with the consultants occurs when the organizational researchers are able to engage and reflect on the transference and countertransference dynamics between themselves, their participants, and their experience of immersion inside an organizational culture.[7] The organizational past becomes more clearly reflected in the challenges of the moment. Organizational participants begin to differentiate past from present, and the work of change becomes more imaginable. What was preverbal is now thoughtfully articulated with words. In "Remembering, Repeating, and Working Through," Freud (2006b) notes, "When the patient speaks of these 'forgotten' things, he rarely fails to add: 'I've always known that really, I've just never thought of it'" (p. 392).

Defensive Resistance and the Unthought Known

Among psychoanalytic researchers and consultants of organizations, the admission of "not knowing" signifies healthy naiveté, curiosity, and imagination. The success of feedback to clients is based on the consultant's empathic articulation of organizational identity without concealing or camouflaging the shared problems and issues. This hermeneutic practice and analytic attitude encourages the participants to think the unthought known. Of course, this quality of feedback does not occur without some defensive resistance. After all, considerable emotional and unconscious effort initially brought about the organizational participants' collective effort to repress their pain and disappointment.

Skillful defensive maneuvers in the form of denial and repression among participants keep the reality of a challenging and sometimes painful work experience out of mind. Employees in many organizations do extraordinary work, even under difficult conditions, including cultures of negativity and complaining. So, when consultants give voice to the reality and the gravity of the situation, and do so in sessions attended by all leaders and subordinates, it is typically experienced by organizational members as being in direct opposition to their efforts to keep such things "away." The notion of "resistance" here is not used in a negative or disparaging way, but rather to indicate the normal and expected reaction of individuals confronted with change—individuals who do not necessarily want to fully acknowledge the difficult issues openly.

In opposition to members' resistance to change, the organizational identity, as presented to participants in feedback sessions, tends to surface a narrative truth embedded in their experiences and perceptions. In so doing, the narrative is an opportunity for authentic as opposed to defensive engagements

around issues and problems of significance and importance to the organization and its stakeholders. Thus, feedback sessions call for an authentic view of
the organization, or the essence of organizational identity, which is necessary
in moving organizations away from excessive defensiveness and toward productive change.

In an effort to deepen our understanding of feedback to workers and to further illuminate resistance to organizational change, I use case examples from
the police department intervention to illustrate the unthought known. It is
worth repeating that it is less the case that organizational members do not
know and more that they have not thought of it. *It* refers to the researchers'
and consultants' articulation of the organizational identity, which is their best
depiction of the organization as a synthesis of unconscious processes, narrative themes, patterns, and points of urgency (Diamond, 1993; Kets de Vries &
Miller, 1984). *It* refers to the organizational identity as a representation of the
results of the consultants' listening deeply (Stein, 1994), observing, participating, and communicating with and back to organizational participants. How
might we think about these unconscious processes in assessing and working
with organizations?

With respect to the case of the police department, some critical observers
or readers might say, "Oh, so you told them what they already knew." This
implies: "What did they need you for if all you did was tell them what they
already knew?" The organizational analysts' response would be to say, "Yes and
no." It may be true that by conveying their observations and interpretations,
consultants communicate something the organizational participants "already
know." This is the case particularly because the feedback is derived from the
organizational members through on-site observations, experiences, and interpretations. Ideally, organizational identity is a declaration in organizational
participants' voice. These data are derived from the participants themselves
and then contained,[8] processed, and formed by the consultants into the organizational identity.

Organizational members had *not thought of it*. They *knew it but they had
not consciously thought* about it. Possibly they felt it but could not articulate
it. Consultants observe behavior and body language contrary to the statement
"We knew it all along." That is, participants sometimes appear anxious and
defensive. They seem to have an assortment of unspoken and unacknowledged
feelings, ranging from shame and guilt to hostility and shock, surrounding the
consultants' presentation of organizational identity. It often feels as if the consultants have surfaced something taboo and too awkward to speak about—the

so-called undiscussable. In fact, frequently the comment is followed by, "Yes, but no one has pulled it [the organizational identity] together in this way; we have not seen it or heard it in this form." They seem to be saying it (organizational identity) is different now, as if its form and meaning were previously unarticulated and without words. Then some courageous members say, "Sure, we knew it, but now it's out in the open and we have to deal with it." This sort of a statement is an acknowledgment of collective responsibility for and validation of the organizational identity—a critical step in moving forward.

Then there are those who, in an apparent state of amazement, say, "I knew there were problems but I didn't know it was this bad!" It is as if the act of surfacing the organizational identity *re-minds* organizational members of the emotional shape and sensations of their embodied and suppressed emotions. Is this an illustration of surfacing the unmentionable, and more particularly the unthought known?

Whatever the nature of their response, the process tends to result in enhanced consciousness of participants' collective experiences and perceptions over time. The seemingly contradictory "no" response to the participants proclaiming that what they heard from the consultants is what they already knew is indicative of the "unthought known."

In the police department in the case example, transference and countertransference dynamics were shaped by the combination of a chain of command and individual proclivities in role. In that case, a narcissistic and dismissive chief surrounded himself with captains hungry for his recognition and approval—what can be described as a mirroring transference. His emotionally (and physically) distant captains then treated the officers in a manner that unconsciously mirrored their treatment by the chief. Police officers at all ranks "knew" this (they could feel it), but they could not discuss it. It was unspeakable, at least until the consultants arrived and presented it openly at the feedback sessions.

The Organizational-Change Agent as Transitional and Transformational Object

Profound change requires a "good enough facilitating environment" for members that provides for a secure, safe, and trustworthy relationship with consultants. This Winnicottian facilitating, or holding, environment permits the confidence and curiosity among members needed for insight, learning, and change. Using the analogy of the mother-infant bond, the participants see the organizational researchers and consultants as transformational objects signifying maturation and change.

If organizational diagnosis unveils a narrative truth in the organizational identity and unspeakable story of organizational membership, then inevitably people will not only have something to say about it but will experience it as well. To say that transference between consultants and organizational members assumes the shape of a "transformational" or "transitional" intersubjectivity refers to an emotional attachment, often in the form of dependency on the part of participants on organizational consultants. This relational bond is derived from trust, empathy, identification, and the eventual production of a potential space, all of which evolves and emerges from the beginning contractual and contact phase of the engagement.

In *The Shadow of the Object* (1987), Bollas develops the idea that in adult life individuals seek others. This is also true for leaders and participants in the process of organizational diagnosis and change. It is generally acknowledged that organizational diagnostic processes stir primitive emotions rooted in experiences of attachment, separation, and loss, which then trigger associated anxieties inside the participants (Diamond, 1984, 1998; Jaques, 1955; Kernberg, 1979; Menzies, 1960; Stein, 1994, 1998, 2001). Executives and their employees somewhat reluctantly open up their systems to inspection, exposing their vulnerabilities and admitting their need for help.

Some participants will not like what they feel or think about the consultants' feedback in the organizational diagnosis. They may displace these bad feelings onto the consultants and project blame upon them for the participants' dysfunctional circumstances: "Well, it really wasn't so bad until you showed up!" The response to anticipated anxiety about organizational diagnosis and feedback leads to splitting good and bad feelings and then projecting typically the bad feelings, perhaps guilt, onto the consultants. This experience would not meet the unconscious expectations and fantasies they hold of consultants' coming in and magically healing the organization. Eventually members confront their anxious feelings about change, loss, and grief. Psychodynamically oriented consultants speak to these expectations and fantasies, minimizing anxieties and defensive retreat resulting from participants' acknowledging the unthought known.

The Methodology of Organizational
Diagnosis and the Unthought Known

In the practice of organizational diagnosis, researcher immersion into the members' organizational culture is essential. Over an unspecified period of time, organizational researchers and consultants become containers of the participants' unthought known by way of transference and countertransference. Observations and experiences of repetitive relational and hierarchic patterns of intersubjectivity in time come into focus (Diamond & Allcorn, 2003). Participants may unwittingly treat consultants as spies and invited intruders, saviors and messiahs, jesters and fools, among other covert roles. Unconscious fantasies are frequently displaced onto the consultant as a transformational object and rendered outside of the participants' awareness.

Organizational researchers and consultants give words and feelings to many things that have been organizationally acted out but unarticulated. This is the nature of the unthought known. Psychoanalytically oriented consultants articulate what appear to be irrational acts by leaders and work groups, acts that, to be sure, have been rationalized in words but can nevertheless be self-destructive to the leader and/or the organization.[9] Organizational members share with consultants their stories in the context of their experiences of themselves, others, groups, and the organization. Consultants assemble these individual and group narratives into feedback shaped by the psychoanalytic data and the process of uncovering of patterns, themes, and points of urgency (Diamond, 1993; Diamond & Allcorn, 2003; Gabriel, 1999; Kets de Vries & Miller, 1984, 1987; Levinson, 1972; Stein, 1994). These data are then interpreted and shared with organizational members in feedback sessions.

The approach taken here assumes that organizational identity resides beneath strategy and structure, behavior and work processes, and mission and power relations connected to hierarchy. Organizational identity is predominantly unconscious and ultimately located at the core of intersubjective relations. These intersubjective dynamics shape assumptions, values, and artifacts held at the surface of organization. The approach presented here highlights these levels of analysis and the idea that organizations are made up of structured relational experiences and perceptions. Organizations comprise psychological and intersubjective realities as well as social, political, economic, and structural realities. Feedback that is meaningful then resonates with the participants—even if resonance means they initially say they "knew it all along."

Transference, the Compulsion to
Repeat, and Process Consultation

Central to the method of organizational diagnosis is the process of constructing organizational identity by arranging data collected (factual, historical, narrative, and experiential) into repetitive patterns, themes, and points of urgency. These stories are coauthored narratives and, if done with sufficient empathy and introspection, are the result of "listening deeply" to groups and individuals (Stein, 1994). Frequently, the collective history and the critical moments in the life of an organization are suppressed, forgotten, and taken for granted by organizational participants. Collective memories may be displaced by a sense of the most immediate and concrete problems and thereby rendered unconscious. Organizational members often rationalize that reflecting on the past is "a waste of time" and therefore "irrelevant to the business at hand." Formal and informal groups may become locked inside polarized and fragmented states of mind, where collective thinking is ahistorical. Consequently, critical moments are much harder to access as data composing the organizational story. The method and processes of organizational diagnosis are intended to elicit these historical data.

The potency of feedback loops in the processes of organizational learning and change (Argyris, 1983) is inherent to the dynamics of transference and countertransference. Participants experience the sharing of the organizational identity with mixed and often conflicting emotions such as recognizing, validating, and confirming of their feelings and perceptions, on the one hand, and anxiously shaming and exposing the participants, on the other. In the latter situation, rather than simply experiencing confirmation of their perceptions, members find themselves face to face with a strange, repressed, denied, and split-off part of themselves as organizational participants. They are confronted by the subjective and objective (internal and external) realities of their performance as acting out repetitively and automatically patterns of interpersonal relations that are at times contrary to their well-being, frequently destructive, and often counterproductive to their tasks, missions, and responsibilities (Diamond, 1985, 1993).

It becomes clear in the course of psychoanalytically informed organizational consultation that the process reaches a critical phase in organizational experience when the time comes to share feedback with participants. By this stage, ideally, the consultants have established good enough trust and empathy through positive transference and countertransference. Once the organizational identity is conveyed and confirmed by participants, the consultants can constructively confront their confirmation by encouraging them to consider why the intervention was necessary to address their organization's issues, problems, themes, and points of urgency. The consultants can ask them to consider the extent of their suppression and denial (of course, not in these precise words), and, further, to consider how their routine defenses work for them and against them simultaneously. Most importantly, however, the researchers have to follow up with them with an on-site intervention that enables the consultants to illustrate these defenses in real time and in their routine daily operations, pointing out, "There it is. Do you see it? Can you claim it?" Lear (2005) explains,

> Psychoanalysis itself is a building up of a practical-cognitive skill of recognizing the fractal nature of one's unconscious conflicts as they are unfolding in the here and now—and of intervening in ways that make a satisfying difference. (p. 52)

Conscious and external acknowledgment on behalf of participants is an important step in the process of change, but it does not necessarily reflect deeper understanding of the patterns and shapes of organized experience that are rendered unconscious and part and parcel of the intersubjective life of an organization—what I refer to as the organizational identity. The psychoanalytically oriented consultant is forever skeptical of the depth of change, based on his awareness of the unthought known and the ritualistic nature of repetition compulsion and acting out discussed in chapter 5. For despite the participants' acknowledgment and agreement with the narrative content of the organizational story, without the capacity to reflect on their actions and practices over time, and without the capacity to observe and experience these patterns and repetitions in the moment, they will not come to understand the emotional shape and nature of their collective past and its impact upon their present and the moment-to-moment routines of their work life. As Freud (2006b) puts it,

> It is now quite plain to us that the start of a patient's analysis does not mean the end of his illness, and that we need to treat the illness not as a matter belonging to the past but as a force operating in the present. (p. 396)

Organizational change is dynamic and of the present. While an organizational diagnosis comprises historical and narrative data, the intervention of researchers and consultants opens up the organizational process to participant observation from the outset. In process consultation (Schein, 1999) as an applied intervention, analysts attend to the organizational dynamics in the here and now in ways that exhibit and confirm historical patterns and institutionalized defensive routines for organizational participants. Interventions such as process consultation are intended to raise the level of awareness in individuals, groups, and organizations about defensive routines that inhibit their capacity to learn and make effective changes. Even the most successful of consultations does not leave the organization radically transformed from dysfunctional to functional or from failing to succeeding. Rather, it enables people to intervene and interrupt repetitive and self-sealing processes before they get completely out of hand. It enables them to put the knowledge of organizational identity to work.

It is the participants' consciousness and capacity to change and to intervene based on what they know from their collective history and organizational identity that makes a difference. Awareness of the compulsion to repeat is possible as participants become more attuned to the signals of unconscious processes taking over the management of an organization. Nevertheless, repetition compulsion, as part of human nature, does not disappear, it is simply better known, thought of, and periodically worked through.

Repression and the Pre-reflective Unconscious

Repression is understood as a process whereby particular configurations of self and object are prevented from crystallizing in awareness. . . . The "dynamic unconscious," from this point of view, consists in that set of configurations that consciousness is not permitted to assume, because of their association with emotional conflict and subjective danger. Particular memories, fantasies, feelings, and other experiential contents are repressed because they threaten to actualize configurations. (Atwood & Stolorow, 1984, p. 35)

Atwood and Stolorow claim that the unconscious was never entirely unconscious. Rather, as Freud indicates, it is the result of repression and splitting of experiences and perceptions of object relations in infancy and early childhood. These repressive and fragmented processes are in defense of the self. Thus, these sensate, autistic-contiguous experiences are forgotten until and unless they are recalled, reconstructed, reenacted, and reexperienced in the course of analysis. Given the emotional and at times traumatic nature of repressed thought, a positive transference is essential for a consultant to be able to put into words that which a client has lost to the unconscious. Thus, these embodied memory traces are facilitated by the consultant's capacity to eventually put into words the past experiences organizational members repress. To say that certain experiences and emotional content are repressed and unconscious, however, does not mean they have no everyday effect on individual relationships. For example, repetition compulsions, as discussed at length in chapter 5, are observable as a result of routine emotional seepage revealed in counterproductive and destructive interpersonal behavior at work.

On the matter of organizational-change processes, some might suggest that defensive denial and undoing are at work among participants during feedback sessions. Some might say that individuals prefer to defensively avoid owning up to "the way things are." Given the frequency with which this defensiveness occurs in feedback sessions, it is more apt to be a defense against painful memories and a lack of readiness to face the collective problems and associated anguish at the institutional doorstep. These organizational participants who reject the narrative feedback are then confronted by others, who proclaim to the consultants, "You nailed it. It's high time we deal with these problems." Eventually, assuming the consultants did "get it," the more overtly resistant individuals relinquish their false selves. This means they abandon the need for denial, disavowal, perfectionism, and false pride. These surrendered defenses are their last-ditch effort to avoid acknowledging responsibility for organizational dysfunction.

False Self, True Self, and Organizational Change

Winnicott (1965) writes about the defensive nature of the false self, "Its defensive function is to hide and protect the true self, whatever that might be." He elaborates: "Observers tend to think it is the real person in relationships; however *the false self begins to fail in situations in which what is expected is a whole person* [emphasis added]. The false self is essentially lacking, the true self is hidden" (p. 144). Organizational diagnosis confronts the researcher and subject-system with the "true self" of the organization, one with a projected self-image of good *and* bad attributes, as opposed to the "false self" of the "party line."[10] This means that participants accustomed to relational systems rooted in suspicious and fragmentary modes of experience in which psychological splitting is incorporated and institutionalized into the status quo will find themselves having to wrestle, emotionally and cognitively, with the concept of integrated whole-objects as opposed to fragmented and part-object relationships.

This means that in telling the organizational story at feedback sessions, researchers are confronting participants with their best articulation of the authentic and actual organizational identity (collective or group self), as in the competing narratives of the case of the police department. This confrontation collides with the defensive and false patina of organizational identity, which participants actively promote, although often unwittingly. Frequently, participants respond defensively to the narrative presentation regardless of how balanced, nonjudgmental, and descriptively written and communicated. In fact, many feel judged and respond by saying, "Well, it can't be that bad!" and "Don't you have anything good to say?" It is as if the guards at the gate of the false self are reassembling to protect the potentially vulnerable participants from within.

Conclusion

In essence, one could say that organizational participants leave behind parts of themselves in their collective organizational history. Organizational members are known to repress, disavow, and deny the meaning and experience of past crises, conflicts, and mistakes, which is precisely what the feedback in organizational diagnosis stands up against. This practice of repression and psychological splitting is familiar to many observers of government agencies and corporations. As noted here and in chapter 5, organizational leaders do not typically appreciate the value of remembering, repeating, and working through as a form of deep learning and change. The collective influences the defensive nature of organizations and organizational identity. Leaders on occasion try to shepherd their organizations into the future in order to escape, rather than confront, the past. Thus, it can be said that organizational participants are regularly discouraged from reparative and integrative processes of grief and mourning (Diamond, 1993; Stein, 1994).

Consequently, individual organizational members experience themselves in relation to their work and organizations as part-objects. That is, they engage in primitive defensive forms of psychological splitting, blaming, and shunning personal responsibility. They are time and again discouraged from examining and reexperiencing negative events. Consequently, they split off bad experiences and render them unconscious. Such organizational cultures facilitate organizations in which participants stress a particular fantasized and omnipotent image of self as good and perfect. Thus, the function of the narrative in organizational diagnosis and change becomes crucial to reintegrating organizational participants with their true selves as more whole and less fragmented, as imperfect and capable of learning and change.

However, the social defense against change, loss, and grief is substantial among participants. Bringing organizational history into the light of present-day operations and human relations in the narrative form of depicting organizational identity is at the heart of psychoanalytically oriented organizational research and consultation. Empathically and effectively confronting workers' defenses and resistances to insight and learning depends upon the consultants' facilitation of a reparative and integrative process. The act of surfacing and attending to seemingly unconscious dynamics is a phenomenon of the un-thought known, which is shaped by repetitive themes, patterns, and points of urgency among organizational members—formed by organizational identity. Once participants are able to transcend routine defenses by linking the narra-tive of the past with present-day circumstances, they develop the emotional, linguistic, and cognitive capacities for assuming responsibility and taking ac-tion to change and resolve conflicts and dysfunctions they have perpetuated at work.

In the approach to organizational study presented here and throughout this book, the goal of organizational consultation is not merely reparative; con-sultants are typically engaged with participants in reformulating linkages and integrations, addressing fragmentations, and confronting the all-too-familiar "us against them" mentality of projection and splitting, which disrupts effec-tive coordination of tasks. The approach to research and consultation present-ed in this book focuses constructively on defenses and in particular on the inevitable defensive resistances to insight and change. Consultants do not see defensive actions as negative; rather, they view them as standard and typical of the reality of organizational identity. In the approach to organizational di-agnosis and change presented in this chapter, researchers address defenses as thematic and characteristic of organizational identity and attend to them in feedback sessions with organizational participants.

The organizational identity presented in feedback to participants is a co-authored narrative drawn from confidential interviews with participants. The meaningfulness and resonance of the organizational identity as feed-back to participants is derived from the consultants' capacity to articulate the collective voice of organizational members. Consequently, this method of organizational diagnosis has consequences for managing the transference-countertransference emotions between consultants and participants as well. By listening deeply and empathically to organizational members with the aim of adequately representing their perceptions, experiences, working relation-ships, and concerns, organizational consultants construct a portrait of organi-zational identity based on the participants' narrative and language, spoken and unspoken, conscious and unconscious. Thus, the discovery of organizational identity is the result of a collaborative and consensual interpretation, which in large part derives out of attending to the nature of defensive resistances against anxiety and the articulation of the unthought known.

Part Three

REFLECTIVE PRACTICE

In this section on reflective practice, I first explore the association between narcissism and leadership from the perspective of challenges posed to organizational analysts, researchers, and consultants. I discuss and critique two case studies of narcissistic leadership and followership. Next, I review the psychodynamics of executive coaching and analyze them with a focus on a relational psychoanalytic perspective and the importance of organizational diagnostic context. Finally, in a concluding chapter I review the processes of discovering organizational identity through relational psychoanalytic organizational theory and practice.

CHAPTER 8

Narcissistic Organizational Leadership

Omnipotence describes a defensive wish, buried in every psyche, that one will have a perfect world, will prevail over time, death, and the other—and that coercion can succeed. (Benjamin, 1988, p. 256)

THROUGHOUT THIS BOOK I endeavor to present methods of acquiring a deeper understanding of human organizations through the lens of psycho-analytic relational theory and the concept of organizational identity. This intersubjective framework locates the psychodynamics of mother-infant attachment during the first eighteen months to three years of childhood as critical to self-identity, and as a metaphor for interpreting organizational identity. This knowledge includes the character of rational and nonrational, conscious and unconscious, human actions in groups, organizations, and politics.[1]

Narcissistic Injuries and Chosen Traumas

The human developmental paradoxes of self-identity and organization-al identity consist of tension between membership and separation. These contradictory processes do not magically dissolve with the transition out of childhood and adolescence. In many cases, these tensions are perceived injuries that become chosen traumas within families, large groups (ethnic, cultural, national, and racial), and organizations. These chosen traumas are emotional wounds that endure over many generations and hundreds of years. Chosen traumas, consciously and unconsciously, can shape group and organizational identity, influencing interactions between self and others, leaders and followers, and workers and managers. Outside of awareness and unconscious, these relational psychodynamics of attachment are passed on. These transferences of emotion move across generations and are observed by psychoanalyst and political psychologist Vamik Volkan (2006), who explains,

> When a large group's traumatization changes function, one result may be its transformation into an exaggerated entitlement ideology that, when the group's identity is threatened, can be manipulated by political leaders to initiate new political programs and/or take new actions supported by this ideology. Exaggerated entitlement provides a belief system that asserts that the group has a right to own what they wish to have, and this can obviously precipitate conflict with others. (p. 174)

Volkan documents many international examples of this phenomenon. While his accounts are not, strictly speaking, organizational, they describe primitive psychological processes of splitting and projection that, as noted previously, occur frequently in work organizations.

Volkan describes the propaganda used in Serbia after Slobodan Milosevic came to power as "very unique, specific, effective, and deadly" (p. 180). He elaborates,

> This propaganda directly targeted the Battle of Kosovo in 1389, a highly mythologized event that came to symbolize the defeat and subsequent suffering of Christian Serbs at the hands of Muslim Ottomans. It is possibly the quintessential chosen trauma—its reactivation caused six hundred years and dozens of generations to collapse into the present; so strong were the inherited tasks that no time seemed to have passed at all. Serbs would avenge their defeat, take back the lands that were "rightfully" theirs, and reverse their victimization at last. (p. 180)

Shared traumas are transmitted through stories and narrative historical accounts of ethnic, cultural, religious, and national large groups, families, societies, institutions, and organizations.[2] In work organizations they can be observed during and following leadership transitions. Based on prior history and collective experience and memory, many workers find it difficult to view new leaders as different or distinctive from past leaders. Despite leaders' pronouncements of new policies and agendas, workers may be skeptical and resistant. This is particularly the case in organizations where there has been a history of violence or abusive treatment of workers.

Narcissism at Work

As noted, at the heart of our joining and associating with groups and organizations is a tension of countervailing needs for membership and dependence versus separateness and independence. These self-oriented, narcissistic needs generate tensions and conflicts that evolve from infantile attachments nourished and tempered by "good enough parenting" and healthy narcissism.[3] The original narcissistic state is a merger between infant and mother (caregiver). Infantile narcissism is reflected in the baby's demands for affection, safety, security, and recognition. Through emotionally attuned mirroring and idealization, the child comes to feel relatively secure and self-confident.

As stated, healthy narcissism and self-confidence are associated with "good enough" parenting (Winnicott, 1971, p. 14).[4] "Good enough" parenting and healthy narcissism are rooted in parental empathy and emotional attunement. Winnicott and Bion, respectively, indicate that when *holding* and *containment* (discussed in chapter 1) are absent or deficient, the child's nascent and developing sense of self becomes anxious, compliant, insecure, and cognitively and emotionally disorganized.[5] Cynical rationalism on the part of parents and later, in adulthood, on the part of leaders can destroy the potential for a secure and balanced attachment between self and object world. Constructive and positive leaders must attend to the productive tension between membership and separateness, dependence and independence, of workers. In addition, they must support the play of imagination, innovation, authenticity, and creativity in their workforce—depicted in chapter 4, with the application of Winnicott's concept of a "potential space." Such progressive leadership requires a leader with self-integrity, maturity, and unselfishness, a leader who relates to workers as human subjects rather than instrumental objects.

Accentuating the critical developmental features of infantile narcissism, Ogden, in his *Projective Identification and Psychotherapeutic Technique* (1982), explains,

> I have described elsewhere (Ogden, 1976, chapter 5) the pressure on an infant to behave in a manner congruent with the mother's pathology, and the ever present threat that if the infant fails to comply, he would cease to exist for the mother. This threat is the muscle behind the demand for compliance: "If you are not what I need you to be, you don't exist for me." Or in other language, "I can see in you only what I put there. If I don't see that, I see nothing." (p. 16)

Such are the origins of the *false self,* and of destructive narcissism evolving out of the relational matrix and *holding environment* between mother (parent) and infant, which results in the young child's formation of a false sense of self and an insatiable hunger for narcissistic nourishment. Alternatively, individuals may abandon this compulsion and accept that they are unworthy of love and admiration. The child's unfulfilled hunger for adoration, love, and affection may be prolonged into adolescence and adulthood. The lost maternal object becomes overvalued and inflated, and the child continues to search for it. Consider the organizational implications for *mirror-hungry narcissists*[6] in search of hierarchic positions of inordinate power and authority.

McWilliams, in *Psychoanalytic Diagnosis* (1994), portrays the characteristics of narcissistic personalities:

> They include a sense of vague falseness, shame, envy, emptiness or incompleteness, ugliness, and inferiority, or their compensatory counterparts: self-righteousness, pride, contempt, defensive self-sufficiency, vanity, and superiority. Kernberg (1975) describes such polarities as opposite ego states, grandiose (all-good) versus depleted (all-bad) definitions of self, which are the only options narcissistic persons have for organizing their inner experience. The sense of being "good enough" is not one of their internal categories. (p. 177)

Thus, narcissistic personalities reject a world of nuance and the very idea of human imperfection as a condition of what it means to be human.

Infantile narcissism is consequential for organizational leadership, followership, and identity. Much like the milieu of abusive families, toxic and oppressive organizational cultures are emotionally abusive and violent relative to participants.

Destructive Narcissism and Leadership: Two Case Examples
In organizational researchers' initial contacts with executives, the leaders frequently assume they do not need to participate in organizational assessments. One might ask, how can this be the case? The concept of narcissism and its association to the unconscious relational dynamics of leadership, power, and authority offer some insight. In public agencies and corporations, leaders (executives at the top) commonly assume that the actual process of organizational change is something that is *done to* their underlings. This common assumption is derived from the mix of human nature and hierarchic relations wherein

self as "superior" views *other* as "inferior."[7] This narcissistic executive cannot imagine—often literally cannot imagine—how she might need to participate in the overall organizational diagnosis. Denial, splitting, projection, and resistance to insight and change, along with some magical thinking on the part of the executive, arise at the outset of a consultation and typically as early as the initial contact.

During the initial contact, the consultants have a dialogue with the executives about the methodology to be used for the organizational consultation, describing it in such a manner that the executives come to appreciate the critical nature of their involvement from start to finish. Agreement upon the scope of work to be done is a part of this process.[8] The expected level of executive involvement in the process is agreed upon along with a description of the process of organizational assessment and diagnosis. Based on the willingness or unwillingness of the executive to participate, these initial discussions sometimes provoke the executive or the consultant to decide not to proceed. One reason that executives may not want to participate is that they are not cognitively and emotionally ready for a reflective learning process, which will inevitably expose their imperfections. Unconsciously, they fear narcissistic injury from appearing to be much like everyone else. Consultants, however, must remain nonjudgmental and empathic to help manage this conflict. It does not matter, nor is it consciously apparent to many narcissistic leaders, that they might not be as perfect and masterful as they assume or desire others to believe. Also, the degree to which leaders are willing to engage in reflective and critical processes, and their anxieties and resistances to doing so, ought to be treated as data[9] for the organizational diagnosis, assuming it proceeds.

Case Example: Destructive Narcissism at a Department of Behavioral Health
Over the past three decades, I have observed many examples of narcissism and leadership as key factors in shaping organizational culture and identity around mirroring and idealizing transferences. One example was a state department of behavioral health. This agency had routinely received poor press coverage and editorials about mismanagement of budgets, mistreatment of patients, and deteriorating residential facilities throughout the state. As a response, state mental health budgets were slashed and the organization disparaged by legislators. The governor's office decided it needed to act.

The department of behavioral health was a large public agency with facilities across its state and with central offices in the state capital. The director held routine weekly meetings with her executive management team and made regular visits to facilities throughout the state. She often referred to her department as a "family." This is a common metaphor that often signifies more about the executive's fantasies and expectations of how she ought to be treated than about what sort of family structure a department might have. Families, like work groups and organizations, can be accepting or rejecting, authoritarian or democratic, functional or dysfunctional.

The organizational consultants promised the agency workers anonymity in individual interviews. As a result organizational members often candidly referred to their department as a "dysfunctional family" headed by a "tyrannical and intimidating mother" who demanded adoration and admiration. Workers described themselves as operating within protective silos (their divisions), frequently illustrating the silo form by gesturing vertically with their hands.[10] Within their silos, members characterized themselves as engaged in withholding information and defending jurisdictional authority. In an attempt to minimize anxieties over loss and uncertainty and under the reign of a tyrannical leader, they unconsciously produced social defense systems.[11] As is the case in many poorly managed bureaucratic organizations (Diamond, 1993; Diamond & Allcorn, 2009), workers felt insecure and anxious about not being able to carry out their responsibilities effectively. They were inadequately empowered and lacked authority (Baum, 1987). Otherwise competent people hired to manage mental health facilities and provide care for patients found themselves feeling incompetent and powerless and trapped in their silos.

The director of the agency was more preoccupied, it appeared, with her public image and, one might conjecture, her private image than with her work role. She was not effectively managing her agency. In practice, she valued loyalty and compliance from management and workers more highly than running the agency well. She unconsciously valued the illusion of perfection and greatness over the realities of daily management and problem solving. The director deeply rejected effective management in the form of learning and problem solving; she was invested in promoting an image of superiority, perfection, and a flawlessly performing agency—an image contrary to what the newspapers reported and what the workers, patients, and constituents knew to be the true situation.

The director rewarded loyal and compliant workers by publicly acknowledging their loyalty, giving them lapel pins with the department's name on them to wear as a sign of their commitment to and identification with "the family." Workers who received this public acknowledgment were, however, ashamed to wear the lapel pins. Following the acknowledgment, they removed the pins, which were never to be worn again. In contrast, the director dealt harshly with her "insubordinate" underlings who showed disloyalty by communicating problems and by poor performance in facility management and patient care. She aggressively confronted these employees, including publicly shaming them. She made it a habit of humiliating people guilty of insubordination by yelling loudly at them in full view of their colleagues. This ritual act led to significant demoralization of organizational members. Turnover was high. Employees came to feel too intimidated to raise issues with their supervisors. They avoided interactions with the director and her inner circle of managers. Some courageous workers leaked problems to the press and news media. This exaggerated the director's paranoia and narcissistic rage. Paradoxically, without these leaks the governor's office would never have called for help.

Relational patterns at an agency like this department of behavioral health are embedded, taken for granted, and routinized. Systemic change requires members' participation and ownership of their actions. These members' attitudes and actions reinforced and mirrored, particularly among the circle of managers around her, the director's expansive and idealized image of executive-self-in-role.

Executive coaching, role analysis, strategic planning, process consultation, and organizational redesign can improve circumstances at an agency like this one. Executive coaching can provide the executive with an opportunity to confront her anxieties around change and loss of control, including the changing nature of her role as director. Some narcissistic leaders are agreeable to such a process, while others are not. Although the director of the behavioral health department had agreed to participate in the process of organizational diagnosis and change after several discussions, it was apparent given the ongoing tension around the issue of her concern about narcissistic injury that it would be a factor in the process. There are limitations to the effectiveness of coaching, as I discuss in the subsequent chapter. Other intervention strategies in a case like this include organizational redesign, which requires more delegation of authority to management and workers, where members are held accountable while being given the necessary authority to match their responsibilities.

Moving people out of their imaginary silos and producing more opportunities for cross-functionality and horizontal movement and flow of information and communication may be helpful as well. These intervention strategies and actions frequently have the effect of defusing the toxicity of narcissistic leadership and of minimizing the emotional impact on employees. Actions such as these occasionally have the effect of encouraging destructive narcissists to resign due to the minimization of idealizing followers desired by narcissistic personalities.

In the case of the department of behavioral health, the director resigned and was replaced by one of her sycophantic deputies, who, predictably, returned the agency to the status quo after the assessment. Such is the repetitive nature of leadership in organizations with many narcissistic leaders. In bureaucratic politics and cultures, abrupt, impulsive, and reactionary decision making at the highest levels, driven by unconscious anxieties and motivations, often blocks genuine learning and change.

Case Example: From Destructive to Constructive Narcissism in the Music and Entertainment Industry

A second case example of destructive narcissism and leadership comes from the entertainment industry. In this case, a vice president described an international organization with a reputation as a major distributor of music as having a culture clash between its marketing department in New York City and its distributions department (order taking and shipping) in the Midwest.

The president of this organization was "a character," according to the employees in both New York and the Midwest. His stories of annual African safaris and big-game hunting were legendary and very much a part of the organizational folklore. His larger-than-life, expansive personality in employees' depictions came through also in his interaction with the consultants. He managed by intimidation and the sheer force of his personality. Twice a year he took managers to upscale retreats—what participants referred to as "boondoggles."

Frequently the boondoggle took place on a Caribbean island, where most participants described the president's behavior as that of "lead performer" and "lecturer-in-chief," relating that he would perform a monologue staged in front of his management team for two full days. For many managers, these events symbolized the president's leadership style as unilateral, one-directional, aloof yet intimidating. He projected an image of superiority, of grand status and prestige, which seemed quite purposeful although likely driven by unconscious needs for love and admiration, omnipotence and grandiosity, in response to expansive narcissism. Based on interviews, he seemed aware of his style of leadership and yet was unaware that he engaged in intimidation and thereby was not mindful of his human toll on his employees and his company.

The president viewed management issues such as dealing personally and directly with the conflicted and demoralized executives of the company's two divisions as beneath his status and prestige. Rather than working to resolve

154

it, he insisted that his vice president fix the problem and report back when he had done so. Dealing directly with management and personnel felt to him too much like joining the ranks of labor, which might deflate the ballooned self-image he had constructed for himself. Behind the grandiose mask, he seemed insecure, anxious, and avoidant. Being loved and adored were what fed his insatiable narcissistic hunger. Nonetheless, there was no getting around the fact that he was a critical piece of the organizational puzzle and had to participate in the consultation.

As in the process described in the previous case example, the president of this company accepted the need for his participation in the organizational diagnosis and consultation. Ironically, and despite his actions and outward appearances, the president actually wanted to hear that the consultants felt his role in solving the problems of the fragmented organization was critical.[12] Beneath the surface he, too, wanted to be taken seriously.

After spending time observing and collecting data on both of the company's sites, in New York and in the Midwest, the consultants presented their organizational diagnosis to both groups at a joint meeting. It was at this meeting that the consultants made a specific request of the president: He was to listen to the presentation and the responses of his managers. He was not to speak. This was a greater demand placed upon him than he was accustomed to. But his listening to the consultants and his managers was critical to his showing flexibility and particularly showing that he understood the intent of the unusual request.

After two days of feedback from and planning by his New York and Midwest groups, which were collaboratively and cross-functionally structured for planning and problem setting, the president was given the opportunity to articulate to both groups what he had heard and learned over the course of the two days. By all appearances, it seemed as if his narcissistic personality had momentarily softened and he had opened to being reparative and constructive rather than destructive.[13] His capacity to listen and to rearticulate what he heard and learned from his employees was poignant. Everyone had an opportunity to experience another part of this man that was humble and appreciative of learning from those who reported to him. This act seemed to temporarily deflate his grandiosity and perfectionistic image, and seemed to reduce the intimidating effect he had on his subordinates. Executive coaching followed simultaneously with the implementation of operational and communication changes between the two divisions. The coaching seemed helpful in addressing the president's capacity to reconceptualize and reimagine his personality-in-role.

Consequently, the president was lauded and rewarded by the company board of directors for his having fixed a significant and costly problem. In actuality, his employees from marketing and operations, working together, repaired the problem in communications and implementation, not the executive. Nevertheless, it is not unusual for a board of directors to assume that the leadership is somehow solely responsible for magically repairing a fractured company. One might cynically say that in the final analysis the company was repaired and the president's grandiosity and omnipotence were merely strengthened and secured. Such is the irony and paradox of organizational analysis and change.

Next, I offer a cautionary note on the narcissistic inclination among researchers and consultants themselves, psychoanalytic and nonpsychoanalytic, to overvalue and overestimate the significance of leaders while undervaluing and underestimating the significance of followers.

Maintaining Perspective: Watching Out for Narcissistic Traps in the Psychoanalytic Study of Organizations

I apply relational psychoanalytic theory and ideas throughout this book, relying on past observations and experiences of leaders and executives of real organizations from dozens of studies and consultations with organizations over the course of thirty-five years. These concepts are intended to inform and describe human actions in organizations rooted in psychosocial development.

Organizational researchers and consultants, given their organizational identifications,[14] frequently enter the task of writing case examples by recollecting the social character of organizational leaders. This tends to personalize the activity, in contrast with initially describing the more abstract and immaterial structures and processes of organizations. The retrospective analysis of case studies of individual leaders opens the organizational theorist's mind, much like opening a metaphoric window to his experiences, associations, observations, and remembrances. This approach to organizational studies is not unusual since individual subjects, in particular individuals with power and authority and, in some instances, with attributes of charisma and narcissism, humanize and invigorate what otherwise are the abstractions and reifications distantly and remotely labeled *organizations*.

Charismatic and, of course, narcissistic leaders[15] (constructive and destructive) are notable and often unforgettable subjects of research, observation, experience, and consultation. Their personalities tap into individual researchers' and consultants' narcissistic desires for status and prestige and for close contact with power and imagined greatness—the transferences and countertransferences of relational matrices discussed throughout this book. The writing of field notes, case studies, and organizational stories is frequently structured around leaders' personalities and their characteristic interactions with followers.

Thus, it may be hard to avoid an overvaluation—an excessive, out-of-proportion, and idealized view of the person in the role of leader—and overestimation of leaders' roles and influences. There is no doubt that the role of leadership and leaders' fantasies, desires, and expectations are critical to the production and reproduction of organizational cultures and identities, narcissistic and otherwise. Yet the study of organizations, as reflected in this book, is relational, experiential, multilayered, multidimensional, and complex, encompassing more than psycho-biographies of individual executives' personalities and charismatic leadership. Explaining organizational behavior and dynamics by the character of one irrational and emotionally blinded human being with inordinate power and authority is at best a rudimentary account for the collective actions of individuals in complex roles and relational networks.

Nonetheless, for organizational analysts who immerse themselves in organizations, it is frequently not the complex relational and cooperative dimension of organizing that grabs their attention and interests. It is of course not the abstraction called "organization" that lures observers' awareness of unconscious transferences of emotions and idealizations. Rather, it is often the psychodrama, the inner theatre of leaders' personalities-in-role,[16] as characters figuratively performing on the organizational stage. This temptation commonly draws the consultant's attention and imagination. The intra- and interpersonal features of organizing, and in particular the leader's position and consumption of inordinate power and authority, entertain researchers and humanize, positively and negatively, the content of organization studies. For those qualitative researchers, fieldworkers, and participant-observers who take an "experience-near" approach to organization studies, focusing on the psychodrama of leadership is understandable and offers a partial, if not seductive, explanation of organizational identity, culture, decision making, and strategic actions. No doubt Lord Acton's 1887 axiom "Power tends to corrupt, and absolute power corrupts absolutely" perseveres as a maxim in the study of organizations and institutions of the twenty-first century.

In a 2003 article about my interview with the organizational psychologist Harry Levinson, who died in 2012, I write how he cautioned colleagues in our field that power, authority, and leadership are seductive forces, not only for leaders themselves but for everyone around them. In particular, organizational consultants, he warned, are fascinated and enchanted, if not instinctively and unconsciously enticed and seduced, by powerful leaders and executives, which has the consequence of distorting more holistic and systemic organizational theories and analyses.

Levinson's concern was with what he viewed as the tendency among organizational consultants to merge and over-identify with organizational leaders. This results in their losing sight of followers and the larger cooperative system of managers and workers. Not managing the psychological boundary between self and other, researcher and subject, consultant and client, and thereby getting caught up in what Levinson viewed as the countertransference trap, jeopardizes researchers' and consultants' capacity to offer and maintain the perspective of a professional stranger and participant-observer.

Psychoanalyst and pioneer of self psychology Heinz Kohut (1984) theorizes of an appropriate and interpretively valuable tension between "experience-near" and "experience-distant" theories. This positional tension is quite relevant when taking into account Levinson's warning and when considering the challenges for the researcher, consultant, or participant-observer immersed as a fieldworker inside the culture of a human organization. Levinson's writings often describe the work of organizational diagnosis and consultation as akin to the encounters of psychological and applied anthropology.[17] Awareness of the dangers and distortions of idealization and idealizing fantasies is critical to researchers and consultants in establishing adequate, "good enough" psychological and emotional distance between themselves and organizational members without losing the capacity for empathy and identification. Empathy and identification are, in combination, crucial concepts for managing and interpreting countertransference reactions in such a way as to develop a deeper understanding of the organizational participant.

The point of this critical reflection on the enigma of leadership in organization studies is to highlight the complexity and nuance of the multiple interacting variables, levels of analysis and consciousness, and contradictory forces (internal and external pressures) that encompass the complexity of organizational and systemic analysis. It is also, more pointedly, suggestive of the need for a relational psychoanalytic concept and idea such as *organizational identity*. Organizational identity emerges from the patterned narrative and data of organizational diagnosis and assessment. It captures the systemic complexity of organizing by defining organizations as relational, experiential, and perceptual. It is a framework that views organizations as made up of repetitive and networked cognitive and emotional psychodynamics.

If organization theorists and researchers are interested in articulating, explaining, and understanding organizations as collective human enterprises, consisting of relational experiences shared by members at all levels of hierarchy, then they, too, must be cautious not to overvalue the presumed effect of individual leaders. They must avoid treating leaders as if they work in a vacuum, thereby lessening the multifaceted and multilayered complexity of actual organizations. Thus, researchers and consultants must avoid treating the subject of leadership out of context, which executive coaches often mistakenly do, as discussed in the next chapter. While organization studies require close attention and analysis of leadership, researchers and consultants must analyze by contextualizing leaders and followers and their roles. This is accomplished by analyzing patterns of intersubjectivity, horizontally and vertically, that motivate and give meaning to the working lives of organizational participants and that affect their mutual capacity to construct cooperative systems. The outcome of these observations, associations, and experiences is organizational identity.

Accordingly, one must take seriously the dyadic and dialectical nature of organizational psychodynamics as a network of relationships, experiences, perceptions, and communications ultimately moving toward an understanding of organizations held in mind, as internalized and introjected images[18] of the meaning of organizational identity. This manner of in-depth exploration demands a level of self-awareness that alerts us to our own narcissism and concomitant tendency for idealization and mirroring. The cautionary point I want to make is that human nature is fundamentally narcissistic and inevitably engaged in varying degrees of idealization of charismatic leaders.[19] Self-awareness and authenticity require organizational researchers and consultants to pay attention to such commonplace human proclivities and thereby to manage tendencies to overvalue and distort leadership by idealizing, perfecting, and romanticizing rather than humanizing the leader as subject. I have attempted to speak to this phenomenon throughout this book by proposing that organizational researchers adopt the relational psychoanalytic framework.

Undoubtedly, any discussion of organizational identity as comprising relational and intersubjective psychodynamics must go beyond the initial problem (or dysfunction) and eventually focus on the character of leadership. Nevertheless, it remains critical to advancing our knowledge of organizations and organizing that researchers and consultants take care to assess and diagnose the whole of complex organizations (groups, constellations, systems, networks). It also remains critical to avoid the reductionistic pitfalls of scapegoating and overdetermining leaders and leadership style as the singular cause of organizational ineffectiveness and deficiencies. Identifying characteristics of leaders and leadership that shape organizational culture and identity is crucial.

And we cannot forget that leadership is dyadic. Leaders do not exist without followers who legitimize and enable them. Organizational change comes about when members understand and claim responsibility in perpetuating to some degree the exploits of leaders and their organizational cultures. Scapegoating and fixing the blame on individual leaders, while emotionally satisfying for some, may not assist participants in transforming organizations in a manner that does not compulsively repeat in self-sealing processes the same psychodynamics under new leadership. In sum, organizational researchers and consultants ought to be fully aware of their own mirroring and idealizing transferences and countertransferences of emotions as they work within and around the psychodynamics of power and authority. They need to establish potential and transitional space.

Return to Freud and Klein: Oedipal and Pre-Oedipal Power and Authority

Freud's concept in his *Group Psychology and the Analysis of the Ego* (1921) of the leader as representing the collective ego ideal of group members as a consequence of their substitution of their individual ego ideals for the symbolic ego ideal of the leader remains persuasive. Freud's position in that work articulates the relational nature of groups and organizations. Followers empower leaders. Followers sacrifice individual liberties to varying degrees to become members of the group. Human desires of membership and separateness are compromised at the point of entry (orientation, socialization, and, in some cases, indoctrination); ego and self-identity are challenged at the admission phase of initiation and collision between the individual recruit and organizational culture.

Given the excessive power and authority that leaders in public and corporate organizations frequently acquire and sustain, it is no surprise that they profoundly affect organizational members, cultures, and identities. The social character of leaders, their personalities, defensive routines, and transferences of emotion, underlie and largely help to explain and answer the researcher's basic query, "What is it like to work here?" After all, leaders are inevitably the target of followers' identifications and idealizations.

As leadership, power, and authority are critical to the discovery of organizational identity presented in this book, and to a deeper understanding of organizational change, so leader-followership with all the caveats thus far discussed is admittedly complicated and complex. Taking object relations theory and relational psychoanalysis as a contemporary framework for studying organizations implies a departure from Freud's historical-era and patriarchal view of leadership and the influence of the oedipal phase. It reflects a paradigmatic shift toward a post-Kleinian maternal and contemporary view of leadership in which the group and organization are analogous to the maternal holding environment, where the influence of the pre-oedipal attachment phase between mother and child is seen as critical to character structure. As discussed throughout this book, the contemporary application of psychoanalytic theory is rooted in the mother-infant dyad, through which we interpret and understand human organizations and leadership as objects of transference and projections of early prerequisite desires for maternal affection and secure attachment.

Destructively Narcissistic Leadership: Role, Organizational, and Political Context

Narcissism as a personality feature does not exist in a metaphorical vacuum. It resides in the person in role and in the organizational and political context. At present in the United States, minimal and neglectful federal, state, and local enforcement and regulation of businesses and executive entitlements, combined with disappearing and weakening labor unions and substantial unemployment, shape the social, economic, and political landscape of unfettered exploitation of powerless workers.

For example, college graduates are expected by business executives to take on years of unpaid internships based on the anticipation of future employment. These same young and inexperienced workers, then, who are "fortunate" to eventually get hired, are employed at minimum wage. In addition, they are expected to work excessively long hours under unusually stressful and unhealthy conditions.

As a result of right-wing antigovernment ideologies and laissez-faire policies that overvalue[20] and idealize[21] free-market capitalism, exploitation of workers is commonplace in the twenty-first-century American economy. Unfair and oppressive political and economic conditions accommodate and indulge psychopathic, arrogant-vindictive, and abusive leaders, executives, and business entrepreneurs.

With little to no legal, governmental enforcement, regulation, and intervention, sadistic and unkind employment practices persist unrestricted. These structural conditions are predisposed for psychologically abusive mistreatment of vulnerable and powerless employees. Without adequately authorized and resourced enforcement agencies, genuine checks and balances, and systemic interventions, these management practices will accelerate. In sum, the present-day American political economy of social and political inequality and widening income disparity indulges destructively narcissistic leaders in positions of inordinate power and authority.

Conclusion

In the final analysis, psychoanalytic theory is predicated on confronting our personal capacity for self-deception and self-other deception and illusions. It is a relational theory of mind, meaning, and motive. With this framework in mind, the study of organizations requires balance, where it takes seriously the power and personality of leaders without overlooking followers' collective actions. In sum, psychodynamically oriented organizational researchers and consultants analyze the relational patterns of interaction and networked interdependencies that compose group and organizational systems.

Given the psychodynamics of reflexive human organizing, psychoanalytic researchers and consultants capture organizational life and the human act of organizing as a moment in time and space, a snapshot of the meaning and significance of relational experiences, perceptions, and narrative patterns and structures. By embracing the passions and desires signified by human action from the theoretical framework presented in this book, I aim to advance our understanding of the emotional life of organizations and the workplace. In the next chapter, I consider the significance of organizational diagnosis and assessment for psychodynamic executive coaching.

CHAPTER 9

Executive Coaching
A Critical Psychoanalytic Perspective

Subjective experience itself is viewed as a construction of human agency. Experience is not simply "there in the mind" waiting to be found and retrieved by objective introspection. Different people tend to construct experiences of the same event differently, each for reasons of his or her own. Many of these reasons originate early in life and therefore give rise to primitive forms of emotional and cognitive experience, and these persist unconsciously and influentially into adult life. They also add individual coloring to otherwise standardized responses to the conventions of one's culture. (Schafer, 1992, pp. xiii–xiv)

I HAVE WORKED WITH hundreds of executive clients from a wide range of professions in public and private organizations. I have found that executive clients frequently have good managerial tools and reasonable strategic ideas for how to handle the technical and operational demands they are confronted with.[1] However, they are often wanting in self-consciousness and self-awareness. In other words, they have not considered the link between their ideas, feelings, and actions and organizational identity. My intention in this chapter is to articulate the relational psychoanalytically informed approach to executive coaching. In so doing, I wish to help cultivate more humaneness, more innovation, and more productivity in organizations by helping executive clients to take more seriously the influence of subjective experience and self-concept on executive-role construction and action. Psychodynamically oriented executive coaching offers potential and transitional space for playful imagination and reflectivity.

One observation of American corporate and public agency executives is that they are often overprotective and defensive about their self-images. They are habitually overcommitted to being seen as omnipotent and beyond reproach. This desire to project grandiosity emboldens many executives to surround themselves with idealizing and adoring subordinates. These workers then re-inforce their executives' superior, flawless, all-knowing self-image. In contrast to this concentration on image, executives often need coaches willing to en-gage them in analyzing their actions and intentions in role[2] and to guide them in the development of greater self-awareness.[3]

Psychodynamically informed executive coaching takes into account three theoretical traditions—classical psychoanalytic theory, psychoanalytic object relations, and systems theory. In this chapter, I explain these three frameworks and also discuss organizational role analysis and group dynamics. Each of these frameworks illuminates different dimensions of what executive consul-tants encounter relative to leadership, groups, and organizational dynamics. Psychodynamically informed executive coaching is, at its core, about promot-ing self-understanding.

This notion of self is a critical concept in promoting executive self-awareness and reflective practice. Psychodynamically informed approaches to executive coaching focus on unconscious processes and relational and group dynamics. Exploring unconscious dynamics facilitates deeper understanding of the in-terpersonal world. The question "How did you feel?" is equally significant to "What were you thinking?" These are the questions discussed in this chapter.

The Development of Psychodynamic Coaching

The psychodynamically informed process of executive coaching moves the consultant's and the executive's attention to the defensive sources of inatten-tion and deficiency in (false, inauthentic, compliant, and reactive) self-other relations at work. I explore the development of psychodynamic coaching by describing approaches to executive coaching in the writings of Levinson (1968, 1970, 1972, 1981, 2002; Levinson et al., 1962), Kets de Vries (1984, 2006, 2007; Kets de Vries and assoc., 1991; Kets de Vries, Guillen, Korotov, and Florent-Treacy, 2010), and Kilburg (2000, 2004a, 2004b, 2005). I chose these three approaches due to their overall influence on psychodynamic coaching and consultation and for their use of different psychoanalytic schools of thought—classical ego psychology, object relations, and an integrated and cross-disciplinary systems model, respectively. I also briefly discuss organiza-tional role analysis (Newton, Long, & Sievers, 2006), which originated with the group-relations traditions of the Tavistock Institute for Human Relations in London and the A. K. Rice Institute in Washington, DC. I apply these psycho-dynamic theories and concepts to understanding organizations and to practic-ing coaching and consultation, to complement and further link the theory and practice of organizational identity presented throughout this book. Indeed, I take liberties with these psychoanalytic approaches to executive coaching and exhibit my own views of their significance along the way. Finally, I present a summary of psychodynamic approaches to coaching and some recommendations for future research.

Psychodynamic Models

Psychodynamic approaches to organizations have evolved most visibly since 1983–1984. This emergence and evolution is rooted in the clinical paradigm of psychoanalysis and in particular in the psychoanalytic study of organizations (see, for example, Czander, 1993; Diamond, 1993; Diamond & Allcorn, 2009; Gabriel, 1999; Kets de Vries & assoc., 1991; Kets de Vries & Miller, 1984; Levinson, 1972, 2002; Sievers, 2009; Stein, 1994). Within psychoanalysis there are a number of competing schools of thought that are also represented in the work of psychoanalytically oriented consultants to organizations. This is reflected in the multiplicity of psychodynamic approaches to executive coaching that integrate ideas and concepts from the main three schools of thought.[4] In the following sections, I discuss the works of Levinson; Kets de Vries; Kilburg; and Newton, Long, and Sievers.

Desires, Needs, and Expectations

Levinson (1962) introduced to the psychoanalytic study of organizations the concept of a *psychological contract*, which he explains is a particular dialogue between employer and employee that shapes mutual expectations and is a key ingredient to successful organizational membership and affiliation. Levinson's notion of a psychological contract encompasses an acknowledgment of conscious and unconscious human needs and desires as well as the complexity of authority relations. Employees are emotionally invested in their relationship to the organization and its leadership—a *transference* of emotions ties individuals and their identities to their work organizations. In psychoanalytic theory and as noted throughout this book, transference dynamics represent the degree to which past experiences from childhood shape and influence perceptions of others, particularly those in positions of authority. Such unconsciously projected emotions from the past frequently distort present relationships. Transference dynamics, for instance, are characterized by mirroring, on the one hand, and idealizing, on the other.[5] Unless management is aware of and attentive to these manifest and latent dimensions of worker motivation and perception, it is unlikely that employees will feel adequately taken care of or recognized by executives. Levinson argues that this managerial oversight and deficiency can lead to demoralization and poor performance.

The psychological contract became a valuable conceptual tool for managers, consultants, and executive coaches as they considered failures of supervision and communication between supervisors and subordinates, executives and their staff. The psychological contract between employer and employee requires perpetual dialogue between the parties, acknowledging the dynamics of mutual emotional needs and expectations, conscious and unconscious. In this regard, Levinson highlights the significance of the *ego ideal* for individual motivation. Defining the ego ideal, as did Freud, as an image of oneself at one's future best, he came to view its management as vital to the psychological contract and crucial to successful mentoring. The psychological contract would be the ongoing dialogue focused on the question of what workers need to feel self-confident and competent and to do their jobs well. The value of this concept was shaped by Levinson's earliest thinking about motivation, career development, mentoring, and emotional well-being at work. Most fundamentally, his emphasis on the ego ideal acknowledges the nature of workers' emotional attachments to and identifications with the workplace.

In his research, Levinson (1964) observed that many supervisors have difficulty managing. In particular, he saw a problem for managers that some individuals understood intuitively yet had no psychological basis for articulating and correcting: managers often feel conflicted, that is, *guilty*, about evaluating subordinates' performance, especially when the evaluation requires negative and critical feedback of the employee's work.

Levinson not only explains the psychodynamics of guilt, he emphasizes the human compassion inherent in and necessary for providing subordinates with unambiguous, direct, and honest feedback in performance evaluation. Through understanding the notion of "management by guilt," the supervisors he worked with came to better appreciate their ambivalent feelings surrounding the act of subordinate evaluation. They also came to appreciate the value of sincere feedback in the development of subordinates' career opportunities. Consultants and executive coaches learned to pay attention to these difficulties of supervision and to provide help to organizational participants. Out of these insights surrounding the individual ego ideal of workers, managers, and executives, Levinson came to stress the leadership's role in mentoring and educating workers and managers.

In his book *Executive* (1981), a revised edition of his 1968 work *The Exceptional Executive*, Levinson directs managers to pay attention to three primary human drives: ministration, maturation, and mastery. In the caretaking practice of *ministration,* needs for gratification, closeness, support, protection, and guidance are served. In supporting human developmental requirements, *maturation* needs for creativity, originality, self-control, and reality testing are supplied. And, given the demands for self-competence and confidence, *mastery* needs that encompass individual demands for ambitious striving, realistic achievement, rivalry for affection, and consolidation are satisfied. With these human needs in mind, executive coaches and consultants might assist executives by encouraging them to engage in more thoughtful and reflective dialogues with their managers and workers, thereby establishing management systems more responsive to individual potential and desire for advancement. Motivation can be understood as multidimensional, and leaders with the assistance of coaches might facilitate growth and maturation in their own executive careers as well as the careers of their employees. One cannot help but reflect on how challenging such sensitivity to the human needs of workers has become in our contemporary global economy of volatility, job insecurity, downsizing, and reengineering.

In *Executive,* Levinson provides a psychoanalytic framework for problem diagnosis. The framework is designed to assist executives and managers in problem solving focused on conflicts and performance issues, providing a template for analyzing troublesome human relations in the workplace and a practical application of a psychodynamic approach to executive coaching.

Starting with the concept of the ego ideal in the workplace, the consultant or executive coach should consider the degree to which individual executives feel they are living up to their ideal self-image, and the degree to which that ideal may or may not be out of reach of what is possible for them given their current self-image and the organizational realities they must contend with. Many consultants and executive coaches can appreciate the frequency with which executives, managers, and workers feel they fall short of their personal goals or are not working at their level of competency and training. A large gap between one's self-image and one's ego ideal may produce low self-esteem, according to Levinson. It also may produce anger and resentment as a consequence of disappointment.

Next, the consultant should consider individual needs for *affection* and the desire to develop closer ties with colleagues and fellow workers. One should reflect on the value of attending to human needs for affection among workers and in their relations with executives. This might entail taking into account an executive's proclivity to "move toward or away from" others, such as his staff and fellow workers. Paying attention to the emotional tensions of transference and countertransference dynamics, as evidenced by the executive's patterns of relationships at work, is critical to accessing insights into what is happening to feelings of affection in the workplace.

Next, the executive coach should consider how the individual executive copes with *aggression* at work. Here the influences of classical psychoanalytic drive theory and ego psychology come through in an implicit acknowledgment of the role of work as a form of sublimation. As executive coaches or consultants, we might look at the degree to which the individual executive "moves against" others in a manner that employees might experience as intimidating, hostile, abrasive, or intrusive.[6] Providing opportunities to observe, discuss, and reflect on these destructive proclivities is a constructive dimension of executive coaching and consultation. Fostering awareness of transference and countertransference dynamics as evidenced and contextualized in patterns of behavior and conflicts between executives and their colleagues, as noted in previous chapters, is critical to self-other awareness.

Finally, Levinson's model encourages paying attention to how executives (managers and workers) manifest human *dependency* needs (1981, p. 33). Given the hierarchic structure of most organizations, the phenomenon of dependency enables executive coaches and consultants to examine once again the psychodynamics of transference and countertransference in the context of super- and subordinate relationships. Is the degree of dependency appropriate or inappropriate, constructive or destructive, progressive or regressive? Codependencies can emerge as well in which executives provoke, often unconsciously, subordinate behavior that renders adult workers in childlike roles—what in psychoanalytic theory is called psychological regression.

In addition to his framework for problem diagnosis, Levinson (1976) formulated a framework for problem analysis that remains helpful to executive coaches and consultants. In the context of a comprehensive consultation (including organizational diagnosis and assessment) with the leader and her organization, the executive coach or consultant considers the following questions: Who is in pain? When did it begin? What is happening to this individual's needs for affection, aggression, and dependency? What is the nature of his ego ideal? Is the problem solvable? How? With this framework, Levinson illustrates how one can arrange and interpret data (in a psychodynamically informed way) around problems and conflicts that might otherwise leave executives and their managers perplexed and seemingly without recourse.

Levinson (1972, 2002) depicts the complexity of diagnosing and assessing organizations with the mishmash of data—factual, historical, generic, and interpretive—that, taken together, reveal (what I call) organizational identity. This diagnostic/clinical framework is an adaptation of an "open systems model"[7] for the purpose of studying and analyzing organizations. If properly contextualized, strategies of intervention and change such as executive coaching ought to be governed in part by organizational diagnosis and assessment. In the case of executive coaching, the organizational diagnosis provides needed context for examining relational and experiential psychological dynamics. As a product of organizational diagnosis, the organizational story, with its thematic patterns and articulated points of urgency, is significant and proffers concrete examples of the executive's key relationships and cognitive-emotional schema. Levinson's legacy for executive coaching and consultation is one that seriously questions coaching without organizational diagnosis and context for reflectivity, which produce more thoughtful and humane leadership. This emphasis on context in the form of independent organizational diagnosis and assessment adds validity, greater opportunities for reality testing, client ownership, claimed action and personal responsibility, and depth and richness of understanding to the examination of transference and countertransference dynamics between executives and staff as well as between psychodynamically oriented executive coaches and their clients.[8]

Character, Narcissism, and the Inner Theatre of Leaders

In contrast with Levinson's application of psychoanalytic ego psychology to executive coaching and his emphasis on the management of human needs and expectations, Kets de Vries (2006) takes psychoanalytic object relations theory (and, to a lesser degree, self psychology) as the clinical paradigm for interpreting executives' character and individual dispositions. He writes, "Character is the sum of the deeply ingrained patterns of behavior that define an individual" (p. 52). Psychoanalytic object relations theory starts from the maturational premise of healthy, primary narcissism as a by-product of good enough parenting during infancy and early childhood. In this developmental schema, discussed throughout this book, the emerging sense of self evolves from a state of attachment and total dependency. Thus, the infant begins life from a symbiotic and undifferentiated position, one in which the child is in fact at the center of the parent-child universe. In this primitive state, cognitive capacity, nascent brain and emotional development, is signified by part-object relationships where the other is experienced and perceived in crude absolutes such as either all good or all bad, always loving or always hating, only accepting or only rejecting. In developmental transition the young child eventually yet ambivalently moves physically, cognitively, and emotionally away from primary caregivers and toward a more independent, holistic, and integrated sense of self—for example, when the child crawls away from the parent and simultaneously turns back toward the parent for cues to see if all is okay. Assuming a positive and reassuring signal, the child continues onward in exploration of the external yet unknown object world. Developmental experiences of separation, differentiation, and individuation confront the child with a jumble of mixed emotions. These maturational realities of separation and loss include acknowledging paradox and an imperfect and depressive object (self and other) world of pain and pleasure, acceptance and rejection, love and hate.

Kets de Vries's clinical paradigm is shaped by the work of several psychoanalytic and developmental theorists, starting with Bowlby's attachment research. Bowlby's (1980) developmental stages of attachment, separation, and loss are critical ideas for interpreting the psychodynamics of nuanced and significant (self-other) adult relationships. Highlighted in these clinical and developmental findings and also found in Levinson's work is the treatment of change as emotional loss—a concept important to working empathically with participants undergoing organizational transitions (addressed in chapter 5).

Kets de Vries's clinical paradigm is also shaped by the groundbreaking theories of Winnicott (1971), who, as does Klein (1959), emphasizes the emotional and developmental significance of self-other (internalized object relations) concepts from infancy and early childhood. As discussed in previous chapters, Winnicott's transformational childhood highlights of "good enough mothering" and a "good enough holding environment" signify object (self-other) relationships that at their best facilitate and nurture psychological safety, interpersonal security, emotional bonding, and maturation—attributes at the core of self-cohesion and integrity. For Winnicott, good enough mothering and adequate holding environments are characterized as *transitional* and *potential spaces* for playing and creativity, which are represented in childhood by *transitional objects* such as teddy bears and blankets. Correspondingly, in adulthood, individuals engage in playing and creative imagination through music, art, entertainment, and culture. Ideally, work and vocation serve as transitional, if not transformational, objects. In addition, Winnicott's ideas of true (authentic) and false (compliant) self, also critical to my perspective, shape Kets de Vries's emphasis on the value of authenticity between leaders and followers, and in the organizational cultures they promote and reproduce. I revisit these values of true and false self and their relevance later in the chapter.

Next, I discuss the concept of narcissism once again, followed by a brief description of leaders' and followers' dispositions in the clinical theory and application of Kets de Vries's object relational approach. Kets de Vries, Korotov, and Florent-Treacy note, "The aim of clinically informed leadership coaching is not a temporary high, but lasting change. They [leaders] want to move beyond reductionistic formulas to sustainable transformation" (2007, p. li).

Narcissism and Executive Coaching

In *The Leader on the Couch: A Clinical Approach to Changing People and Organizations* (2006), Kets de Vries reviews narcissism in leaders, and in particular examines the nuance of constructive versus reactive narcissism (the latter I referred to in the previous chapter as "destructive narcissism"). In the psychoanalytic literature the degree to which narcissism is constructive or reactive is frequently identified by the idea of "primary narcissism" typical of early life and "malignant narcissism" as defining compensatory and pathological forms of narcissism in adulthood. Ironically, narcissism is a relational concept and therefore it ought to be seen through the lens of a two-person psychology such as object relations theory and self psychology. A key concept in the interpretation of narcissism is the psychoanalytic idea of transference—what Kets de Vries (2006) calls the "t-word."

Similar to the approach presented throughout this book, in his clinical application of object relations theory to organizations and their leaders, Kets de Vries (1984, 2006) draws on Klein's (1946, 1959) important discovery of the infantile roots of adulthood (paranoid-schizoid and depressive positions) and on Kohut's (1977) notion of the prevalence of narcissistic personalities manifesting through *mirroring and idealizing transference* dynamics. On the matter of mirroring, Kets de Vries (2006) writes,

> Within organizations, the mirroring process between leaders and followers can become collusive. Followers use leaders to reflect what they want to see, and leaders rarely resist that kind of affirmation. The result is a mutual admiration society. Leaders . . . tend to take actions designed to shore up their image rather than serve the needs of the organization. In times of change, embedded mirroring processes can be fatal to the organization. (pp. 43–44)

And on the complementary matter of idealizing transference, he writes,

> Through this idealizing process, we hope to combat feelings of helplessness and acquire some of the power of the person admired. Idealizing transference is a kind of projective shield for followers. Reactive narcissists are especially responsive to this sort of administration, often becoming so dependent upon it that they can't function without the emotional fix. It's a two-way street, of course: followers project their fantasies onto their leaders, and leaders mirror themselves in the glow of their followers. (2006, p. 44)

Mirroring and idealizing transference dynamics represent an inescapable paradox of narcissism and leadership. Leaders require followers who legitimize their power and authority (real or imagined), and of course followers need leaders who direct and inspire them. Mirroring and idealizing transference is a dyadic relationship in which the leader defines the character and emotionality of the follower and vice versa. In sum, narcissistic leaders demand idealizing and adoring followers who reinforce their defensive and compensatory need for idealization and grandiosity. Whether leaders are constructive or reactive narcissists depends on the nature and quality of these transference dynamics and the degree to which organizational strategies and structures minimize unilateral, expansive, and grandiose leadership style.

In particular, the degree to which the personality of the narcissistic leader is driven by infantile narcissistic injuries and associated rage and hostility matters when it comes to the character of executives-in-role. Discovering leaders with flexibility and the capacity to openly reflect and consider change, as opposed to leaders who react with rigidity and inflexibility as manifested in persistent resistance, distinguishes constructive from reactive narcissists. Constructively narcissistic leaders are transformational and inspiring role models. They are capable of assuming responsibility for their actions and are less prone to blaming others. Their vision extends beyond themselves. In contrast, reactive narcissists are troubled by inadequacies, bitterness, anger, depressive thoughts, and lingering feelings of emptiness and deprivation. Attempting to master feelings of inadequacy and insecurity, they construct an exaggerated sense of self-importance and self-grandiosity along with an associated desire for admiration. Reactive narcissists lack empathy and are unable to understand what others feel and experience. This latter observation may be critical in one's expectations about the value of executive coaching with reactive narcissists. If empathy is seemingly absent in executive clients, one might ask whether it is sufficient and helpful to engage in coaching rather than recommending psychotherapy. As does Kernberg, who has written on the subject of regression in leadership and organizations (1998), Kets de Vries (2006) suggests "downsizing" the negative and potentially destructive impact of narcissistic leaders on workers and organizations. Writing specifically of boards of directors, he states,

> Organizations need not be helpless in the face of reactive narcissistic leadership. They can take action, both preemptive and follow-up. Strategies include distributing decision-making and erecting barriers against runaway leadership; improving the selection, education, and evaluation of board members; and offering coaching and counseling to executives showing signs of excessive narcissism. (p. 46)

In working with varying degrees of narcissism in leaders, executive coaches and consultants might consider the following questions: How dependent is this executive on the admiration of his staff through the mirroring transference? To what degree is this staff dependent on their need to admire and aggrandize their leaders through idealizing transference? To what degree are the followers in this organization responsible for projecting omnipotent qualities onto their executives? To what extent do these leaders move against or away from followers as opposed to moving toward followers in the form of cooperation and collaboration as opposed to unilateralism and deception?

Executive Dispositions and Coaching

Finally, on the spectrum of personalities in the dispositions of leaders and followers, Kets de Vries (2006) notes, "Prototypes aren't depictions of mental disorders: each one includes a range of human behavior, from normal to dysfunctional, because normality and pathology are relative concepts, positions on a spectrum" (p. 57). Reflecting on their proclivities for leadership and followership, Kets de Vries identifies eleven prototypes on a continuum of personalities. These are (1) the *narcissistic* disposition, which has very high leadership tendencies and low followership tendencies; (2) the *dramatic* disposition, with medium leadership tendencies and high followership tendencies; (3) the *controlling* disposition, with high leadership tendencies and high followership tendencies; (4) the *dependent* disposition, with very low leadership tendencies and high followership tendencies; (5) the *self-defeating* disposition, with very low leadership tendencies and high followership tendencies; (6) the *detached* disposition, with medium leadership tendencies and medium followership tendencies; (7) the *depressive* disposition, with low leadership tendencies and low followership tendencies; (8) the *abrasive* disposition, with medium leadership tendencies and low followership tendencies; (9) the *paranoid* disposition, with high leadership tendencies and medium followership tendencies; (10) the *negativistic* disposition, with very low leadership tendencies and medium followership tendencies; and (11) the *antisocial* disposition, with high leadership tendencies and low followership tendencies (pp. 130–132).

In this approach to executive coaching, these dispositions, or core conflictual relational themes, have consequences not only for relations between leaders and followers but also for productive and counterproductive strategizing, decision making, delegating, and structuring, as well as organizational identity. In the end, beyond individual proclivities and character, when true to the ethic of psychoanalytic theory, psychodynamic approaches to executive coaching and consultation (as moral psychology) value authenticity and truth. In that spirit, practitioners of psychodynamic approaches are engaged in the removal of individual and organizational defensive screens, which typically distort the quality and reality of cooperative relationships at work. Unconscious collusive relationships are exposed and critically reconsidered. Next, I examine an integrated and comprehensive approach to psychodynamic executive coaching by Kilburg.

Systems Complexity and Chaos

Kilburg's *Executive Coaching: Developing Managerial Wisdom in a World of Chaos* (2000) is a detailed and comprehensive articulation of psychodynamic executive coaching. His model is complementary to Levinson's focus on needs and expectations and Kets de Vries's focus on the character and inner theatre of executives and their organizations. In contrast to these concepts, Kilburg places greater emphasis on systemic chaos and complexity in addition to internal psychodynamics. Kilburg constructs a seventeen-dimension model of systems and psychodynamics, an elaborate conceptual framework joining external components of systems with internal components of psychodynamics. This linkage between systems and psychodynamics is supported by the notion of the executive character as a complex self-organizing adaptive system. Here is a model for executive coaching grounded in psychodynamic and systemic processes, which incorporates the conceptual and contextual complexity of leadership in contemporary organizations, public and private, along with the challenges of helping executives become more reflective and thereby better equipped for adapting to changing and unpredictable environments.

For Kilburg, psychodynamically informed executive coaching demands a "fully connected" (2000, p. 44) overarching dimensional model that links open systems and psychodynamic processes. Being aware of these connected components of people and systems, consultants and coaches, means paying attention to organizational structure, process, content, input, throughput, and output, along with psychodynamic components such as psychological and social defenses, relational dynamics (past and present), transference of emotions, instinctual dynamics, conflicts, idealizing dynamics, focal relationships, cognition, and conscience. Ultimately, beyond the complexity and chaos of this plethora of variables, Kilburg is after what he calls "foci for executive coaching" (p. 61). This mutual spotlight is on open systems (structure, process, content, input, throughput, and output) and on increasingly reflective, self-aware executives (rational self, conscience, idealized self, instinctual self, cognition, emotion, defenses, conflict, knowledge, skills, abilities, personality styles, jobs, roles, and tasks), producing a mediated focal point on relationships (past, present, focal) and behavior (system, whole organization, subunit, organizational work unit, group, individual). It is at this psychosocial, systemic, intervening hub of participant relationships that the work of executive coaching and consultation occurs in practice.

Kilburg's notion of a mediated focus is rooted in contemporary psychoanalytic object relations theories. These psychodynamic theories are presently shaped to some extent by attachment research and by theories of postmodernism and complexity, as well as by findings in neuroscience and brain research. Fundamentally, Kilburg's mediated focus has much in common with the object relations concepts discussed and applied throughout this book, in particular the idea of intersubjectivity and potential space. As noted, for Winnicott (1971), these concepts signify a psychological reality embedded in the mother-baby dyad. "Good enough mothering" means adequate holding and containment of the baby's toxic feelings and emotions. With this foundation for secure attachment, the child learns to adapt to the coming and going of mother and the shifting emotions of love and hate, good and bad, acceptance and rejection. Maturation for the child requires containment of projected emotions displaced from the "contained" infant onto the "container" mother (Bion, 1962, 1967). Holding and containing, as noted earlier, are considered critical caregiving object functions of the parent in the emotional and cognitive development of the child.

In Winnicott's (1971) thinking, a "facilitating environment" as characteristic of "good enough" parenting provides the child with the interpersonal security and safety necessary for healthy separation and individuation. As noted, the critical nature of the quality of earliest attachments is supported by research in attachment theory and neuroscience (Fonagy, 2001; Leffert, 2010; Siegel, 2001). Winnicott refers to a "facilitating environment" that fosters a transitional and potential space for the emergence of play and imagination, curiosity and reflectivity.

Transitional and potential space so vital to infant development represents, according to Winnicott, the psychosocial location of culture—culture as derived from play and imagination, culture as the area of human experience situated in between reality and fantasy, the source of imagination and creativity, art and music, the reflective practices of theorizing and problem solving. The effectiveness of Kilburg's comprehensive model of open systems and psychodynamics depends on seeing and working with executives as self-organizing complex systems. Consistent with the ideas and functions of containment and transitional or potential space in object relations theory, Kilburg's concept of "reflective containment" is at the core of his method of psychodynamic executive coaching (2000, p. 72).

Awareness of one's sense of self in the world of work requires paying attention to the effect of organizational roles, which I briefly review next.

Psychodynamic Coaching and Organizational Role Analysis

The genesis of organizational role analysis (ORA) was the Tavistock and A. K. Rice traditions of group-relations education and training, wherein the analysis of authority, responsibility, and roles in groups, and the combination of open systems theory and psychodynamics, are prominent features of method and application. ORA is influenced by the original thinking of Bion in his book *Experiences in Groups and Other Papers* (1959b). As I discussed in chapter 3, Bion's psychodynamic model for understanding groups emphasizes the parallel processes of work groups. His hypothesis is that groups operate on two levels of consciousness, conscious and unconscious. At the manifest level of group activity is the task of the group—the group's purpose or mission. Concurrently, at the latent level of group activity are three basic underlying assumptions: fight/flight, dependency, and pairing (or utopia). This model provides analysts, consultants, coaches, and facilitators with a richer and deeper appreciation of the complexity of group psychology. For instance, it is observed that groups come together behind a leader to engage in fight against or flight from some designated scapegoat or enemy. It is also observed that groups emerge behind a leader whom members collectively believe they can depend upon, one who makes them feel comforted and safe in following her lead. Finally, it is observed that within groups, individual members are frequently attracted to pairings of members who offer hope and a sense of a better future for members in contrast to a disturbing or disappointing present. These are Bion's basic assumptions, which in some instances support the primary task of the work group and in other instances work against the task or pull groups into unproductive, destructive, and psychologically regressive, spiraling psychodynamics.

Newton, Long, and Sievers, in their work *Coaching in Depth: The Organizational Role Analysis Approach* (2006), proffer a collection of papers on the theory and practice of ORA. Practitioners stress the value of staying in role and on task by expanding their awareness of underlying basic assumptions. Many of the proponents of ORA claim the approach is intended to focus on the role, not on an individual's character. Thus, ORA is a process for clarifying roles within organizations. It is a peer-driven inquiry that focuses on the systemic dimension of work problems and role performance. It is a psychodynamic approach that "assists the client to examine the dynamic process of finding, making, and taking up their organizational role" (p. xiv). ORA attends to "the interaction between the psychological and sociological pressures on the person in role as the consultant assists the client to discern his/her organization-in-the-mind and test this against the aim of the system" (p. xiv). It is a process of in-depth coaching and exploring how the organization becomes "an object in the inner world of a client, entangled with the authority structures derived from her childhood experience and made accessible through the use of work drawings within the ORA process" (p. xiv).

It appears that roles are peculiarly shaped by character and therefore one can imagine conflicted and ambivalent relationships to organizational roles. Thus, one might expect frequent tensions between the external organizational demands for belonging, affiliation, adaptation, and compliance and the internal individual needs for independence, autonomy, self-identity, and authenticity (Diamond, 1991). This phenomenon reflects the core dilemma between membership and separateness at the heart of organizational identity presented throughout this book. The idea of authenticity is a critical theme of the self-narrative in psychodynamic executive coaching.

I conclude this section with a note of reservation on the matter of "research evidence."

As part of the social and human sciences, theories of psychodynamic executive coaching are rooted in what Aristotle in *The Nicomachean Ethics* called *phronesis,* or practical wisdom. Phronesis differs from *episteme* (epistemology as basic science and predictive theory) and *techne* (technical skills and crafts). Phronesis is the reflective practitioner's ability to deliberate between the universal and the particular by drawing from a wealth of universal knowledge, which is then practiced in everyday situations. "The goal of the phronetic approach becomes one of contributing to society's capacity for value-rational deliberation and action" (Flyvbjerg, 2001, p. 167). The study of organizations and individuals who lead and reproduce systems, and who are in turn shaped by these very same cultures, is the study of reflective human subjects, not of dead objects (Flyvbjerg, 2001). Constructing meaning and mutual understanding, not prediction, is the aim. The goal of increasing self-consciousness, by attending to what Bollas (1987) calls the "unthought known," or unconscious thoughts and emotions, distinguishes psychodynamic executive coaching. Developing executives' and leaders' cognitive and emotional capacity for reflective action is at the heart of this enterprise of organizational intervention.

Case examples and qualitative approaches to the study of organizations and their leaders are critical to advancing the psychodynamic paradigm in executive coaching and consultation as they are important to more deeply understanding human organizations and their executive leaders in pursuit of value-laden action, power, and interests.

Executive Coaching as Organizational Intervention

I covered the development of psychodynamic approaches in executive coaching in the section on psychodynamic models, with reviews of Levinson; Kets de Vries; Kilburg; and Newton, Long, and Sievers. I continue this reflection with the discussion below that addresses the heart of psychodynamically informed executive coaching in theory and practice, and by further articulating its paradigmatic origins in object relations theory and the contributions of Winnicott, as mentioned at the beginning of this chapter and elsewhere in this book, in particular the ideas of true and false self, the holding environment, and potential and transitional space, discussed elsewhere.

However, it is critical at this juncture to articulate this epistemological position: executive coaching is a form of organizational intervention. It is a step in a larger process of working with organizations and individuals. Executive coaching is an idea situated within a larger conceptual framework that links theory and practice. And while there are varied approaches to executive coaching, the psychodynamic approach as presented here combines psychoanalytic theory and practice with systems and group-relations theory. Psychoanalytic theory is over a hundred years old and continues to experience evolution rooted in clinical, historical, cultural, and global tensions—one might say it has advanced both despite and because of internal and external pressures.

Psychoanalytic theory is a school of thought with competing paradigms. Many scholars and practitioners believe this state of affairs represents a healthy and productive paradigmatic tension. Beyond the paradigmatic conflicts and tension, all the psychodynamic approaches discussed in this chapter on executive coaching concern themselves with minimizing defensiveness, enhancing awareness of self and others, and promoting authenticity. Levinson's approach emphasizes the value in understanding executives' desires, needs, and expectations, not in isolation but in the context of organizational diagnosis and assessment. Kets de Vries's approach debunks the rational economic man model and proffers categories of character disposition and individual executive proclivity rooted in the realities of the workplace. His extensive typology of dispositions provides insights into the characteristics that shape key relationships, organizational strategies, decision making, and performance. Kilburg's systemic approach to psychodynamics and organizations stresses complexity and chaos, and the challenges of self-organizing adaptive systems. Finally, organizational role analysis highlights the significance of analyzing roles over individual character and stresses the importance of group-level (over individual-level) analysis. An integration of these approaches may be preferable.

From a psychodynamic perspective, executive coaching is an exercise in reflecting upon organizational identity, conflict, and character. That is why Winnicott's notion of authenticity, true and false self, is critical to a psychoanalytic approach to executive coaching, particularly one that takes organizational identity as an organizing frame of reference.

Executive Coaching and the Challenge of Authenticity: True versus False Self

The Winnicottian value of authenticity and the idea of a true self hidden behind the veil of a false self is a starting point. The false self, like the ego, is a stable and recurring, continuously operative structure. Winnicott (1971) repeatedly asserts the critical idea that this separation of self into true and false is normal and commonplace. Authenticity is an element of the idea of true self; it requires self-consciousness and attentiveness to the executive's impact on others and in turn others' effect on the executive-in-role.

Winnicott's (1965) theory of infancy and childhood development describes a nascent self of potential spontaneity and authenticity. This emerging true self, however, fades away behind the defensive forces of an acquiescent and reactive false self where inadequate, "not good enough" parenting and holding are present. This phenomenon of false self is present in adulthood and in particular is commonplace among narcissistic executives unconsciously defending themselves against the pain and discomfort of conflict (internal and external) and against the threat of rejection by underlings who might question the "wisdom" of their leadership, thus causing them to lose subordinates' idealization and reinforcement of their need for aggrandizement.

Employees are frequently required, implicitly and explicitly, by managers and executives to be submissive and obedient. This compliance compels subordinates to function psychologically from behind the fortress of a false self. Simultaneously, managers and executives shun personal responsibility for their actions and tend to blame subordinates for failed or flawed organizational strategies whenever necessary and convenient despite the reality that workers often lack the authority to assume actual responsibility for the implementation of managerial and executive strategies. Workers under these stressful and alienating conditions experience demoralization and become disgruntled.

Under conditions of stress and demands for change, executives find, with the assistance of psychodynamically oriented executive coaches and consultants, that reactive and defensive solutions to their anxiety are no longer manageable or efficacious. They also find that secrecy and withholding of information is ineffective and that it merely further deflates workers' sense of self-confidence and competence. Executives with rigid dispositions are challenged by circumstances in which resilience and openness to change in the status quo are imperative yet seemingly absent. Profound change can come about with mutual authenticity, respect, and shared responsibilities among leaders and followers (executives, managers, and workers). Followers (or subordinates), despite having limited power and authority, need to assert themselves as well. They need to acknowledge their shared responsibility for perpetuating inauthentic and defensive leadership and culture. Executive coaches and consultants help by supporting and facilitating a *transitional space* or *reflective containment* for participants engaged in change. As noted in previous chapters, *potential space* refers to the need to provide a safe and creative emotional and psychological virtual room for people in their attempt to produce radical change and solve complex problems. By directing feedback to address unconscious reactive and defensive behavior patterns and dispositions that block positive change, psychodynamically oriented executive coaches work to enhance participants' self-awareness and emotional intelligence. Heightened self-awareness and consciousness in executives is the first step toward minimizing the toxic consequences of reactive narcissism and giving voice to the true self of authentic leaders and followers while limiting the prevalence of the false self and the negative impact of excessively defensive operations on organizational culture and identity.

In the next and concluding section, I address the advancement of the study of psychodynamic executive coaching by promoting organizational ethnographic and action research.

Conclusion

The study of psychodynamic executive coaching is advanced by qualitative and idiographic approaches to the study of organizations and leadership, and by the interpretive power of case examples. Not simply more but better case illustrations of psychodynamic coaching in theory (conceptual frameworks) and practice (concrete applications) are required. Reconstructing narratives between coaches and clients might proffer a better understanding and illustration of psychodynamically oriented coaching and consulting. It might provide us with insight into the manner and degree to which psychodynamic coaches take into consideration the importance of organizational culture, diagnosis, and assessment. If they do so, examples depicting the influence of independent organizational diagnoses on executive coaching sessions and the sorts of psychological issues and dynamics discussed would be helpful. How do coaches manage the anticipated transference and countertransference dynamics? Psychodynamic executive coaching differs from psychoanalytic psychotherapy. These differences and commonalities need to be better clarified and further explored.

While some might argue that the practice of psychodynamic executive coaching ought to be grounded in current organizational circumstances supported and informed by organizational diagnoses and assessments, other practitioners might argue about this requirement and might articulate the value added for clients in processes in which organizational assessments are not a precondition. Psychodynamic executive coaching and, for that matter, other forms of executive coaching are intervention strategies that can increase reflective learning among executives, managers, and workers, and therefore can contribute to positive organizational change. However, when executive coaching is not a component of comprehensive organizational-change efforts, there might be a tendency to take executive issues and psychodynamics out of context, providing little assistance to the collective whole of the organization, its members, and executives. Without the benefits of independent organizational diagnoses, I argue, executive coaching efforts carry serious limitations and ought to carry, at best, modest expectations.

Psychodynamic approaches to executive coaching as principally influenced by the works discussed in this chapter and other works referenced abound with case examples and illustrations. Works by Stein (1994, 2001), Zaleznik (1984a, 1984b, 1989, 1991), Sievers (2009), Stapley (2002), Diamond (1993, 2007), and Diamond and Allcorn (2009) offer case illustrations and vignettes that support conclusions drawn and interpretations espoused. These examples are instructive and could benefit from more elaborate organizational ethnographies and case narratives that better depict and account for the actual interpersonal dynamics between coaches and clients in particular organizational interventions. Psychodynamic theories and approaches to organizational consultation and executive coaching are not intended as theories for prediction; rather, they are designed for more deeply understanding and interpreting the significance and meaning of complex human relationships and work roles, groups, and organizations. The psychodynamic approaches to executive coaching outlined and briefly discussed in this chapter offer researchers and consultants a more profound understanding and consideration of the impact of psychological reality on organizational roles and working relationships; they are intended to help leaders and executives by engaging them in authentic and reflective dialogue that expands awareness and consciousness of self and others in the workplace—the essence of organizational identity.

CHAPTER 10

Conclusions

We have to discover what the situation is *in the course of* our intervention in the situation. One way to discover what a situation is (so obvious, and yet frequently not done), is to convene in the one place, at the one time, the set of people we have good initial reason to suppose compose the key elements of the situation. (Laing, 1969, p. 35)

As THE PRECEDING chapters have indicated, the theory and practice of contemporary relational psychoanalytic organizational research and consultation requires an intervention in the situation of a dysfunctional organization. This intervention can produce potential space. The opening up of and making room for this reflective and transitional psychological space starts with the initial contact between psychodynamically oriented organizational researchers and the organization's leadership. It proceeds with the consultant's entering the field of the organization (figure 2, level 2). The process of opening potential space moves ahead with the development and presentation of the organizational narrative (diagnosis and assessment) and the provision of feedback and subsequent confirmation of the story with organizational members. These steps are followed by planned reparative interventions and change. The process concludes with an eventual exit and follow-up months later.

The Four Phases of the Consultative Process

In retrospect this is an observational and experiential process of enhancing consciousness, insight, and learning. It is a research and consultative process experienced by participants in four phases: (1) disruption, (2) confrontation, (3) demystification, and (4) transparency.

First, *disruption* refers to a process of opening and exposing organizational participants as part of a relational network. This process of opening and exposing signifies for participants an intrusion by outsiders (researchers and consultants) and an associated vulnerability for insiders (organizational participants). *Disruption* also refers to chaos, which is, on the one hand, disorganizing and, on the other hand, essential to deep learning, creativity, and reflective practice.[1]

Second, *confrontation* denotes the initial and inevitable defensiveness and resistance among participants to consultants' feedback in the organizational narrative (diagnosis) and the subsequent depiction of organizational identity. Such defensive resistance to insight and change is typical and at the heart of relational challenges to opening space for participants' reflection and agency. The nature of confrontation as a component of intervention is that of the unthought known (see chapter 7), as in telling the participants something they already know at a deep and profound level of consciousness. Yet, it is a narrative that has taken these participants' and their predecessors' psychological effort to suppress and disavow. So the confrontational presence of consultants is not an entirely welcome sight.

Third, *demystification* refers to the process of working through participants' resistance to feedback and to overcoming the inevitable social denial and defensiveness, which blocks members' recognition and ownership of the unthought known. Repression and denial are eventually weakened by exposure of a collective or group false self and a destructive, counterproductive narrative. Once claimed by organizational participants, the unthought known can be replaced with a narrative truth and authenticity at the heart of organizational well-being. The collective false self can be exchanged with a true self embodied in participants' resonance with and confirmation of the publicly articulated organizational identity. This is what is meant by participants' finding agency through claimed action and mutual responsibility.

Fourth and finally, with acknowledgment of the unthought known, a degree of *transparency* results in melting down and otherwise minimizing the rigidity of shared defenses such as splitting and projection, which are the frequent products of "us against them" social structures and the Manichean mind-set. Following demystification and greater transparency, members and leaders come to accept the value and lightness of authenticity and humility over the heaviness of inauthenticity and destructive narcissism.

At the moment of the psychodynamically oriented researchers' first contact with organizational leaders and participants, they start collecting data from their experiences, observations, and associations. As they cross personal and organizational boundaries, their individual and shared experiences demand processing of transference and countertransference emotional responses to organizational participants and leaders. Empathy and identification are possible but only as a consequence of consultants' willingness to explore their thoughts and feelings about organizational members and their predicament, periodically asking themselves: "What is it like to work here?"

In the interests of elevating insights and reflective processes, organizational consultants need supervision and consultation themselves. As a critical dimension and additional layer of consciousness, supervision enables consultants to process transference and countertransference dynamics among themselves as a research team and with the organizational participants as they engage in the collection of psychoanalytic data and the pursuit of organizational identity (see appendix).[2]

Next I summarize the idea of organizational identity and relational psychoanalytic theory for clarity and further consideration.

Organizational Identity and Relational Psychoanalytic Theory

Organizational identity has been offered as a uniquely psychodynamic frame of reference for understanding organizations as relational modes of experience and action. Organizational identity is the unconscious result of transference and countertransference dynamics between members and their organizations, leaders and followers, executives and workers, and consultants and organizational participants. As an aim of psychodynamically informed organizational research and consultation, organizational identity assists in answering the question "What is it like to work here?"

Organizations, regardless of their highly rationalized structures and designs, are human, and humans are frequently irrational and unaware of their motives and actions. This reality lends itself to a psychodynamic approach to understanding organizations and organizational identity. The contemporary relational psychoanalytic approach is rooted in the mother-baby attachment and the governing assumption that human beings are object-seeking creatures. Thus, in its application to organizations, contemporary psychoanalytic theory accentuates the significance of organizational identity as a psychological reality—the intersubjective and narrative structure of individuals' actual experience of groups and organizations.

Thus, organizational identity is a theory and product of organizational narrative, which emerges from diagnosis and assessment. It encompasses systemic complexity (figure 2) and defines organizations as relational, experiential, and perceptual systems (Diamond & Allcorn, 2009). Organizational identity comprehends organizations as repetitive and networked, cognitive and emotional, psychodynamic systems. Organizational identity is a narrative (as noted above) that is ultimately the authoritative voice of organizational participants' experiential and perceptual world. Therefore, the goal of the practice of psychoanalytic organizational research and consultation is reparative and integrative. Once articulated, organizational identity has the potential to reformulate linkages while addressing fragmentations such as "us against them" social structures and the Manichean mind-set derived from unconscious acts of splitting and projection.

It has been my intention to provide readers with a rationale and outline for a contemporary psychoanalytic organizational theory. This model gives heuristic centrality to the idea of organizational identity. I have presented relational psychoanalytic organizational research and consultation as a dialectical framework of organizational theory and practice, a praxis aimed at reaching a deeper understanding of organizational membership via organizational identity.

As developed in chapter 4, organizational identity is situated in the transitional area of intersubjectivity and potential space. This metaphoric mental space is located between archetypal concepts of objective reality and subjective illusion. In other words, organizational identity by way of potential space is situated in between objectivity and subjectivity and located within the actual participant experiences of play and imagination, creativity and chaos. Finally, and I assume in contrast with a large majority of management and organization theory, organizational identity describes a psychological and experiential place where we truly live (Winnicott, 1971).

Key Concepts and Reflective Practice

The contemporary relational psychoanalytic approach to the study of organizations presented here depicts a framework of reflective practice for organizational researchers, scholar-practitioner consultants, executives, managers, and workers. It is based on the value of self-awareness and self-consciousness in our daily lives and the associated desire for a healthier and more humane workplace. The following review of key concepts is meant to leave the reader with critical parts of the whole of organizational theory and practice presented in this book.

The psychosocial context for discovering organizational identity (discussed in chapter 4 and table 2) is found in the ideas of intersubjectivity and potential space. It is the location from which psychoanalytic consultants observe, experience, and interpret leadership, followership, and organizational well-being and effectiveness. It is, as noted above, the potential space between subject and object, self and other (as illustrated by figure 4). The nature of organizational identity depicted from this psychological space is often represented in the leadership's capacity or incapacity to provide good enough holding and containment of members' anxieties and toxic emotions.

Repetition, and the compulsion to repeat (discussed in chapter 5), is shown to be an important factor in organizational identity, learning, and change. Distinguishing between passive and active repetition (table 3) is critical for the organizational researcher and consultant in developing a deeper understanding of the degree to which transference and countertransference traps—between leaders and followers, between consultants and organizational participants, and among organizational members—are contributing to organizational deterioration and ineffectiveness. Breaking out of the vicious circle of passive and destructive repetition requires members' awareness of relational routines such as transference and countertransference that perpetuate unthinking defensive rigidity and routinization. Repetition is not exclusively destructive. In the form of active rather than passive repetition, it is critical to developing a more reflective practice and to learning from experience.

As all humans do, organizational members and leaders think in terms of organizational images and metaphors. These metaphors shape how participants view the multilayered model of organization (figure 2) and organizational identity. In addition to understanding metaphors as images of organizations as machines, organisms, brains, and psychic prisons, among others, people need to see metaphors as psychological and linguistic processes (Diamond, 2014; Morgan, 2006). Fluid processes tend to produce imaginative, creative, fearless, experimental, and inventive workers who are capable of innovating and confronting complex problems. In contrast, frozen processes tend to block communication and interactions across divisional boundaries and tend to inhibit progress and change (for example, the silo metaphor discussed in chapter 6).

A contemporary relational psychoanalytic model takes into account the influence of unconscious processes on the coordination of tasks and leader-follower relationships that shape organizational identity. The concept of the unthought known (chapter 7) takes unconscious processes as embodied in memory such that the individual comes to know something as true, as having resonance and feeling right. Unconscious processes are stored in the sensations of the body, and intersubjective insights depend on the depth of awareness and consciousness. We often know something is "true" when we feel it to be so, such as when participants feel resonance with the presentation of organizational identity. During feedback sessions where consultants share the organizational narrative (organizational diagnosis), participants are known to proclaim, "We knew that! We just hadn't thought of it." This signifies the unthought known, which is a good indicator of a shift in the collective level of consciousness from relatively unconscious to conscious awareness. This shift is a positive sign that organizational members are reflective and conscious. They are thinking about their counterproductive and defensive routines. Reflective practice is a productive counterweight to expansive narcissism.

The concept of narcissism is critical to a psychoanalytic organizational framework. It is particularly helpful in understanding and assessing organizational leadership and followership, power and authority, and the nature of transference and countertransference. Narcissism is not always negative and destructive. Constructively narcissistic leaders foster the confidence and loyalty of their followers. They typically are visionaries and capable of visualizing a triumphant future organization. They attend to great ideas and ignore everyday operations and details, which is why they need effective and competent managers. Nevertheless, they demand the adoration and aggrandizement of their followers. When environmental, political, and economic circumstances change, and require altering or dispensing of these leaders' grand plans for the organization, they resist, possibly to the point of bringing down the organization along with them. Positively and constructively narcissistic leadership can turn negative, aggressive, and destructive with changing environmental circumstances that are no longer consistent with the leader's vision.

The construct of narcissism in leadership is a reasonable barometer for assessing organizational well-being and effectiveness. Destructively narcissistic leaders acquire executive positions of inordinate power and authority. They tend to perpetuate hierarchic systems of dominance and submission, superior and inferior relational dynamics. Consequently, organizational members feel oppressed, disrespected, and abused. Organizational identity is often shaped by experiences and relationships in the service of narcissistic leaders and their demands for personal grandiosity and omnipotence.

Finally, reflective practice is defined in part by psychodynamic executive interventions. Coaching executives is merely one small part of the puzzle. As a psychoanalytically informed practice, coaching is contextualized by way of understanding organizational identity. This means taking into account the relational patterns and transference dynamics of intersubjectivity, which reflect workers' vertical and horizontal organizational experiences. Issues of attachment, narcissism, and the executive's capacity to provide a good enough holding environment for employees are critical to assessing potential success or failure. Knowledge of organizational identity is instructive when working with executives who struggle with empathy and identification with workers' perceptions and experiences.

* * * * *

The future of the social and organizational sciences depends upon their relevance and application to society's perplexing problems. These challenges require an interdisciplinary scholar-practitioner model that addresses systems complexity and authenticity through theory and practice. Advances in organizational scholarship, in particular, depend on case studies, organizational immersion and diagnosis, organizational stories, fieldwork and ethnography, and the application of a relational psychoanalytic theory to groups and organizations. They rely on observations and field notes from psychodynamically oriented researchers who take an experience-near approach in which empathy and identification offer insight into the meaning of organizational membership. These researchers and consultants position themselves in organizations within the third dimension of intersubjectivity and potential space. Many psychodynamically oriented action researchers will combine understanding the character of organizations with assisting leaders and followers with transitions and reparations. As Lewin (1946) concluded long ago, there is much to be learned about human beings and social problems from the intervention action-research model.

It is difficult to imagine understanding an organization in depth without researchers' immersion into the actual situation. It is also hard to imagine a theoretical framework better suited to studying organizations in depth than relational psychoanalytic theory. It is my hope that readers take away an insightful perspective for making sense of organizations, and that they come to appreciate the typical anxieties and uncertainties surrounding organizational membership and change discussed throughout this book.

The relational psychoanalytic theory and method for discovering organizational identity explained in this book represents thirty-five years of studying, learning from, listening to, and working with struggling and dysfunctional organizations and their leaders. It is my hope that the framework presented here supports organizational scholars and thoughtful consultants who want to better understand the psychosocial meaning of organizational experiences. Finally, it is my intent that the application of this psychoanalytic model of theory and practice results in the promotion of a more satisfying, less oppressive, and more reflective and humane work life.

APPENDIX

In this appendix, I offer some practical ideas about relational psychoanalytic organizational research and consultation on matters of (1) interviewing, (2) fieldwork and note taking, (3) participant observation, (4) psychoanalytic data, and (5) research/consultant team processing.

Interviewing

On the value of interviewing and free association, there is an interesting dialogue, I submit, that ought to occur among psychoanalytic organizational researchers about the interpretive benefits and weaknesses of interviewing organizational participants in structured and semistructured fashion, and immersing oneself in the organization to allow for more spontaneous dialogue and free associating on the part of consultants and organizational members. *Free association* here refers to the facilitation of participants' saying whatever comes to mind in the context of their work experience and in relation to the intervention. In the final analysis, there is something to be said in favor of some combination of formal interviewing and free associating.

Fieldwork and Note Taking

One might consider structuring field notes in a manner that organizes note taking into the dimensions of consciousness and experience indicated by the following questions and advice. (1) Am I aware of myself as an instrument of research and consultation? Am I conscious of my countertransference reactions? Can I write them down and keep them in perspective? How do I feel I am treated in my role as researcher/consultant? (2) What do I observe? Write it down. (3) What do I hear? Write it down. (4) What do I feel? Write it down. (5) Am I aware of my tendency to judge organizations and individual participants from the outset? If so, can I suspend judgment for the duration by writing down my opinions and judgments? (6) Am I spending most of my time listening and very little time talking? If so, good. If not, reverse your priorities by shutting your mouth.

Participant Observation

I have often described the phenomenon of participant observation as that of "one foot in and one foot out" of the organization. One might be critical of taking this position because it might appear to signify ambivalence of the researcher/consultant and thereby might interfere with acquiring empathy and identification. I do not see it that way, however; rather, I find the idea (one foot in and one foot out) heightens attention to role and psychosocial boundaries between insiders and outsiders, self and other, and thereby assists in avoiding the greater problem of overidentification with organizational participants. Also, participant observation takes place in the area of intersubjectivity and potential space (chapter 4).

Psychoanalytic Data

I introduced the idea of psychoanalytic data (historical, observational, associative, experiential, and empathic [HOAEE]) in the study of organizations earlier in this book. Assuming a hermeneutic approach to one's work with organizations, there is much to the practice of fieldwork and observation that requires confirmation and validation, particularly from participants. Efforts at depicting the organization are ultimately centered on a combination of data that tell a story, a narrative truth, which thereby confirm a psychological reality that captures and resonates with participants' living and working experiences. Knowing and understanding the participants' experiences are critical to articulating and vocalizing organizational identity and to assisting in positive transformations.

In addition to the collection of uniquely psychoanalytic data described above, organizational diagnosis as originally outlined by Harry Levinson includes the collection of factual data, generic data, structural and process data, and operations data, as well as historical, narrative, and interpretive data. Psychoanalytic data as presented in this book take the researcher deeper into the unconscious and unacknowledged layers of organizational experience.

Research/Consulting Team Processing

Supervision of research and consulting teams engaged in the fieldwork of psychoanalytic organizational diagnosis is crucial for learning and relational perspective. As they are for participants, holding and containment are necessary for researchers and consultants while they are immersed in organizations. Assistance in processing emotional reactions, judgments, and unconscious assumptions requires someone with a tad more psychological distance— someone not immersed in the organization.

This process often enhances consultants' capacity for empathy and identification, which as discussed earlier is invaluable to the discovery of organizational identity and the capacity for productive change. Working in research and consulting teams is always preferable to flying solo as it supports cognitive and emotional processing of the psychoanalytic data and facilitates the dispensation, management, and interpretation of transference and countertransference dynamics between researchers and organizational members.

NOTES

Introduction

1. Referring to organizations as transformational objects is intended to highlight the concept of organizations as extensions of our individual ego ideal, which is Freud's concept of our sense of ourselves at our future best. This concept of transformational objects, which I took from the work of Bollas (1987) and redefined for application to organizations, is also meant to highlight the fact that organizational members hold expectations of their organization and its leadership. Frequently, these members assume they will change and be transformed through the capacity to work creatively, productively, and imaginatively. All too often, they are disappointed and angry when this does not come to fruition.

2. Winnicott's (1971) notion of *potential space* is what he and other psychoanalysts consider the intersubjective third, the area between self and object, the space in which the subject gains perspective with an additional degree of psychological distance and the capacity to observe, experience, associate, and reflect. In psychoanalytic organizational studies this area is opened up for participants by researchers' and consultants' intervention in organizational systems.

3. I use *object* here to represent the nature of self and object relations, as in the meaningful relationship between oneself and the organization as an object of idealization or deserving of contempt, for instance.

4. I am referring here to the post-Kleinian object relational work of Winnicott, particularly *The Maturational Processes and the Facilitating Environment* (1965) and *Playing and Reality* (1971), a collection of seminal papers covering many of his key concepts and major contributions to psychoanalytic theory.

5. The word *it* here refers not only to unarticulated and unconscious emotional baggage but also to the Freudian "it," or id, as representing primitive, unconscious processes and motives.

6. When I speak of "real," I am referring to the notion of "real" as shared psychological reality and experience. Some refer to this as "actuality" and "authenticity," as in Winnicott's notion of the true self. This notion of "real" can be described as the figurative space where we actually live (as in lived experience). Often this notion of "real" describes the psychological space between objective reality and illusion or fantasy. Some (Spence, 1982) view this notion of "real" as a narrative truth in contrast with a historical truth. My preference and the way I use the notion of

"real" or "true" implicitly throughout this book is as in psychological reality and shared experience—the location of intersubjectivity, potential space, and organizational identity.

Chapter 1: Psychoanalytic Organizational Theory

1. Winnicottian *potential space* refers to the mental and transitional area of imagination and invention, the psychological space between objective reality and fantasy. For Winnicott this is the area of play and the location of culture, art, music, theatre. It is also the location of an intersubjective third and, in my view, organizational identity, discussed here and in subsequent chapters.

2. *Introjections* and *projections* refer to the psychological processes that shape internal object relations whereby experiences of self and others are internalized as good or bad, loving or rejecting, and subsequently affect normal projections of the self, rooted in those experiences and put onto others.

3. On ongoing change throughout the life cycle of adolescence, early adulthood, midlife, and old age, see Erikson, *Identity: Youth and Crisis* (1968). It is, however, important to note that the concept of identity suggests that while things change and humans adapt to changes, they simultaneously remain the same in their core character and sense of self.

4. "Much of what interests psychoanalysts about unconscious mental content does not, as we have seen, really involve *unconsciousness*; it rather involves the nature and relations of the mental activity present in the two cerebral hemispheres and includes the interplay, dominance, and connectedness of their very different kinds of consciousness. Repression, as we know it, is nowhere to be found; it does not denote some single process but is the outcome of many processes acting and interacting on different mental functions and contents in different parts of the brain" (Leffert, 2010, p. 249).

5. The concept of boundaries is critical in psychoanalytic organizational theory as it refers to the psychological and psycho-geographical delineation between oneself and others as well as the maintenance of horizontal and vertical organizational divisions, roles, power, and authority.

6. See the pioneering work of Volkan (1997, 2004, 2006).

7. While Winnicott emphasizes mothers in their initial caregiving role during attachment, it is clear that fathers provide caregiving as well and are critical to the establishment of secure attachments and a secure base for childhood development.

8. See Bingley (2003), who argues that we know ourselves through the coexistence of inner and outer realities.

9. As Benjamin (2004) states, "Thirdness is about how we build relational systems and how we develop the intersubjective capacities for such co-creation" (p. 7). She later goes on to equate "thirdness" with Winnicott's potential space. See also Diamond (2007) for the application of the analytic third as akin to potential space in the context of organizational change.

10. The clinical notion of containment seems to have been mentioned for the first time when Bion, in his 1959 article "Attacks on Linking," refers to the mother's aptitude to deal with the baby's "primary aggression and envy." Bion (1967) uses several words to describe the mother's reaction: "unreceptiveness," to "remain balanced," "comfortable state of mind"; finally, when describing transference--countertransference interaction with a patient, he says, "Projective identification makes it possible for him to investigate his own feelings in a personality powerful enough to *contain* [emphasis added] them" (p. 106).

11. Baum (1987) coined the term *invited intruder* as a way of describing the ambivalent relationship between research and researched.

Chapter 2: Self Identity and Organizational Identity

1. In psychoanalytic organizational research and consultation, the self is also an instrument of research and participant observation. Identification and empathy with research subjects and clients becomes an avenue of deeper understanding of members' predicament rather than a distortion and presumption of their subjective experience of work and organizational life.

2. When using the concept of "personal knowledge," I am referring to the manner in which the philosopher and chemist Michael Polanyi uses this notion in his *Personal Knowledge: Towards a Post-Critical Philosophy* (1958).

3. Harquail and King (2010) describe three traditions of organizational identity: discursive, constructionist, and social actor. Then they add their own contribution to the organizational identity literature with their intriguing and complementary notion of embodied cognition.

4. Humphreys and Brown (2002) focus on issues of identity and identification. The authors suggest that identity, individual and collective, and the process of identification that binds people to organizations are illustrated in personal and shared narratives.

5. Whetten (2006) clarifies organizational identity as an analogue of individual identity and thus in taking a social-actor perspective seems to acknowledge organizational identity as projected identity.

6. Corley et al. (2006) distinguish organizational identity from organizational culture and climate.

7. Pratt and Foreman (2000) examine multiple organizational identities and suggest that these identities can be managed by manipulating dimensions of plurality and synergy. They identify four types of managerial responses.

8. The term *critical* here is used in the spirit of "critical theory" and the dialectical tradition of the Frankfurt School of Germany and the Institute for Social Research (as represented by theorists Herbert Marcuse and Erich Fromm, among others).

9. See Brown and Starkey's (2000a, 2000b) commentary in the special edition of the *Academy of Management Journal*. The authors address every article in the

edition and comment on the notions of multiple organizational identities, meta-identities, the benefits of identity fluidity, identity creation, and social identity. They suggest that the contributors could benefit from psychodynamic insights that take into account the irrationality and emotionality of organizational life.

10. One among many good articles on the nonpsychoanalytic approach to organizational identity is a piece by Dutton and Dukerich (1991) that addresses how individuals make sense of their organizational responses to a nontraditional and emotional strategic issue. Their research concerned what they call "microprocesses of organizational adaptation," which they derived from a case study of the Port Authority of New York and New Jersey and the challenge of homeless people at their facilities. This led to a description of a new perspective on organizational adaptation. They conclude that image and identity guide and activate individuals' interpretations of an issue and motivations for action. The article develops the constructs of organizational identity and image and then uses them to link ideas from work on impression management with ideas about organizational adaptation.

11. I use Winnicott's (1971) thinking on *holding* to conceptualize the quality of secure attachment which in organizations manifests in the leader's capacity to manage members' anxieties and insecurities about loss and separation and Bion's (1962, 1967) thinking on *containment* to conceptualize the capacity of leaders and their organizational cultures to be able to process toxic emotions and anxieties so that at a future point in time members can learn from and better manage these difficult emotions.

Chapter 3: Group Dynamics

1. *Transference* and *countertransference dynamics* refer to the phenomenon of relational psychodynamics, where one projects emotions onto the other and the other then responds to the projections with counterprojections.

2. *Repression* refers here to acts of disavowal, denial, undoing, and generally forcing reality outside of awareness.

3. Persecuted work groups, personality cults, vulnerable ethnic groups, and insecure nation-states are known to insulate and isolate themselves behind boundaries and borders from an external world they perceive as hostile and dangerous. The tyrannical and Stalinist totalitarian regime of North Korea exemplifies this mass phenomenon. Individual leaders and their dispirited societies figuratively resign and emotionally retreat from the external object world. While the large group reacts to preserve itself, in so doing it slips into a collective fantasy and delusional state.

4. Turquet's (1975) notion of "oneness" is similar to my concept of a "homogenized" work group, and both concepts add to Bion's (1959b) model of basic assumption groups.

5. Idealizing and mirroring transferences are two sides of the relational coin. Narcissistic leaders engage in mirroring, wherein they unconsciously surround themselves with adoring followers whose idealization mirrors the leader's image of grandiosity and omnipotence. The adoring followers look to satisfy their need to idealize by attaching themselves to grandiose and omnipotent leaders, and when they do so, they feel comforted and safe in being close to imagined greatness.

6. The autocratic group is admittedly and intentionally based on the Freudian patriarchy and thereby the rule of the father as steeped in the historical moment of the early twentieth century. It is therefore distinctive from what we might characterize as a matriarchy. The overarching psychoanalytic organizational theory presented throughout this book is rooted in a post-Kleinian model, with the mother-infant unit as the foundation for greater understanding of organizational dynamics. Thus, it places the pre-oedipal period and infantile roots as most critical and primary and the oedipal phase prioritized by the Freudian patriarchy as critical and secondary as developmental precursors to the meaning of organizational identity and membership among adult workers.

7. I described the autistic-contiguous phase in chapter 1 and discuss it elsewhere throughout this book. In this reference I am speaking of a regressive collapse into the most primitive of preverbal and symbiotic infantile states.

8. Reflective practice involves authenticity in which members intervene in their own group processes, particularly when those processes become regressive and counterproductive. This intervention could be asking a simple question, such as, what are we doing? Or making an observation, such as, look at us, we are behaving like children; what is the matter with us?

Chapter 4: Intersubjectivity and Potential Space

1. See the pioneering work of Winnicott, followed by the contemporary ideals of Ogden.

2. The idea of the third in psychoanalytic theory signifies the intersubjective dimension, the production of a third subject as a consequence of two subjects' coming together. The third subject signifies the combination and outcome of a human interaction or merger. Psychologically, we view this phenomenon as an intersubjective (rather than individual psychological) structure, what Kohut (1977) calls the self-object.

3. Potential space is a space critical in the well-being and development of the child, and it is derived from a "good enough holding environment," what I have earlier referred to as the attachment phase and mother-baby unit. For Winnicott (1971), the potential space is also the location of culture, and in my own thinking the potential space is that mental space facilitated by a psychoanalytic intervention that enables clients to come to terms with their shared organizational identity.

4. *Reflective action* here refers to what Anna Freud (1966) calls the "observing ego"—a self-consciousness that enables one to observe and process without having to react in the present moment. It also refers to the capacity to articulate observation of self and other as well as experience of self and other as in the nature of countertransference and empathy. In sum, identification ought to gain clarity by taking up the position of the intersubjective dimension.

5. Displaced projected emotions from the past onto the present object are not exclusively negative; they are sometimes positive and constructive.

6. What I am referring to here as "an expanding potential space" is the depth of experience, insight, and self-consciousness that comes from a good enough holding environment.

7. Referring back to figure 4, I often imagine this process as participants unconsciously lifting the two upper sides of the equilateral triangle up out of the linearity and assumed causality of the straight line from subject to object, constructing the third position, from which they can see the dialectical, intersubjective structure of nonlinear relations—the organizational identity.

8. Minolli and Tricoli (2004) argue that the notion of the third was created to solve the Hegelian problem of duality. For Hegel, self-consciousness is the avenue to resolve the limitations of duality.

Chapter 5: Repetition, Remembering, and Change

1. See Schon, *The Reflective Practitioner* (1983); see also Diamond, "Organizational Change and the Analytic Third: Locating and Attending to Unconscious Organizational Psychodynamics" (2007).

2. I submit that organizations and groups in conflict often have competing narratives, each representing the perspective organized around conscious and unconscious feelings specific to their group identification.

3. Hopefully it is obvious that questions during feedback are more concrete, absent of technical jargon, and nonpsychoanalytic, that what typically occurs is a description of the organization as, as in this case, broken in two and fragmented. Consultants seek confirmation or rejection of their findings. Once the participants provide confirmation, a dialogue proceeds in which a deeper understanding of the dysfunctional organizational dynamics is possible, and then the researchers work with the participants to generate a commitment to change.

4. Notions of grief and mourning are critical to our understanding the emotional processes of change, particularly when change is understood as the breaking of an attachment.

5. Change as emotional loss, along with processes of grief and mourning, depicts the positive and developmentally progressive aspects of the depressive position.

6. Some negative aspects of these organizations can become clear, however, as with community policing in the United States, which is getting more attention

in the media as more evidence of abusive and discriminatory policing practices throughout the country comes to light.

7. Such contentment is often indicated by comments such as, "We've always done it this way!"

8. See Lear's use of the concept of "primordial struggle" in his book *Freud* (2005), in which he uses the term in describing "structures of repetition" in the "compulsion to repeat."

9. Argyris and his colleagues see organizations as brains, hard-wired to reinforce the status quo. While change in the status quo is problematic, this ignores the findings of neural plasticity and thereby the possibility of change in the structure of the brain resulting from intense relations and events (see Vaughan, *The Talking Cure* [1997]).

10. Paranoid-schizoid modes of experience were first described by Klein as the initial position of the infant in relation to the mother. This concept later came to describe the infantile roots of adulthood characterized by fragmented thinking (part-objects), projected aggression, and what is called "projective identification," in which the individual projects unwanted parts of him- or herself onto the other and experiences them vicariously through the other.

11. See Loewald's (1971) article on repetition for an introduction to these concepts of productive re-creation and passive reproduction.

Chapter 6: Metaphor and Metaphoric Processes

1. See Levinson, *Organizational Assessment* (2002), on "organizational assessment" as a framework for studying and intervening in organizations; see also Diamond and Allcorn, *Private Selves in Public Organizations: The Psychodynamics of Organizational Diagnosis and Change* (2009). Initially Levinson (1972) labeled his model "organizational diagnosis."

2. *Transference* and *projective identification* refer to the associative interaction whereby one individual or group of individuals displaces idealizing desires onto a leader or executive, who responds by mirroring the expansiveness and grandiosity unconsciously wished for. Thus, an emotional knot between superior and subordinate (inferior) is created. In the idealizing transference, subjects are in search of and attracted to narcissistic leaders whom they can idealize and in whose presence they can feel comforted. In the mirroring transference, subjects are in search of and attracted to followers who will support their need to feel expansive, grandiose, and omnipotent. Idealizing and mirroring transferences are complementary psychodynamics with psychologically regressive features. See Kohut (1984) for an elaboration of idealizing and mirroring transference.

3. Generally speaking, positive transferences (compassionate) are representative of the transfer of positive emotions onto the other as the object of transference, in contrast with negative transferences, which are representative of the transference

of negative (often hostile, aggressive) emotions onto the other.

4. Regressive action serves the defensive function of protecting individual organizational members from persecutory (and/or separation) anxiety by constructing unconscious fantasies of withdrawal into a safe and secure inner space—a space in time symbolized by the "holding environment" of infancy.

Chapter 7: The Unthought Known

1. See Bollas, *The Shadow of the Object: Psychoanalysis of the Unthought Known* (1987). See also Bollas's *Forces of Destiny* (1989), in which he explains that the term *unthought known* "refers to any form of knowledge that as yet is not thought. . . . Infants also learn rules for being and relating that are conveyed through the mother's logic of care, much of which has not been mentally processed. Children often live in family moods or practices that are beyond comprehension, even if they are partners in the living of such knowledge" (pp. 213–214).

2. This narrative feedback is data gathered from observation, participation, interviews, historical documents, factual information, etc.

3. Contemporary psychoanalytic theory stresses the intersubjective and interpersonal. It is therefore more applicable than Freudian theory to organizational research as a study of cooperative and collaborative endeavors.

4. Historical, observational, associative, experiential, and empathic data, as discussed earlier.

5. See Levinson (1972, 2002) for systematic presentation of an organizational diagnosis.

6. This confrontation with the undiscussable may be in contrast to some versions of organizational change, such as Appreciative Inquiry.

7. See Diamond, "Organizational Change and the Analytic Third" (2007).

8. See chapter 1 for discussion of Bion's (1962) notion of the dyad of *container* and *contained*.

9. I wish to acknowledge helpful correspondence on this subject with Howard F. Stein and Seth Allcorn, 2007.

10. From correspondence with Howard F. Stein.

Chapter 8: Narcissistic Organizational Leadership

1. From the perspective of ego psychology, the organizational psychologist Harry Levinson (1981) conceptualizes the unconscious dimensions of management and executive actions rooted in human development with three categories: maturation, ministration, and mastery (discussed in chapter 9). In addition, the need for dependency and the nature of the individual ego ideal as one's view of oneself at her future best play a key role.

2. See Volkan's *Killing in the Name of Identity* (2006) and *Enemies on the Couch* (2013). His concept of "the large group identity" is an insightful, powerful framework for analyzing the relational dynamics between polarized and frequently

deadly conflicts between ethnic and religious groups.

3. Kohut (1977) refers to early self-object needs for narcissistic supplies from parental self-objects, feeding the baby's healthy (stage-appropriate) narcissistic demands for mirroring, grandiosity, omnipotence, and exhibitionism. "Good enough" versus "not good enough" narcissism refers to Winnicott's (1965) language of the "good enough holding environment," from which the self emerges sufficiently gratified and secure or inadequately taken care of, anxious, and insecure.

4. I use *good enough mothering* and *good enough parenting* synonymously at times. While the role of the mother in shaping the baby's well-being is critical, it is also important to understand "mothering" as a "parenting" role and one that fathers participate in. Attachments, while primarily formed at the outset with the mother, are further secured and emotionally supported by nurturing and *holding* fathers.

5. See Hedges's *In Search of the Lost Mother of Infancy* (1994) for a cogent description of the resulting anxiety, dissociation, and disorganization.

6. See Kohut (1984) and self psychology for discussion of "mirror-hungry" and "ideal-hungry" narcissists, where the former project an exaggerated need for others who are willing to mirror their sense of greatness and perfection and the latter project a need to locate themselves close to others, particularly leaders, where they project an exaggerated need to imagine the perfection and greatness of the other and feel comforted and secure in doing so.

7. See Fromm's *The Sane Society* (1955), where he discusses superior-inferior, manager-worker dynamics.

8. It is important to remind the reader that the method of organizational research and consultation in this book is not the typical business-consulting model, where the consultant works in behalf of the executive client; what I describe is a research model based on a contemporary psychoanalytic framework, so people in all positions are naturally integral to the process.

9. Psychoanalytic data include historical (narrative), observational, associative, experiential, and empathic data.

10. The silo metaphor was also presented by members of the public works department discussed in chapter 6. The critical nature of metaphoric processes and the frozen metaphor of the silo were significant in this case, as they were in that department.

11. See the classic works in the field by Menzies (1960) and Jaques (1955) to better understand how organizations design structures and routines that operate as defenses against anxiety.

12. Gaining the involvement and full participation of the president may, admittedly, have come at the cost of reinforcing his image of grandiosity and omnipotence; nevertheless, it did provide an opportunity to give him feedback on a routine basis as the organizational study proceeded, and if there was a possibility of his being open to insight and change based on the consultants' observations,

it was without a doubt critical to have his support of the study and methodology.

13. Readers might consider the following contrast helpful: Saddam Hussein and Adolf Hitler were clearly destructively narcissistic leaders, while Mohandas Gandhi and Martin Luther King Jr. were reparatively and constructively narcissistic leaders.

14. Identification is a key idea and ought to be thought of as a description in part of the psychological processes of joining and becoming an organizational member as well as a key concept for psychoanalytic organizational researchers and consultants as they immerse themselves in organizational cultures and, via transference, countertransference, and empathy, come to deeply understand the research subject or client.

15. Charismatic leaders are not necessarily narcissistic, yet narcissistic leaders are frequently charismatic. These are not synonymous categories.

16. McDougall, *Theaters of the Mind: Illusion and Truth on the Psychoanalytic Stage* (1982).

17. See the work of medical and psychoanalytic anthropologist Howard F. Stein (1994, 1998).

18. Internalization and introjection are critical ideas in the object relational view of early human development and of the emergence of a sense of self in relation to others. These concepts are key to understanding the development of internal object relations as an organizing force that shapes experience and perception.

19. The extremes of idealization we know historically on a grand scale with Adolf Hitler and Nazi Germany or on a less grand scale with Jim Jones and the Peoples Temple. There are also many examples from the world of business and capitalism, such as Enron and AIG, and from the world of government, such as Reagan's fiasco in the Iran-Contra affair and Nixon's Watergate.

20. *Overvalue* here is used politically, economically, and in particular psychoanalytically.

21. *Idealize* here refers to the psychological process of idealization that fosters a blind faith in free-market capitalism.

Chapter 9: Executive Coaching

1. I have also observed many circumstances in which executives simply do not have background or skills in leadership or management and had simply been appointed to positions for which few if any recruits were available.

2. Consider Doris Kearns Goodwin's *Team of Rivals*, about Lincoln and his inner circle.

3. See Zaleznik et al. (1965) on the concept of "executive role constellation." Here I use the concept to promote reflective leadership organized around the exploration of leaders' resistances to change, paying attention to key concepts and psychological processes discussed in this book, such as repetition, metaphor, taking up the position of the analytic third, and the unthought known in giving

feedback based on historical and narrative data, observations, associations, transferences and countertransferences, and empathy.

4. Psychoanalytic theory includes at minimum three major schools of thought: classical psychoanalytic theory (and ego psychology), rooted in Freud's drive and structural model; psychoanalytic object relations theory, rooted in a Kleinian and Winnicottian relational object-seeking model; and Kohut's self psychology, rooted in a mixed model with a particular focus on the developmental lines (mirroring, idealizing, twinship) of narcissism and self-organization. One of the better overviews of the evolving psychoanalytic paradigms and schools of thought is Greenberg and Mitchell, *Object Relations in Psychoanalytic Theory* (1983).

5. It should be noted that Levinson did not apply the more contemporary object relational transference terminology of *mirroring* and *idealizing*. I have taken the liberty of doing so in the interest of clarifying my presentation of his pioneering work in organizational psychology and consultation. As noted in the previous chapter, *mirroring transference* refers to the individual unconscious desire for others to reinforce a need to be seen as omnipotent and grandiose, as seen in the narcissistic leader who requires admiring and adoring followers and who views himself as godlike. Idealizing transference is the complement to mirroring, whereby followers are in search of leaders to idealize and admire—this is the unconscious need for an all-powerful leader by whom followers are made to feel safer and grander simply by being in her proximity.

6. See Horney's *Our Inner Conflicts* (1945) for concepts of moving toward, moving against, and moving away from people and her notion of the idealized image. Horney's Neo-Freudian sociocultural perspective is particularly relevant in its application to the workplace.

7. See Harrison's *Diagnosing Organizations: Methods, Models, and Processes* (2005) for an application of the open systems model.

8. I wholeheartedly endorse the critique of mainstream executive coaching as frequently absent of context in the executive's professional role relationships and organization.

Chapter 10: Conclusions

1. See Stacey, *Complexity and Creativity in Organizations* (1996).

2. I typically insist on supervising researchers and research teams immersed in organizational assessment and diagnosis. Our weekly sessions provide an excellent opportunity for learning and developing insight.

REFERENCES

Abram, J. (1997). *The language of Winnicott.* Northvale, NJ: Jason Aronson.

Agar, M. H. (1996). *The professional stranger* (2nd ed.). San Diego, CA: Academic Press.

Albert, S., Ashforth, B. E., & Dutton, J. E. (2000). Organizational identity and identification: Charting new waters and building new bridges. *Academy of Management Review, 25*(1), 13–17.

Alford, C. F. (1994). *Group psychology and political theory.* New Haven, CT: Yale University Press.

Alvesson, M., & Willmott, H. (2002). Identity regulation as organizational control: Producing the appropriate individual. *Journal of Management Studies, 39,* 619–644.

Argyris, C. (1983). *Reasoning, learning, and action.* San Francisco: Jossey-Bass.

Argyris, C. (2004). *Reasons and rationalizations.* New York: Oxford University Press.

Argyris, C., Putnam, R., & Smith, D. (1985). *Action science: Concepts, methods, and skills for research and intervention.* San Francisco: Jossey-Bass.

Argyris, C. & Schon, D. (1974). *Theory in practice.* San Francisco: Jossey-Bass.

Argyris, C., & Schon, D. (1978). *Organizational learning.* Reading, MA: Addison-Wesley.

Argyris, C., & Schon, D. (1996). *Organizational learning II.* Reading, MA: Addison-Wesley.

Aristotle. (1976). *The Nicomachean ethics* (J. A. K. Thomson, Trans.). Harmondsworth, UK: Penguin.

Arlow, J. (1979). Metaphor and the psychoanalytic situation. *The Psychoanalytic Quarterly, 48*(3), 363–385.

Arnaud, G. (2003). A coach or a couch? A Lacanian perspective on executive coaching and consultation. *Human Relations, 56*(9), 1131–1154.

Aron, L., et al. (1998). *Relational perspectives on the body.* Hillsdale, NJ: Analytic.

Atwood, G. E., & Stolorow, R. D. (1984). *Structures of subjectivity: Explorations in psychoanalytic phenomenology.* Hillsdale, NJ: Analytic.

Baum, H. S. (1987). *The invisible bureaucracy.* New York: Oxford University Press.

References

Baum, H. S. (1990). *Organizational membership.* Albany, NY: State University of New York Press.

Benjamin, J. (1988). *The bonds of love.* New York: Pantheon.

Benjamin, J. (2004). Beyond doer and done to: An intersubjective view of third-ness. *The Psychoanalytic Quarterly, 73*(1), 5–46.

Bingley, A. F. (2003). In here and out there: Sensations between self and land-scape. *Social and Cultural Geography, 4*(3), 329–345.

Bion, W. R. (1959a). Attacks on linking. *International Journal of Psycho-Analysis, 40*(5-6), 308.

Bion, W. R. (1959b). *Experiences in groups and other papers.* London: Tavistock.

Bion, W. R. (1962). *Learning from experience.* London: Karnac.

Bion, W. R. (1965). *Transformations.* London: Tavistock.

Bion, W. R. (1967). *Second thoughts.* London: Karnac.

Bollas, C. (1987). *The shadow of the object: Psychoanalysis of the unthought known.* New York: Columbia University Press.

Bollas, C. (1989). *Forces of destiny: Psychoanalysis and human idiom.* Northvale, NJ: Jason Aronson.

Bollas, C. (2006). Perceptive identification. *The Psychoanalytic Review, 93*(5), 713–718.

Book, H. E. (1998). *How to practice brief psychodynamic psychotherapy: The core conflictual relationship theme method.* Washington, DC: American Psychological Association.

Borbely, A. F. (1998). A psychoanalytic concept of metaphor. *International Journal of Pscyho-analysis, 79,* 923.

Borbely, A. F. (2008). Metaphor and psychoanalysis. In J. Raymond & W. Gibbs (Eds.), *Cambridge handbook of metaphor and thought* (pp. 412–424). New York: Cambridge University Press.

Bowlby, J. (1969). *Attachment.* New York: Basic Books.

Bowlby, J. (1973). *Separation: Anxiety and anger.* New York: Basic Books.

Bowlby, J. (1980). *Loss: Sadness and depression.* New York: Basic Books.

Britton, R. (2004). Subjectivity, objectivity, and triangular space. *The Psychoanalytic Quarterly, 73*(1), 47–62.

Brown, A. D., & Starkey, K. (2000a). Organizational identity and learning: A psychodynamic perspective. *Academy of Management Review, 25*(1), 102–120.

Brown, A. D., & Starkey, K. (2000b). Toward integration. *Academy of Management Review, 25*(1), 148–150.

Brown, T. J., Dacin, P. A., Pratt, M. G., & Whetten, D. A. (2006). Identity, intend-ed image, construed image, and reputation: An interdisciplinary frame-work and suggested terminology. *Journal of the Academy of Marketing Science, 34*(2), 99–106.

References

Castoriadis, C. (1987). *The imaginary institution of society.* Cambridge, MA: MIT Press.

Castoriadis, C. (1997). *World in fragments.* Stanford: Stanford University Press.

Cavell, M. (1998). Triangulation, one's own mind, and objectivity. *International Journal of Psychoanalysis, 55,* 349–357.

Chodorow, N. J. (1999). *The power of feelings.* New Haven, CT: Yale University Press.

Cooperrider, D. L., & Whitney, D. (2005). *Appreciative inquiry: A positive revolution in change.* San Francisco: Berrett-Koehler.

Corley, K. G., & Gioia, D. A. (2004). Identity ambiguity and change in the wake of a corporate spin-off. *Administrative Science Quarterly, 49*(2), 173–208.

Corley, K. G., Harquail, C. V., Pratt, M. G., Glynn, M. A., Fiol, C. M., & Hatch, M. J. (2006). Guiding organizational identity through aged adolescence. *Journal of Management Inquiry, 15*(2), 85–99.

Crozier, M. (1964). *The bureaucratic phenomenon.* Chicago: University of Chicago Press.

Czander, W. M. (1993). *The psychodynamics of work and organizations.* New York: Guilford.

Diamond, M. A. (1984). Bureaucracy as externalized self-system: A view from the psychological interior. *Administration & Society, 16*(2), 195–214.

Diamond, M. A. (1985). The social character of bureaucracy: Anxiety and ritualistic defense. *Political Psychology, 6,* 663–679.

Diamond, M. A. (1988). Organizational identity: A psychoanalytic exploration of organizational meaning. *Administration & Society, 20*(2), 166–190.

Diamond, M. A. (1991). Stresses of group membership: Balancing the needs for independence and belonging. In M. F. R. Kets de Vries and Associates (Eds.), *Organizations on the couch: Clinical perspectives on organizational behavior and change.* San Francisco: Jossey-Bass.

Diamond, M. A. (1993). *The unconscious life of organizations: Interpreting organizational identity.* Westport, CT: Quorum Books, Greenwood.

Diamond, M. A. (1998). The symbiotic lure: Organizations as defective containers. *Administrative Theory & Praxis, 20*(3), 315–325.

Diamond, M. A. (2003). Organizational immersion and diagnosis: The work of Harry Levinson. *Organisational and Social Dynamics, 3*(1), 1–18.

Diamond, M. A. (2007). Organizational change and the analytic third: Locating and attending to unconscious organizational psychodynamics. *Psychoanalysis, Culture & Society, 12*(2), 142–164.

Diamond, M. A. (2008). Telling them what they know: Organizational change, defensive resistance, and the unthought known. *The Journal of Applied Behavioral Science, 44*(3), 348–364.

Diamond, M. A. (2014). Metaphoric processes and organizational change: A contemporary psychoanalytic perspective. *Organisational and Social Dynamics, 14*(1), 104–129.

Diamond, M. A., & Allcorn, S. (1985). Psychological responses to stress in complex organizations. *Administration & Society 17*, 217–239.

Diamond, M. A., & Allcorn, S. (1987). The psychodynamics of regression in work groups. *Human Relations, 40*(8), 525–543.

Diamond, M. A., & Allcorn, S. (2003). The cornerstone of psychoanalytic organizational analysis: Psychological reality, transference and countertransference in the workplace. *Human Relations, 56*(4), 491–514.

Diamond, M. A., & Allcorn, S. (2004). Moral violence in organizations: Hierarchic dominance and the absence of potential space. *Organisational and Social Dynamics, 4*(1), 22–45.

Diamond, M. A., & Allcorn, S. (2009). *Private selves in public organizations: The psychodynamics of organizational diagnosis and change.* New York: Palgrave Macmillan.

Diamond, M. A., Allcorn, S., & Stein, H. F. (2004). The surface of organizational boundaries: A view from psychoanalytic object relations theory. *Human Relations, 57*(1), 31–53.

Diamond, M. A., Stein, H. F., & Allcorn, S. (2002). Organizational silos: Horizontal organizational fragmentation. *Journal for the Psychoanalysis of Culture & Society, 7*(2), 280–296.

Driver, M. (2009). Struggling with lack: A Lacanian perspective on organizational identity. *Organization Studies, 30*(1), 55–72.

Dutton, J. E., & Dukerich, J. M. (1991). Keeping an eye on the mirror: Image and identity in organizational adaptation. *Academy of Management Journal, 34*(3), 517–554.

Edelman, G. M. (2006). *Second nature: Brain science and human knowledge.* New Haven, CT: Yale University Press.

Erikson, E. H. (1963). *Childhood and society.* New York: Norton.

Erikson, E. H. (1964). *Insight and responsibility.* New York: Norton.

Erikson, E. H. (1968). *Identity: Youth and crisis.* New York: Norton.

Fairbairn, R. D. (1952). *An object relations theory of personality.* New York: Basic Books.

Fairfield, S., Layton, L., & Stack, C. (Eds.) (2002). *Bringing the plague: Toward a postmodern psychoanalysis.* New York: Other Press.

Flyvbjerg, B. (2001). *Making social science matter.* New York: Cambridge University Press.

Fonagy, P. (2001). *Attachment theory and psychoanalysis.* New York: Other Press.

Fonagy, P., et al. (1991). Thinking about thinking: Some clinical and theoretical considerations in the treatment of a borderline patient. *International Journal of Psycho-Analysis, 72*, 1–18.

Freedman, A. M., & Bradt, K. H. (2009). *Consulting psychology: Selected articles by Harry Levinson.* Washington, DC: American Psychological Association.

Freud, A. (1966). *The ego and the mechanisms of defense* (2nd ed.). New York: International Universities Press.

Freud, S. (1920). *Beyond the pleasure principle.* New York: Norton.

Freud, S. (1921). *Group psychology and the analysis of the ego.* New York: Norton.

Freud, S. (1927). *The future of an illusion.* New York: Norton.

Freud, S. (1930). *Civilization and its discontents.* New York: Norton.

Freud, S. (1933). *The new introductory lectures on psychoanalysis.* New York: Norton.

Freud, S. (1938). Splitting of the ego in the process of defense. In *The standard edition of the complete psychological works of Sigmund Freud* (Vol. 23, pp. 271–278). London: Hogarth.

Freud, S. (1989). The unconscious. In P. Gay (Ed.), *The Freud Reader* (pp. 572–584). New York: Norton. (Original work published 1915)

Freud, S. (2006a). Mourning and melancholia. In A. Phillips (Ed.), *The Penguin Freud Reader* (pp. 310–326). New York: Penguin. (Original work published 1917)

Freud, S. (2006b). Remembering, repeating, and working through. In A. Phillips (Ed.), *The Penguin Freud Reader* (pp. 391–401). London: Penguin. (Original work published 1914)

Fromm, E. (1955). *The sane society.* New York: Fawcett World Library.

Frosch, J. (1983). *The psychotic process.* New York: International Universities Press.

Gabriel, Y. (1999). Organizations-in-depth. London: Sage.

Gay, P. (Ed.) (1989). *The Freud reader.* New York: Norton.

Gedo, J. (1999). *The evolution of psychoanalysis: Contemporary theory and practice.* New York: Other Press.

Gerson, S. (2004). The relational unconscious: A core element of intersubjectivity, thirdness, and clinical process. *The Psychoanalytic Quarterly, 73*(1), 63–98.

Ghent, E. (1990). Masochism, submission, surrender. *Contemporary Psychoanalysis, 26,* 169–211.

Gioia, D. A., Price, K. N., Hamilton, A. L., & Thomas, J. B. (2010). Forging an identity: An insider-outsider study of processes involved in the formation of organizational identity. *Administrative Science Quarterly, 55*(1), 1–46.

Gioia, D. A., Schultz, M., & Corley, K. G. (2000). Organizational identity, image, and adaptive instability. *Academy of Management Review, 25*(10), 63–81.

Glass, J. M. (1995). *Psychosis and power.* Ithaca, NY: Cornell University Press.

Goodwin, D. K. (2005). *Team of rivals.* New York: Simon and Schuster.

Green, A. (2004). Thirdness and psychoanalytic concepts. *The Psychoanalytic Quarterly, 73*(1), 99–136.

Greenberg, J., & Mitchell, S. (1983). *Object relations in psychoanalytic theory.* Cambridge, MA: Harvard University Press.

References

Grinberg, L., Sor, D., & Tabak de Bianchedi, E. (1993). *New introduction to the work of Bion* (Rev. ed.). Northvale, NJ: Jason Aronson.

Grotstein, J. S. (1985). *Splitting and projective identification.* Northvale, NJ: Jason Aronson.

Guntrip, H. (1969). *Schizoid phenomena, object relations and the self.* New York: International Universities Press.

Harlow, H. (1958). The nature of love. *American Psychologist, 13,* 673–678.

Harquail, C. V., & King, A. W. (2010). Construing organizational identity: The role of embodied cognition. *Organization Studies, 31*(12), 1619–1648.

Harrison, M. I. (2005). *Diagnosing organizations: Methods, models, and processes* (3rd ed.). Thousand Oaks, CA: Sage.

Hatch, M. J. & Schultz, M. (2002). The dynamics of organizational identity. *Human Relations, 55*(8), 989–1018.

Hawkes, T. (1972). *Metaphor.* London: Methuen.

Hedges, L. E. (1994). *In search of the lost mother of infancy.* Northvale, NJ: Jason Aronson.

Hegel, G. W. F. (1807). *The phenomenology of mind* (J. B. Baille, Trans.). London: George Allen & Unwin; New York: Humanities Press.

Hinshelwood, R. D. (1991). *A dictionary of Kleinian thought* (2nd ed.). Northvale, NJ: Jason Aronson.

Hodgson, R. C., Levinson, D. J., & Zaleznik, A. (1965). *The executive role constellation: An analysis of personality and role relations in management.* Boston: Harvard University Graduate School of Business Administration.

Hoffman, I. Z. (1998). *Ritual and spontaneity in the psychoanalytic process: A dialectical-constructivist view.* Hillsdale, NJ: Analytic.

Horney, K. (1945). *Our inner conflicts.* New York: Norton.

Humphreys, M., & Brown, A. D. (2002). Narratives of organizational identity and identification: A case study of hegemony and resistance. *Organization Studies, 23*(3), 421–447.

Hunt, J. C. (1989). *Psychoanalytic aspects of fieldwork.* London: Sage.

Jaques, E. (1955). Social systems as defense against persecutory and depressive anxiety. In M. Klein et al. (Eds.), *New directions in psychoanalysis* (pp. 478–498). New York: Basic Books.

Jurist, E. L., Slade, A., & Bergner, S. (Eds.). (2008). *Mind to mind: Infant research, neuroscience, and psychoanalysis.* New York: Other Press.

Kampa-Kokesch, S., & Anderson, M. Z. (2001). Executive coaching: A comprehensive review of the literature. *Consulting Psychology Journal: Practice and Research, 53*(4), 205–228.

Kandel, E. R. (2006). *In search of memory: The emergence of a new science of mind.* New York: Norton.

Karen, R. (1998). *Becoming attached.* New York: Oxford University Press.

References

Kernberg, O. (1979). Regression in organizational leadership. *Psychiatry, 42*, 24–39.

Kernberg, O. (1980). *Internal world and external reality: Object relations theory applied.* New York: Jason Aronson.

Kernberg, O. (1998). *Ideology, conflict, and leadership in groups and organizations.* New Haven, CT: Yale University Press.

Kets de Vries, M. F. R. (Ed.). (1984). *The irrational executive: Psychoanalytic explorations in management.* New York: International Universities Press.

Kets de Vries, M. F. R. (2001). *The leadership mystique.* New York: Financial Times Prentice Hall.

Kets de Vries, M. F. R. (2006). *The leader on the couch: A clinical approach to changing people and organizations.* West Sussex, ENG: Wiley.

Kets de Vries, M. F. R. (2007). Executive complexes. *Organization Dynamics, 36*(4), 377–391.

Kets de Vries, M. F. R., & assoc. (Eds.). (1991). *Organizations on the couch: Clinical perspectives on organizational behavior and change.* San Francisco: Jossey-Bass.

Kets de Vries, M. F. R., Guillen, L., Korotov, K., & Florent-Treacy, E. (2010). *The coaching kaleidoscope: Insights from the inside.* New York: Palgrave Macmillan.

Kets de Vries, M. F. R., Korotov, K., & Florent-Treacy, E. (2007). *Coach and couch: The psychology of making better leaders.* New York: Palgrave Macmillan.

Kets de Vries, M. F. R., & Miller, D. (1984). *The neurotic organization.* San Francisco: Jossey-Bass.

Kets de Vries, M. F. R., & Miller, D. (1987). Interpreting organizational texts. *Journal of Management Studies, 24*(3), 233–247.

Kilburg, R. R. (1996). Toward a conceptual understanding and definition of executive coaching. *Consulting Psychology Journal: Practice and Research, 48*, 134–144.

Kilburg, R. R. (2000). *Executive coaching: Developing managerial wisdom in a world of chaos.* Washington, DC: American Psychological Association.

Kilburg, R. R. (Ed.). (2004a). Trudging toward Dodoville, 1: Conceptual approaches and case studies in executive coaching [Special issue]. *Consulting Psychology Journal: Practice and Research, 56*(4), 203–213.

Kilburg, R. R. (2004b). When shadows fall: Using psychodynamic approaches in executive coaching. *Consulting Psychology Journal: Practice and Research, 56*(4), 246–268.

Kilburg, R. R. (Ed.). (2005). Executive coaching: The road to Dodoville needs paving with more than good assumptions [Special issue]. *Consulting Psychology Journal: Practice and Research, 57*(1), 90–96.

Klein, G. S. (1976). *Psychoanalytic theory: An exploration of essentials.* New York: International Universities Press.

References

Klein, M. (1946). Notes on some schizoid mechanisms. *International Journal of Psychoanalysis, 27*, 99–110.

Klein, M. (1959). Our adult world and its roots in infancy. *Human Relations, 12*, 291–303.

Klein, M. (1975). *Envy and gratitude and other works 1946–1963.* New York: Delacorte.

Klein, M. (1986). *The selected Melanie Klein* (J. Mitchell, Ed.). New York: Free Press.

Klein, M., & Riviere, J. (1964). Love, hate and reparation. New York: Norton.

Kohut, H. (1977). *The restoration of the self.* New York: International Universities Press.

Kohut, H. (1984). *How does analysis cure?* (A. Goldberg, Ed.). Chicago: University of Chicago Press.

Kunda, G. (1992). *Engineering Culture: Control and Commitment in a High-Tech Corporation.* Philadelphia: Temple University Press.

LaBier, D. (1980, February 17). Uncle Sam's working wounded. *The Washington Post Magazine.*

LaBier, D. (1983a). Bureaucracy and psychopathology. *Political Psychology, 4*, 223–243.

LaBier, D. (1983b). Emotional disturbance in the federal government. *Administration & Society, 14*, 403–448.

LaBier, D. (1986). *Modern madness: The emotional fallout of success.* Reading, MA: Addison-Wesley.

Lacan, J. (1991). The seminar of Jacques Lacan, Bk. 1: 1953–1954 (J. Forrester, Trans.). New York: Norton. (Original work published 1975)

Laing, R. D. (1969). *The politics of the family and other essays.* New York: Pantheon Books.

Lakoff, G., & Johnson, M. (1980). *Metaphors we live by.* Chicago: University of Chicago Press.

Laplanche, J., & Pontalis, J. B. (1973). *The language of psycho-analysis.* New York: Norton.

Lear, J. (2005). *Freud.* New York: Routledge, Taylor & Francis.

Lear, J. (2007). Working through the end of civilization. *International Journal of Psycho-Analysis, 88*, 291–308.

Leffert, M. (2010). *Contemporary psychoanalytic foundations: Postmodernism, complexity, and neuroscience.* New York: Routledge, Taylor & Francis.

Levine, D. (2006). *Attack on government: Fear, distrust, and hatred in public life.* Charlottesville, VA: Pitchstone.

Levine, D. (2010). *Object relations, work and the self.* New York: Routledge.

Levinson, H. (1964). *Emotional health in the world of work.* New York: Harper & Row.

References

Levinson, H. (1968). *The exceptional executive.* Cambridge, MA: Harvard University Press.

Levinson, H. (1970). *Executive stress.* New York: Harper & Row.

Levinson, H. (1972). *Organizational diagnosis.* Cambridge, MA: Harvard University Press.

Levinson, H. (1976). *Psychological man.* Cambridge, MA: The Levinson Institute.

Levinson, H. (1981). *Executive* (Rev. ed.). Cambridge, MA: Harvard University Press.

Levinson, H. (2002). *Organizational assessment.* Washington, DC: American Psychological Association Press.

Levinson, H., et al. (1962). *Men, management, and mental health.* Cambridge, MA: Harvard University Press.

Lewin, K. (1946). Action research and minority problems. *Journal of Social Issues, 2*(4), 34–46.

Loewald, H. (1971). Some consideration on repetition and repetition compulsion. *International Journal of Psycho-Analysis, 52,* 59–66.

Lopez-Corvo, R. E. (2003). *The dictionary of the work of W. R. Bion.* New York and London: Karnac.

Lowman, R. L. (2001). Constructing a literature from case studies: Promise and limitations of the method. *Consulting Psychology Journal: Practice and Research, 53*(2), 119–123.

Lowman, R. L. (2005). Executive coaching: The road to Dodoville needs paving with more than good assumptions. *Consulting Psychology Journal: Practice and Research, 57*(1), 90–96.

Maccoby, M. (1976). *The gamesman.* New York: Simon and Schuster, Bantam Books.

Mahler, M. S., Pine, F., and Bergman, A. (1975). *The psychological birth of the human infant: Symbiosis and individuation.* New York: Basic Books.

Marucco, N. C. (2007). Between memory and destiny: Repetition. *International Journal of Psycho-Analysis, 88,* 309–328.

McDougall, J. (1982). *Theaters of the mind: Illusion and truth on the psychoanalytic stage.* New York: Basic Books.

McWilliams, N. (1994). *Psychoanalytic Diagnosis : Understanding Personality Structure in the Clinical Process.* New York: Guilford.

Meissner, W. W. (1991). *What is effective in psychoanalytic therapy: The move from interpretation to relation.* Northvale, NJ: Jason Aronson.

Menzies, I. E. P. (1960). A case in the functioning of social systems as a defense against anxiety: A report on the nursing service of a general hospital. *Human Relations, 13,* 95–121.

Merton, R. (1963). Bureaucratic structure and personality. *Social Forces,* 18(4), 560–568.

References

Mills, J. (2000). Hegel on projective identification: Implications for Klein, Bion, and beyond. *The Psychoanalytic Review, 87*(6), 841–874.

Minolli, M., & Tricoli, M. L. (2004). Solving the problems of duality: The third and self-consciousness. *The Psychoanalytic Quarterly, 73*(1), 137–166.

Mitchell, S. A. (1988). *Relational concepts in psychoanalysis: An integration.* Cambridge, MA: Harvard University Press.

Mitchell, S. A., & Aron, L. (1999). *Relational psychoanalysis.* New York: Analytic.

Modell, A. (1984). *Psychoanalysis in a new context.* New York: International Universities Press.

Modell, A. (1993). *The private self.* Cambridge, MA: Harvard University Press.

Modell, A. (2006). *Imagination and the meaningful brain.* Cambridge, MA: MIT Press.

Moore, B. E., & Fine, B. D. (1990). *Psychoanalytic terms and concepts.* New Haven, CT: Yale University Press.

Morgan, G. (2006). *Images of organization.* Thousand Oaks, CA: Sage.

Newton, J., Long, S., & Sievers, B. (Eds.). (2006). *Coaching in depth: The organizational role analysis approach.* London: Karnac.

Ogden, T. H. (1982). *Projective identification and psychotherapeutic technique.* Northvale, NJ: Jason Aronson.

Ogden, T. H. (1989). *The primitive edge of experience.* Northvale, NJ: Jason Aronson.

Ogden, T. H. (1994). *Subjects of analysis.* Northvale, NJ: Jason Aronson.

Ogden, T. H. (2004). The analytic third: Implications for psychoanalytic theory and technique. *The Psychoanalytic Quarterly, 73*(1), 167–196.

Person, E. (1995). *By force of fantasy.* New York: Basic Books.

Pierce, C. (1972). *Charles S. Pierce: The essential writings* (E. C. Moore, Ed.). New York: Harper & Row.

Phillips, A. (Ed.). (2006). *The Penguin Freud reader.* New York: Penguin.

Polanyi, M. (1958). *Personal knowledge: Towards a post-critical philosophy.* Chicago: University of Chicago Press.

Pratt, M. G., & Foreman, P. O. (2000). Classifying managerial responses to multiple organizational identities. *Academy of Management Review, 25*(1), 18–42.

Pratt, M. G., Rockman, K. W., & Kaufmann, J. B. (2006). Constructing profession identity: The role of work and identity learning cycles in the customization of identity among medical residents. *Academy of Management Journal, 49* (2), 235–262.

Ravasi, D., & Schultz, M. (2006). Responding to organizational identity threats: Exploring the role of organizational culture. *Academy of Management Journal, 49*(3), 433–458.

Richards, I. A. (1955). *Speculative instruments.* Chicago: University of Chicago Press.

References

Richards, I. A. (1965). *The philosophy of rhetoric.* New York: Oxford University Press.

Ricoeur, P. (2012). *On psychoanalysis.* Cambridge, UK: Polity.

Roberts, V., & Brunning, H. (2007). Psychodynamic and systemic coaching. In S. Palmer & A. Whybrow (Eds.), *Handbook of coaching psychology* (pp. 253–277). London and New York: Routledge.

Rosenzweig, S. (1936). Some implicit common factors in diverse methods of psychotherapy. *American Journal of Orthopsychiatry, 6*(3), 412–415.

Rycroft, C. (1968). *Critical dictionary of psychoanalysis.* London: Penguin.

Schafer, R. (1976). *A new language for psychoanalysis.* New Haven, CT: Yale University Press.

Schafer, R. (1983). *The analytic attitude.* New York: Basic Books.

Schafer, R. (1992). *Retelling a life.* New York: Basic Books.

Schein, E. (1985). *Organizational culture and leadership.* San Francisco: Jossey-Bass.

Schein, E. (1999). *Process consultation revisited.* Reading, MA: Addison-Wesley.

Schnell, E. R. (2005). A case study of executive coaching as a support mechanism during organizational growth and evolution. *Consulting Psychology Journal: Practice and Research, 57*(1), 41–56.

Schon, D. (1983). *The reflective practitioner.* New York: Basic Books.

Schwartz, S. J. (2005). A new identity for identity research: Recommendations for expanding and refocusing the identity literature. *Journal of Adolescent Research, 20*(3), 293–308.

Scott, S. G., & Lane, V. R. (2000). A stakeholder approach to organizational identity. *Academy of Management Review, 25* (1), 43–62.

Searle, J. R. (1995). The mystery of consciousness, Pt. 2. *The New York Review of Books, 42*(18), 4–61.

Segal, H. (1957). Notes on symbol formation. *International Journal of Psycho-Analysis, 38,* 391–397.

Senge, P. (1990). *The fifth discipline: The art and practice of the learning organization.* New York: Doubleday Currency.

Siegel, D. (2001). Toward an interpersonal neurobiology of the developing mind: Attachment relationships, mindsight, and neural integration. *Infant Mental Health Journal, 22*(1–2), 233–247.

Sievers, B. (Ed.). (2009). *Psychoanalytic studies of organizations: Contributions from the International Society for the Psychoanalytic Study of Organizations (ISPSO).* London: Karnac.

Spence, D. P. (1982). *Narrative truth and historical truth.* New York: Norton.

Spence, D. P. (1987). *The Freudian metaphor.* New York: Norton.

Stacey, R. D. (1992). *Managing the unknowable.* San Francisco: Jossey-Bass.

Stacey, R. D. (1996). *Complexity and creativity in organizations.* San Francisco: Berrett-Koehler.

References

Stapley, L. F. (2002). *It's an emotional game: Learning about leadership from the experience of football.* London: Karnac.

Stein, H. F. (1994). *Listening deeply.* Boulder, CO: Westview.

Stein, H. F. (1998). *Euphemism, spin, and the crisis in organizational life.* Westport, CT: Greenwood.

Stein, H. F. (2001). *Nothing personal, just business.* Westport, CT: Greenwood.

Stein, H. F. (2004). *Beneath the crust of culture.* Amsterdam and New York: Rodopi.

Stern, D. N. (1985). *The interpersonal world of the infant: A view from psychoanalysis and developmental psychology.* New York: Basic Books.

Stern, D. N. (2004). *The present moment in psychotherapy and everyday life.* New York: Norton.

Sullivan, H. S. (1953). *The interpersonal theory of psychiatry.* New York: Norton.

Summers, F. (2013). *The psychoanalytic vision: The experiencing subject, transcendence, and the therapeutic process.* New York and London: Routledge.

Tauber, A. I. (2013). *Requiem for the ego: Freud and the origins of postmodernism.* Stanford, CA: Stanford University Press.

Turquet, P. (1975). Threats to identity in the large group. In L. Kreeger (Ed.), *The large group: Dynamics and therapy* (pp. 87–144). London: Constable.

Vaughan, S. C. (1997). *The talking cure.* New York: Owl Books, H. Holt.

Volkan, V. (1997). *Bloodlines: From ethnic pride to ethnic terrorism.* New York: Farrar, Straus, and Giroux.

Volkan, V. (2004). *Blind trust: Large groups and their leaders in times of crisis and terror.* Charlottesville, VA: Pitchstone.

Volkan, V. (2006). *Killing in the name of identity.* Charlottesville, VA: Pitchstone.

Volkan, V. (2013). *Enemies on the couch.* Charlottesville, VA: Pitchstone.

Wampold, B. E. (1997). Methodological problems in identifying efficacious psychotherapies. *Psychotherapy Research, 7,* 21–43.

Wampold, B. E. (2001). *The great psychotherapy debate: Models, methods, and findings.* Mahwah, NJ: Erlbaum.

Weber, M. (1947). *The theory of social and economic organization.* New York: Free Press.

Whetten, D. A. (2006). Albert and Whetten revisited: Strengthening the concept of organizational identity. *Journal of Management Inquiry, 15*(3), 219–234.

Winnicott, D. W. (1958). The capacity to be alone. *International Journal of Psychoanalysis, 39,* 416–420.

Winnicott, D. W. (1960). The theory of parent-infant relationship. *International Journal of Psychoanalysis, 41,* 585–595.

Winnicott, D. W. (1965). *The maturational processes and the facilitating environment.* New York: International Universities Press.

Winnicott, D. W. (1971). *Playing and reality.* London: Tavistock.

References

Zaleznik, A., et al. (1965). *The executive role constellation.* Cambridge, MA: Harvard University Press.

Zaleznik, A. (1984a). Charismatic and consensus leaders: A psychological comparison. In M. F. R. Kets de Vries (Ed.), *The irrational executive* (pp. 112–131). New York: International Universities Press.

Zaleznik, A. (1984b). Power and politics in organizational life. In M. F. R. Kets de Vries (Ed.), *The irrational executive* (pp. 315–343). New York: International Universities Press.

Zaleznik, A. (1989). *The managerial mystique.* New York: Harper & Row.

Zaleznik, A. (1991). Leading and managing: Understanding the difference. In M. F. R. Kets de Vries and assoc. (Eds.), *Organizations on the couch: Clinical perspectives on organizational behavior and change* (pp. 97–119). San Francisco: Jossey-Bass.

Zweibel, R. (2004). The third position: Reflections about the internal analytic working process. *The Psychoanalytic Quarterly, 73*(1), 215–265.

INDEX

Note: Page numbers followed by *fig* and *t* indicate figures and tables, respectively.

acting out, 102, 110, 111–112, 139, 140
active re-creative repetition, 101, 111–113,
    113*t*, 117, 187
Acton, Lord, 157
affection, 167–168
aggression
    in autocratic work group, 68
    executive coaching and, 168
    in institutionalized work groups, 65–66
    projection of, 59
Allcorn, S., 182, 201n1, 202n9
Alvesson, M., 47
antisocial disposition, 174
Argyris, C., 104, 105, 106, 107, 132
Aristotle, 178
associative data, 35, 36, 44–45, 53, 192
atonement, 68
attachment theory, 4, 6, 22–26, 40, 108,
    170. *See also* mother-infant bond
Atwood, G. E., 141
authenticity, 177, 179–181
autistic-contiguous mode of experience, 7,
    28–29, 31, 33–34, 70, 76, 128
autocratic work groups, 7, 56, 67–70, 75*fig*,
    77

basic assumption groups, 198n4
Baum, H. S., 197n11
Benjamin, J., 196n9
Bergman, A., 6
Bergner, S., 6
Bingley, A. F., 196n8
Bion, W.
    basic assumption groups and, 198n4
    on compulsive repetitiveness, 107
    on container and contained, 30, 84, 149,
        198n11, 202n8

dependency and, 122
    ORA and, 176–177
    psychological regression and, 41, 55,
        127–128
Bollas, C., 9, 130, 137, 178, 195n1, 202n1
boundaries, 196n5
Bowlby, J., 6, 23
Brown, A. D., 197–198n9
bureaucracies, 101–102, 107

case examples
    destructive narcissism, 150–156
    feedback, 131–133
    frozen metaphor, 120–121
    identification with the aggressor, 70
    potential space and, 88–92
    repetition, 98–99
    schizoid withdrawal, 63–64
    social defenses, 66–67
    transitioning from negative to positive
        transferences, 73–74
    unthought knowns, 131–133
categorical imperative, 47
change
    anxiety and, 103–104
    as emotional loss, 170
    metaphor and, 119–121
    organizational diagnosis and, 114–116
    organizational learning and, 104–106
    resistance to, 8, 89, 104–105
    transformational objects and, 136–137
chaos, 174–176
charisma, 156, 159
Chodorow, N., 52
chosen traumas, 147–148
Civilization and Its Discontents (Freud), 21

Coaching in Depth (Newton, Long, and Sievers), 177
codependency, 168
cognitive-behavioral approach to learning, 105–106
collapse, 31, 32, 33–34, 70
Complexity and Creativity in Organizations (Stacey), 205n1
compromise formations, 7–8, 21, 53, 70, 75–76, 75*fig*
compulsion to repeat, 10*fig*, 12*t*, 14, 100–101, 106–108, 116–117, 140–142, 187. *See also* repetition
confrontation, 16, 183, 184
consensual validation, 9
constructive narcissism, 154–156, 172, 188
consultative process, phases of, 183–185
containment, 30, 31–32, 34, 54, 84, 175, 202n8
control, containment versus, 31–32
controlling disposition, 173
Corley, K. G., 46, 47, 197n6
countertransference
    about, 13
    Bion on, 197n10
    compulsion to repeat and, 100
    description of, 35
    dynamics of, 14, 55
    intersubjectivity and, 8
    metaphoric nature of, 126–127
    organizational diagnosis and, 37
    process consultation and, 138–141
    reflective practice and, 42–44
    relational psychoanalytic theory and, 34
    repetition and, 108–111
    researcher's/consultant's experience of, 126
cross-disciplinary systems model, 164

data, psychoanalytic, 34–37
death instinct, 106, 112
defensive organizational identifications, 101–104
defensive reactions, 57–58, 59, 104, 106, 142–143, 144
defensive resistance, 134–136
defensive work-group subcultures, 7, 13

demystification, 16, 183, 184
denial, 24, 27
dependency, 168, 176–177
dependent disposition, 173
depressive disposition, 174
depressive mode of experience, 7, 27, 30, 31–32, 77, 85–86, 112
depressive position, 23–24, 26–27, 47, 68
destructive narcissism, 154–156, 188
detached disposition, 174
developmental crises, 40
Diagnosing Organizations: Methods, Models, and Processes (Harrison), 205n7
dialectical interplay, 29–31
dialectical modes of experience, 7, 26–31
Diamond, M. A., 182, 196n9, 200n1, 201n1, 202n7
Dictionary of Kleinian Thought, A (Hinshelwood), 24
disruption, 16, 183–184
division versus fragmentation, 32–33
double-loop learning, 105, 106–108
dramatic disposition, 173
Dukerich, J. M., 198n10
Dutton, J. E., 198n10

ego ideal, 57, 62, 68, 122, 160, 166, 167
ego psychology, 164
ego/"I"
    awareness of, 3
    Freud's model of mind and, 20–21
embodied cognition, 46, 197n3
empathic data, 35, 37, 44–45, 53, 192
empathy, 42–44, 49
Enemies on the Couch (Volkan), 202n2
episteme, 178
Erikson, E., 40, 41, 196n3
evaluations, performance, 166
Executive (Levinson), 166–167
executive coaching
    about, 163–164
    authenticity and, 179–181
    case example and, 153, 155
    development of, 164–165
    executive dispositions and, 173–174
    narcissism and, 10–11, 171–173

as organizational intervention, 178–179
psychodynamic approaches to, 16
psychodynamic models for, 165–178
summary of, 188–189
Executive Coaching (Kilburg), 174
executive dispositions, 173–174
experience, subjective, 163
experience-near methodology, 45, 158
Experiences in Groups and Other Papers
    (Bion), 176
experiential data, 35, 37, 44–45, 53, 192
external environment, 50*fig*, 51

facilitating environment. *See* holding/
    facilitating environment
false self, 42–43, 46–47, 48, 142–143, 150,
    170, 179–181
feedback, 98–99, 133–134, 144
feedback sessions, 129–134
fieldwork, 191–192
fight/flight, 176–177
Fine, B. D., 22, 124
first-order processing, 104
Florent-Treacy, E., 171
fluid metaphor, 119, 120, 121, 123, 187
Fonagy, P., 6
Forces of Destiny (Bollas), 202n1
Foreman, P. O., 197n7
forgiveness, 68
formless dread, 29
fragmentation, division versus, 32–33
free association, 191
Freud (Lear), 115, 201n8
Freud, A., 200n4
Freud, S.
    on compulsion to repeat, 106–107
    on concept of leader, 160
    on death instinct, 112
    drive and structural model of, 205n4
    ego ideal and, 195n1
    empathy and, 37
    as foundation for psychoanalytic theory,
        13, 19–22
    group dynamics and, 41, 62, 68
    Kant and, 47
    on melancholia, 23
    metaphoric processes and, 122

on psychological regression, 55
psychological splitting and, 132
rational-drive model of, 77
regression and, 128
on repetition, 110
on transference, 110
on treatment, 116, 140
unconscious and, 141
on unthought knowns, 134
Winnicott compared to, 25
Fromm, E., 3, 203n7
frozen metaphor, 119, 120, 123, 128, 187

Gioia, D. A., 46, 47
goals, 51
Goodwin, D. K., 204n2
Greenberg, J., 205n4
grief, 23, 100, 114, 143
group dynamics, 7, 10*fig*, 12*t*
group membership, 56–60
*Group Psychology and the Analysis of the
    Ego* (Freud), 21, 62, 68, 122, 160
group regression, 57
group transition, psychodynamics of,
    74–76, 75*fig*
guilt, 68, 69, 137, 166
Guntrip, H., 61–62, 63

Harquail, C. V., 46, 197n3
Harrison, M. I., 205n7
Hawkes, T., 125
Hedges, L. E., 203n5
Hegel, G. W. F., 200n8
Hinshelwood, R. D., 24
historical data, 35–36, 44–45, 53, 192
HOAEE, 35, 44–45, 53, 192
holding/facilitating environment. *See also*
    potential space
    case example and, 86–87
    change and, 136
    dialectical interplay and, 29–30
    integration and, 34
    Winnicott's concept of, 23, 25–26, 39, 40,
        44, 46, 58, 176
homogenized work groups, 7, 56, 60–64,
    74–75, 75*fig*, 76
Horney, K., 21, 205n6

Index

idealizing transference, 68, 72, 74, 165, 171, 172, 201n2
identification, 42–44, 49
identification with the aggressor, 69
identity. *See also* organizational identity
  psychological roots of, 39
  role of, 19
  sense of, 40–41
Identity: Youth and Crisis (Erikson), 196n3
id/"it," Freud's model of mind and, 20–21
Images of Organization (Morgan), 119
"in and out" programme, 63
In Search of the Lost Mother of Infancy (Hedges), 203n5
incorporations, 43
infant research, 6, 22–23
infantile narcissism, 149, 150
institutionalized work groups, 7, 56, 64–67, 75*fig*, 76–77
integration versus isolation, 33–34
internalization, 22, 43
intersubjective awareness, 89, 95
intersubjective dimension, 82
intersubjectivity/intersubjective third. *See also* potential space
  application of theory of, 13–14
  change and, 87–92
  concept of, 81, 82–85
  context for, 81–82
  context of, 34
  discovery of organizational identity and, 9–10, 10*fig*, 12*t*
  emerging organizational identity ad, 85–87
  narrative processes and, 92–93
  organizational identity and, 86*t*
  potential space, 195n2
  potential space and, 26
  reflecting on, 93–94
  reflective practice and, 8
  summary of, 186–187
  visualization of, 83*fig*
interviewing, 191
introjections, 19, 22, 23, 28
invited intruders, 36
isolation, 33–34, 59

Jaques, E., 203n11
Jurist, E. L., 6

Kant, I., 47
Kernberg, O., 59, 64–66, 101, 107, 150, 173
Kets de Vries, M. F. R., 164, 165, 169–171, 173, 179
Kilburg, R. R., 164, 165, 174–176, 179
Killing in the Name of Identity (Volkan), 202n2
King, A. W., 46, 197n3
Klein, M., 22–25, 26, 28, 47, 59, 68, 132, 170, 171, 201n10, 205n4
Kohut, H., 6–7, 158, 171, 201n2, 203n3, 203n6, 205n4
Korotov, K., 171

Lane, V. R., 45
Language of Psycho-Analysis, The (Laplanche and Pontalis), 21
Laplanche, J., 21
Leader on the Couch, The (Kets de Vries), 171
Lear, J., 103, 107, 110, 112, 115, 116–117, 140
learning for insight and change, 100–101
Levinson, H., 34, 157–158, 164, 165–168, 170, 179, 192, 201n1, 202n1, 202n5
Lewin, K., 189
Loewald, H., 101, 111–112, 201n11
Long, S., 165, 177

Mahler, M. S., 6
Marucco, N. C., 107
mastery, 167
maturation, 167
Maturational Processes and the Facilitating Environment, The (Winnicott), 195n4
McDougall, J., 204n16
McWilliams, N., 150
mediated focus, 175
mediating ego, 21
melancholia, 23
membership, attachment theory and, 6
memory, collective, 138–139

Menzies, I. E. P., 107, 203n11
merger, 56
metaphor/metaphoric processes, 8–9, 10*fig*, 12*t*, 14–15, 119–128, 187
mind, Freud's model of, 20–22
ministration, 167
Minolli, M., 200n8
mirror-hungry narcissists, 150
mirroring, 68, 72, 136, 165, 171, 201n2
mistreatment of subordinates, 4
Mitchell, S., 205n4
Mitchell, S. A., 25
Modell, A., 22
modes of organizing, 31–34
Moore, B. E., 22, 124
Morgan, G., 119
mother-infant bond, 4, 6, 25–26, 28, 39, 41, 58, 175, 197n10. *See also* attachment theory
mourning, 23, 100, 114, 143
Mourning and Melancholia (Freud), 23
multilayered model, 49–52, 50*fig*, 187

narcissism, 10–11, 10*fig*, 12*t*, 149–156, 161–162, 169–173, 188
narcissistic disposition, 173
narcissistic gratification, 6–7
narcissistic injuries, 147–148
narcissistic organizational leadership, 15–16
narcissistic traps, 156–160
narrative processes, 92–93
negativistic disposition, 174
New Introductory Lectures on Psychoanalysis, The (Freud), 20
Newton, J., 165, 177
Nichomachean Ethics (Aristotle), 178
nondefensive work-group subcultures, 7
note taking, 191–192

object relations, 164
Object Relations in Psychoanalytic Theory (Greenberg and Mitchell), 205n4
object relations theory, 6, 20, 22–26, 108, 169–171, 175

object world, 41
observational data, 35, 36, 44–45, 53, 192
observing ego, 200n4
Oedipal power and authority, 160–161
Ogden, T., 7, 26–31, 47, 74, 82, 149
"oneness," 198n4
open systems model, 169
organizational analysis and multilayered model, 49–52
Organizational Assessment (Levinson), 201n1
organizational control, 47
organizational culture, 50*fig*, 52
organizational diagnosis, 98–99, 114–116, 137–140
organizational identity
    definition of, 44–45
    discovering, 7–9, 10*fig*, 12*t*
    essence of, 4–6
    intersubjectivity and, 85–87, 86*t*
    management and, 45–48
    multilayered model and, 49–52
    organizational culture and, 52–53
    potential space and, 9–10
    psychoanalytic concept of, 13
    reflecting on, 93–94
    role of, 3, 158–159
    self-identity and, 41–42
    summary of, 185–186
    theories of influence on, 6–7
organizational learning, 104–106
organizational narrative, 53, 89–90, 92–93, 98, 113–115, 133, 138–139
organizational role analysis (ORA), 164, 176–178, 179
organizational strategies, 50*fig*, 51–52
organizational structure, 50*fig*, 51–52
organizing, modes of, 31–34
ossification, 32
Our Inner Conflicts (Horney), 205n6

pairing (utopia), 176–177
paranoid disposition, 174
paranoid-schizoid mode of experience, 7, 27–28, 31, 32–33, 64, 76–77, 112

paranoid-schizoid position, 23, 24, 26–27, 47–48
participant observation, 192
passive reproductive repetition, 101–104, 111–113, 113*t*, 117, 187
persecutory transference, 62, 66, 72
Personal Knowledge: Towards a Post-Critical Philosophy (Polanyi), 197n2
phronesis, 178
Pine, F., 6
Playing and Reality (Winnicott), 195n4
Polanyi, M., 197n2
Pontalis, J. B., 21
potential space. *See also* holding/facilitating environment; intersubjectivity/intersubjective third
  about, 14
  description of, 19, 26, 81–82, 84
  dialectical interplay and, 29–30
  dialectical model of group dynamics and, 77
  dialectical modes of experience and, 31
  discovery of, 85
  emerging organizational identity and, 85–87
  executive coaching and, 180–181
  opening up of, 53
  organizational identity and, 9–10, 10*fig*, 12*t*
  questions involving, 6
  reflecting on, 93–94
  reflective practice and, 8
  role of, 5
  summary of, 186–187
  visualization of, 83*fig*
  Winnicott's concept of, 170, 176
Power of Feelings, The (Chodorow), 52
practical wisdom (phronesis), 178
Pratt, C. V., 197n7
pre-Oedipal power and authority, 160–161
pre-reflective unconscious, 141–142
primitive aggression, 61–62
primordial struggle, 103
Private Selves in Public Organizations (Diamond and Allcorn), 201n1
process consultation psychodynamics, 116–117

projection of aggression, 59
projections, 19, 22–23, 24, 27–28
projective identification, 28, 59, 65, 84, 85, 95, 201n2, 201n10
Projective Identification and Psychotherapeutic Technique (Ogden), 149
propaganda, 148
psychoanalytic data, 192
Psychoanalytic Diagnosis (McWilliams), 150
psychoanalytic organizational theory, 13
psychoanalytic theory, as framework, 4
psychodynamic coaching, 164–165
psychodynamic models, 165–178
psychological contract, 165–166
psychological regression, 55, 56–57, 59–60, 127–128, 168
psychological splitting, 22–23, 24, 27–28, 59, 103, 132–133, 143
Putnam, R., 104, 105

rational-drive model, 77
reactive narcissism, 171, 172–173, 181
"real," notion of, 195–196n6
reflective action, 82
reflective containment, 176, 180
reflective practice, 111–113, 186, 188
Reflective Practitioner, The (Schon), 200n1
reflectivity, 8
regression
  group, 57
  psychological, 55, 56–57, 59–60, 127–128, 168
regressive work groups, 60–71
relational psychoanalytic perspective, 49, 84
relational psychoanalytic theory, 34–37, 185
repetition
  about, 14, 97–98
  compulsion for, 10*fig*, 12*t*, 14, 100–101, 106–108, 116–117, 140–142, 187
  compulsions and, 100–101
  countertransference and, 108–111
  destructive cycle of, 98–99
  destructive versus constructive, 101

interrupting, 116–117, 141
organizational learning and, 104–106
organizational narrative and, 113–114
structure of, 108–109
summary of, 187
transference and, 108–111
repression, 22, 57, 141–142, 143
research/consulting team processing,
    192–193
resilient work groups, 7, 56, 71–74, 75*fig*, 77
resistance to change, 8, 89, 104–105
Rice Institute, A. K., 164, 176
Richards, I. A., 124
routinization, 101–102
Rycroft, C., 58

sabotage, 90
Sane Society, The (Fromm), 203n7
schizoid organizational identity, 102–103
schizoid retreat, 63
Schon, D., 104, 105, 106, 107, 132, 200n1
Schultz, M., 46, 47
Scott, S. G., 45
second-order processing, 105
self psychology, 6–7
self-awareness, 47, 163–164
self-defeating disposition, 173–174
self-identity
    about, 13
    group membership and, 58–60
    in institutionalized work groups, 65
    introduction to, 40–41
    organizational identity and, 41–42
self-sealing processes, 99, 100–101, 104,
    106, 112, 117, 141
sense of identity, 40–41
separateness, attachment theory and, 6
separation, 23
separation anxiety, 27, 33, 57, 60, 64–65,
    67, 70, 74
Shadow of the Object, The (Bollas), 137,
    202n1
Sievers, B., 165, 177, 182
silo metaphor, 14–15, 121–123, 124–126,
    128, 152
single-loop learning, 104–105, 106–108, 132
Slade, A., 6

Smith, D., 104, 105
social constructionist perspective, 45
Stacey, R. D., 32, 205n1
Stapley, L. F., 182
Starkey, K., 197–198n9
Stein, H. F., 182, 202n9, 202n10, 204n17
Stern, D. N., 6
Stolorow, R. D., 141
subcultures, 52
superego/"I-above," 20–21
symbol formation proper, 27
systems complexity, 174–176

task environment, 51
Tavistock Institute for Human Relations,
    164, 176
Team of Rivals (Goodwin), 204n2
techne, 178
Theaters of the Mind (McDougall), 204n16
theories of action, 104–105
"thirdness," 196n9
transference
    Bion on, 197n10
    compulsion to repeat and, 100
    discovery of organizational identity and,
        35, 37, 42–44
    dynamics of, 55, 75–76, 127–128
    group dynamics and, 13
    idealizing, 201n2
    metaphoric nature of, 126–127
    as metaphoric process, 124–126
    mirroring, 201n2
    narcissism and, 171
    process consultation and, 138–141
    psychological contract and, 165
    reflective practice and, 8
    repetition and, 108–111
    unthought knowns and, 130–134
transformational objects, 136–137, 195n1
transitional objects, 170
transitional space, 180
transparency, 16, 183, 184
traumas, chosen, 147–148
Tricoli, M. L., 200n8
true self, 42–43, 46–47, 142–143, 170,
    179–181
trust, 40, 44

Turquet, P., 198n4
twinship transference, 71–72, 74

unconscious, pre-reflective, 141–142
unconscious processes, 4, 20–21
unreflective practice, 111–113
unthought knowns
  about, 15
  awareness of, 92, 114
  concept of, 9, 129–130
  defensive resistance and, 134–136
  demystification and, 184
  discovery of organizational identity and,
    10*fig*, 12*t*
  self-consciousness and, 178
  summary of, 144, 187–188
  transference and, 130–134

Volkan, V., 148, 196n7, 202n2

Weber, M., 64
Whetten, D. A., 197n5

Willmott, H., 47
Winnicott, D. W.
  executive coaching and, 178
  on facilitating environment, 23, 39, 40,
    44, 58, 149, 176
  "good enough" phrasing and, 203n3
  holding and, 198n11
  Kant and, 47
  Kets de Vries and, 170
  mother-infant bond and, 175
  object relations theory of, 25–26
  overview of theories of, 6
  on potential space, 30, 53, 77, 81–82,
    195n2, 196n1
  psychoanalytic theory of, 205n4
  true versus false self and, 42–43, 46, 48,
    142–143, 170, 179–181
worker exploitation, 161–162
work-group subcultures, 7–8, 13, 60–71

Zaleznik, A., 182, 204n3